Oracle10gR2
Recovery Manager

Oracle10gR2 Recovery Manager

The Concise Treatise

Ramesh Raghav
Sr. Oracle10g OCP dba, IBM Corporation

iUniverse, Inc.
New York Lincoln Shanghai

Oracle10gR2 Recovery Manager
The Concise Treatise

iUniverse books may be ordered through booksellers or by contacting:

iUniverse
2021 Pine Lake Road, Suite 100
Lincoln, NE 68512
www.iuniverse.com
1-800-Authors (1-800-288-4677)

The views expressed in this work are solely those of the author and do not necessarily reflect the views of the publisher, and the publisher hereby disclaims any responsibility for them.

ISBN-13: 978-0-595-42027-8 (pbk)
ISBN-13: 978-0-595-86372-3 (ebk)
ISBN-10: 0-595-42027-3 (pbk)
ISBN-10: 0-595-86372-8 (ebk)

Printed in the United States of America

This book is dedicated to the unparalleled spiritual heritage of India.

Table of Contents

Preface

Conventions used in this book:

Each chapter begins with a list of objectives defined at the outset.
Boxed items highlight some of the key features.
All the SQL statements are provided in uppercase.
All the RMAN commands are presented in lowercase.
The target database(s) are assumed to be in archivelog mode.
The use of recovery catalog is emphasized at every possible opportunity since it is one of THE BEST PRACTICES.
The actual server output is always made available whenever warranted.
The deployment of ASM based storage is demonstrated wherever possible.
The significant concepts are recapitulated at the end of every chapter.

References:

http://technet.oracle.com
IBM Tivoli Storage Manager—Data Protection for Oracle Unix Guide
NetBackup for Oracle v6.0 System Administrator's Guide: Symantec Corp.

Acknowledgements:

I fully appreciate the wonderful support of my wife & son during the challenging manuscript preparation phase. I also extend my sincere thanks to Mary Carey of iUniverse for getting me started on this publishing journey.

Chapter 1 Objectives

- Backup & Recovery Defined
- Types of Solutions
- Physical Structures
- Recovery Explained

Chapter 1
Oracle Database Backup & Recovery

Backup & Recovery functions are the backbone of any enterprise Information Systems strategy to assure business continuity under all conditions.

What is Backup?

Backup is the set of processes to ensure the database data is archived securely to prevent any loss of data should some disaster strike.

As DBAs we all know protecting vital enterprise data is extremely important. Since Murphy's Law ("If anything can go wrong it will") is always true Oracle data backup can not be jeopardized in any manner!

What is Recovery?

Recovery is the set of processes aimed at salvaging or resurrecting the database data after a disaster has struck.

Media failure like disk crashes is one of the most common situations requiring recovery of data from backup.

Logical backups like export are of limited use at the hour of crisis. So it is imperative that database is backed up physically.

> Recovery is more often a stressful and challenging activity for the database administrator. The importance of having a sound **VALIDATED** backup & recovery strategy in place need not be overstated.

1.1 Types of Solutions

Broadly we have 2 kinds of physical Oracle Database Backup and Recovery. We will briefly evaluate both of them now. This book is devoted to the deployment of Oracle's very own **Recovery Manager (RMAN)**. Needless to say we can look forward to a richer set of features in the upcoming releases of Oracle Database for this tool!

1.1.1 Recovery Manager: a comprehensive powerful command-line client tool (like SQL*Plus). RMAN is Intelligent, Native & Free. It is the preferred solution for database backup and recovery. For Very Large Databases (VLDB) it provides an excellent solution by way of its ability to perform incremental backups. With its continually upgraded functionality RMAN is essential gear for any Orcale data center. Many of the Oracle10g new features are available only through RMAN.

1.1.2 User-managed: This involves the use of both host operating system & SQL*Plus commands. Certain backup & recovery tasks can NOT be performed employing this methodology.

Let us contrast these two approaches now:

Feature	Recovery Manager	User-managed
Cold backup	Yes (db in mounted stae)	Yes
Hot backup	Yes – NO need to put db in backup mode	Yes - need to put db in backup mode
Incremental backup	YES	NO
Automatic record keeping	YES	Manual specification of files to be backed up
Recovery catalog	YES	NO
Platform-independence	YES	NO
ASM based storage	YES	NO
Cross platform transport	YES	NO
Encryption	YES	NO

Table 1-1 Comparison of RMAN & User-managed Backup Methods

1.2 Physical Structures

An Oracle database backup essentially backs up controlfiles, datafiles & archived redo logs. It is a good practice to backup the server parameter file(spfile) also.

1.2.1 Controlfiles

These are crucial files that contain vital information like db name, db id, datafile names, checkpoints, redo log sequence, SCN etc.

RMAN backs these up automatically whenever a full db backup is done. For db recovery the control file is the reference point used.

1.2.2 Datafiles

We know that each tablespace in a database consists of one or more datafiles which are physical files of the host(server).

Backups of datafiles are the basic blocks upon which db recovery is performed. While undo tablespace datafiles are a part of this set the temp files of temporary tablespace would be exempt.

1.2.3 Archived Redo Logs

Redo logs record all changes made to the database. The changes are recorded in the online redo log FIRST and THEN applied to the datafiles.

The database engine cycles through the online redo log groups using them in a circular manner overwriting the old contents with the new.

Hence archiving the used redo logs is absolutely essential for reconstructing the db in the event of a disaster. Once archived they can be backed up to other disks or on tape for long term storage. They can then be pressed into service for db recovery if called upon.

Note: The undo segments (of undo tablespace) are used to undo the effects of uncommitted transactions after all the archived redo logs have been applied to the datafiles.

The relevant background processes & physical/logical structures are schematically depicted here for clarity.

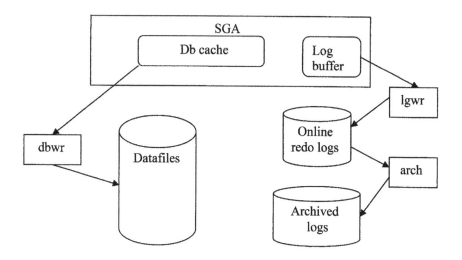

Figure 1-1 A subset of an operational Oracle database

1.3 Recovery Basics

Reconstructing or resurrecting the database from a backup is made up of 2 distinct sub-tasks: Restore & Recovery.

Restore: this is the first (and usually more time consuming) function of retrieving a copy of the database from a backup. Normally this backup would be housed in tape media.

Recovery: all the database changes preserved in the archived logs are applied to the database since the time of the backup (which has been restored).

The database can be successfully opened ONLY if the recovery process completes without errors. Once the DBA is able to open the database the world becomes a better place once again!

It is very strongly recommended that a validation of the enterprise backup & recovery strategy be done annually at the minimum. It is also not uncommon to have this process done every quarter in some organizations.

Lessons learned from these exercises will have to be incorporated subsequently in order to have a very high comfort level.

Chapter 1 Recapitulation

Backup is the set of processes to ensure the database data is archived securely to prevent any loss of data should some disaster strike.

Recovery is the set of processes aimed at salvaging or resurrecting the database data after a disaster has struck.

The importance of having a sound VALIDATED backup & recovery strategy in place need not be overstated.

Broadly we have 2 kinds of physical Oracle Database Backup and Recovery: RMAN & User-managed.

RMAN is the preferred solution for database backup and recovery.

An Oracle database backup essentially backs up controlfiles, datafiles & archived redo logs.

Reconstructing or resurrecting the database from a backup is made up of 2 distinct sub-tasks: Restore & Recovery.

Chapter 2 Objectives

- Disk & Tape Media
- Backup Formats
- Environment Components
- Flash Recovery Area

Chapter 2
RMAN Architecture

We know RMAN is a robust backup & recovery tool which is tightly integrated with the Oracle database engine. Let us briefly study its framework now.

2.1 Disk & Tape Media

RMAN can perform backups to disk or tape.
As a result it can restore backed up database files from either disk or tape.

Backing up data of Very Large Data Bases (VLDB) poses a serious challenge for a disk based solution. Tapes come in very handy in this scenario. Even for archiving or long term retention of data tapes present the perfect strategy. They can also be stored in remote locations for increased security. Maximum availability is assured even in the unfortunate event of database server crash or failure of disks.

RMAN can seamlessly work with various tape storage systems with the aid of Media Management Layer (MML) software. We will explore the two most common tape library environments later in chapter 4:

IBM's Tivoli Storage Manager & Veritas NetBackup

Oracle provides the sbttest utility as a simple mechanism to test the installation & configuration of the Media Manager. In the following example we are checking if RMAN can send a byte stream of a file to the Media Manager and receive it back. The diagnostic messages of this operation are captured in the log file.

Example: sbttest test.dbf -trace sbtio.log

This utility can be supplied several other switches as under:

$ sbttest

Error: backup file name must be specified
Usage: sbttest backup_file_name
          <-dbname database_name>
          <-trace trace_file_name>
          <-remove_before>
          <-no_remove_after>
          <-read_only>
          <-no_regular_backup_restore>
          <-no_proxy_backup>
          <-no_proxy_restore>
          <-file_type n>
          <-copy_number n>
          <-media_pool n>
          <-os_res_size n>
          <-pl_res_size n>
          <-block_size block_size>
          <-block_count block_count>
          <-proxy_file os_file_name bk_file_name
                  [os_res_size pl_res_size block_size block_count]>
          <-libname sbt_library_name>

The only required switch is the backup_file_name which is the backup file created by this program. After the operation completes this file will be removed.

2.2 Backup Formats

RMAN can backup database files as backup sets or image copies.

A backup set is always made in proprietary RMAN-specific format.
It is made up of units called backup pieces. Each such piece may hold one or more database files.

> RMAN tape backups can ONLY be in this format. These backup sets can be managed only by RMAN and are not available to any host OS.

Image copies are like OS replicas of database files. Though these can also be made using operating system commands like cp, dd etc. (in Unix) they need to be cataloged into the RMAN repository before use.

2.3 Environment Components

The target database is the structure on which RMAN performs various backup & recovery tasks.

The RMAN client is the command line interface (CLI) used by the DBA to input various native & SQL commands.

> RMAN can use either the target database controlfile or a separate entity called the **recovery catalog** as a repository to store the entire backup & recovery related information.

The contents of the control file are used in a circular manner. When all the available record slots are filled up the database can either enlarge the control file or overwrite the oldest records in a ring like fashion. The CONTROL_FILE_ RECORD_KEEP_TIME initialization parameter specifies the minimum age (in integer days) of a record before it can be reused. While the default value is 7 days it can take on a range from 0 (never expand) to 365 (maximum of a year). It can also be dynamically configured.

SQL> ALTER SYSTEM SET CONTROL_FILE_RECORD_KEEP_TIME = 30 SCOPE = BOTH;

The best practice is to house the repository in a recovery catalog rather than the target database control file. The recovery catalog is an external Oracle database which can be used to retain extended periods of backup historical information. There are also a few features of RMAN that necessitate the use of a recovery catalog. A good example of such a feature would be RMAN stored scripts which are DBA-created RMAN commands packaged as a capsule.

In a nocatalog situation if the controlfile is recreated all the RMAN repository information will get wiped out.

Please be aware that a single recovery catalog can act as the repository for multiple target databases. This is another major benefit of utilizing a separate catalog. You can register multiple target databases in a single recovery catalog if they do not have duplicate DBIDs. RMAN uses the DBID to distinguish one database from another. If needed DBID can be changed by running the DBNEWID utility.

Note that you can also register a single target database in multiple recovery catalogs.

Note: Standby databases can be backed up ONLY when a recovery catalog is employed.

The recovery catalog contains information like datafile and archived redo log backup sets and backup pieces, datafile and archived redo logs copies, tablespaces and datafiles of the target database, stored scripts, persistent RMAN configuration settings etc.

RMAN creates a snapshot control file, which is a consistent backup of the target database control file (snapcf_<dbname>.f in $ORACLE_HOME/dbs by default) when it performs a full resynchronization of the recovery catalog. This is the process of RMAN propagating information about the database structure, archived redo logs, backup sets, and datafile copies into the recovery catalog from the target database control file.

The command below calls the RMAN client attaching to both the target database & catalog database to execute the statements contained in the cmdfile.rcv file & redirecting the output to a log.

$ rman target/catalog rman/rwoman@rman4all cmdfile cmdfile.rcv log cmdfile.log

The dynamic view V$RMAN_STATUS has metadata about RMAN jobs in progress as well as completed.

2.4 Flash Recovery Area—Concept

In addition to enabling database flashback configuring the flash recovery area is markedly superior to other disk based backups.

Database files marked obsolete by RMAN with respect to the predefined retention policies are considered eligible for deletion and are deleted automatically when space pressure arises.

This also eliminates the need for DBA intervention and any human error thereof. The flash recovery area can be set up using a file system directory or Automatic Storage Management disk group as the container to hold the database files.

Note: You can NOT use any raw file system.

Two parameters need to be defined: firstly DB_RECOVERY_FILE_DEST_SIZE which is the disk quota (maximum space available) and then DB_RECOVERY_FILE_DEST denoting the actual destination (physical location).

Needless to say it is strongly recommended to place the flash recovery area in a separate disk storage away from active database files to eliminate any exposure to media failures that can wipe out both the areas.

Typically this area will hold control files, datafile copies, online redo logs & archived redo logs (not backed up to tape yet), flashback logs (if database is enabled for flashback) etc.

V$RECOVERY_FILE_DEST may be queried to obtain the information about this area.

LOG_ARCHIVE_DEST_10 will be used as DB_RECOVERY_FILE_DEST if no other local archiving destinations are specified (and recovery area is configured).

Chapter 2 Recapitulation

RMAN can perform backups to disk or tape.

RMAN can seamlessly work with various tape storage systems with the aid of Media Management Layer (MML) software.

RMAN can backup database files as backup sets or image copies.

The best practice is to house the repository in a recovery catalog rather than the target database control file.

You can register multiple target databases in a single recovery catalog if they do not have duplicate DBIDs. RMAN uses the DBID to distinguish one database from another.

For configuring the flash recovery area two parameters need to be defined: firstly DB_RECOVERY_FILE_DEST_SIZE which is the disk quota (maximum space available) and then DB_RECOVERY_FILE_DEST denoting the actual destination (physical location).

Chapter 3 Objectives

- Implement Recovery Catalog
- RMAN Client
- Persistent Configurations
- Stored Scripts
- Flash Recovery Area

Chapter 3
Setup & Configuration

RMAN connects to target databases ONLY through a dedicated server process. Even if the target database is configured for shared servers the DBA has to ensure RMAN obtains a dedicated server connection. This will avoid any attempt by RMAN to attach to a shared server dispatcher which would fail anyway.

How do we accomplish this? We will resort to a solution provided by Oracle Net naming services. In the tnsnames.ora file we can have 2 different service entries.

Suppose rmanelse is the value of SERVICE_NAMES initialization parameter for the target database.

```
RMANELSE_dedi =
  (description=
   (address=(protocol=tcp)(host= 192.168.203.11)(port1521))
   (connect_data=(service_name=RMANELSE)(server=dedicated))
  )

RMANELSE_shar =
  (description=
   (address=(protocol=tcp)(host= 192.168.203.11)(port1521))
   (connect_data=(service_name=RMANELSE)(server=shared))
  )
```

RMAN> connect target sys/r24rman@RMANELSE_dedi;

connected to target database: RMANELSE (DBID=1826602558)

RMAN> connect catalog rman/rwoman@rman4all;

connected to recovery catalog database

We can confirm this also from within the target database.

SQL> SELECT SERVER FROM V$SESSION WHERE USERNAME='RMAN';

SERVER

DEDICATED

We clearly understand the recovery catalog is distinctly superior as the RMAN repository of choice over the target database control file. Now let us create the catalog to service all our backup & recovery needs. The following workshop will step us through the entire process.

3.1 Workshop—Implement Recovery Catalog

Ideally the database housing the catalog should be running on a different server (in a different geographical location too) from the target database.

Please ensure the initialization parameter **remote_login_passwordfile** is set to the value of 'exclusive' for the target database. This will be used by the password file being created now. You can create the password file like this: ($ORACLE_HOME/dbs is the default location)

$ orapwd password=r24rman file=orapwRMANELSE force=y

Oracle Net connectivity should be available for both the target & catalog instances.

Step 1 Create the catalog database "RMAN4ALL". This database has a small footprint size on the host server. You may create an initialization parameter file (pfile) with some parameter values as under:

db_block_size=8192
db_file_multiblock_read_count=16
open_cursors=100
db_name=RMAN4ALL
background_dump_dest=/u01/app/oracle/admin/RMAN4ALL/bdump
core_dump_dest=/u01/app/oracle/admin/RMAN4ALL/cdump
user_dump_dest=/u01/app/oracle/admin/RMAN4ALL/udump
db_create_file_dest=+MY_DG2

```
db_create_online_log_dest_1=+MY_DG1
job_queue_processes=10
compatible=10.2.0.1.0
processes=50
sga_target=100000000
audit_file_dest=/u01/app/oracle/admin/RMAN4ALL/adump
pga_aggregate_target=11000000
undo_management=AUTO

$ export ORACLE_SID=RMAN4ALL

SQL> startup nomount

SQL> CREATE DATABASE rman4all
  CONTROLFILE REUSE
  LOGFILE
    GROUP 1 SIZE 10M,
    GROUP 2 SIZE 10M,
    GROUP 3 SIZE 10M
  ARCHIVELOG
  MAXLOGFILES 6
  MAXLOGHISTORY 100
  MAXDATAFILES 10
  MAXINSTANCES 2
  CHARACTER SET AL32UTF8
  NATIONAL CHARACTER SET AL16UTF16
  DATAFILE SIZE 500M AUTOEXTEND ON MAXSIZE UNLIMITED
  EXTENT MANAGEMENT LOCAL,
  SYSAUX DATAFILE SIZE 250M AUTOEXTEND ON MAXSIZE 500M
  DEFAULT TEMPORARY TABLESPACE TEMP_TS TEMPFILE SIZE 100M
  UNDO TABLESPACE UNDO_TS DATAFILE SIZE 250M
  USER SYS IDENTIFIED BY RMAN2U
  USER SYSTEM IDENTIFIED BY RMAN2U;
```

Note: In the above script db_create_file_dest set in the parameter file is the container for all the datafiles. We are also using ASM based disk storage for both the datafiles & the online redo logs.

You may update the parameter file with the actual location of the control file created like this:

control_files=("+MY_DG1/rman4all/controlfile/current.273.592851635")

SQL> $ORACLE_HOME/rdbms/admin/catalog.sql
SQL> $ORACLE_HOME/rdbms/admin/catproc.sql

Step 2 Create an exclusive tablespace for the catalog.

SQL> CREATE TABLESPACE RMANCAT DATAFILE SIZE 500M
EXTENT MANAGEMENT LOCAL UNIFORM SIZE 1M;

Step 3 Create an exclusive schema

SQL> CREATE USER RMAN IDENTIFIED BY RWOMAN
DEFAULT TABLESPACE RMANCAT TEMPORARY TABLESPACE TEMP;

SQL> ALTER USER RMAN QUOTA UNLIMITED ON RMANCAT;

SQL> GRANT **RECOVERY_CATALOG_OWNER** TO RMAN;

Note: This role is made up of these 11 privileges.
create type
create view
create table
alter session
create cluster
create session
create synonym
create trigger
create sequence
create procedure
create database link

Step 4 Attach to both the target & catalog databases

$ export ORACLE_SID=RMANLESE

RMAN> connect target;

connected to target database: RMANELSE (DBID=1826602558)

The dbid is a unique identification number assigned when the database is created. The DBA can query the dynamic V$DATABASE view or the RC_DATABASE recovery catalog view for this integer.

RMAN> connect catalog rman/rwoman@rman4all;

connected to recovery catalog database

Step 5 Now create the recovery catalog & register the target database

RMAN> **create catalog**;

recovery catalog created

Note: You can create the recovery catalog without connecting to target database also but for the next task of registering a connection has to be established with it.

RMAN> **register database**;

database registered in recovery catalog
starting full resync of recovery catalog
full resync complete

We will now find the snapshot controlfile snapcf_RMANELSE.f in the default location of $ORACLE_HOME/dbs. This file is used to resynchronize the recovery catalog with the target database control file.

Note: In a Real Application Clusters (RAC) environment you may also find as many snapshot controlfiles as the number of nodes/instances.

Using this 5 step process we have now successfully implemented the recovery catalog. Now we are ready to start backing up the database.
The following 53 views are installed in the recovery catalog:

RC_ARCHIVED_LOG
RC_BACKUP_ARCHIVELOG_DETAILS
RC_BACKUP_ARCHIVELOG_SUMMARY
RC_BACKUP_CONTROLFILE
RC_BACKUP_CONTROLFILE_DETAILS
RC_BACKUP_CONTROLFILE_SUMMARY

RC_BACKUP_COPY_DETAILS
RC_BACKUP_COPY_SUMMARY
RC_BACKUP_CORRUPTION
RC_BACKUP_DATAFILE
RC_BACKUP_DATAFILE_DETAILS
RC_BACKUP_DATAFILE_SUMMARY
RC_BACKUP_FILES
RC_BACKUP_PIECE
RC_BACKUP_PIECE_DETAILS
RC_BACKUP_REDOLOG
RC_BACKUP_SET
RC_BACKUP_SET_DETAILS
RC_BACKUP_SET_SUMMARY
RC_BACKUP_SPFILE
RC_BACKUP_SPFILE_DETAILS
RC_BACKUP_SPFILE_SUMMARY
RC_CHECKPOINT
RC_CONTROLFILE_COPY
RC_COPY_CORRUPTION
RC_DATABASE
RC_DATABASE_BLOCK_CORRUPTION
RC_DATABASE_INCARNATION
RC_DATAFILE
RC_DATAFILE_COPY
RC_LOG_HISTORY
RC_OFFLINE_RANGE
RC_PROXY_ARCHIVEDLOG
RC_PROXY_ARCHIVELOG_DETAILS
RC_PROXY_ARCHIVELOG_SUMMARY
RC_PROXY_CONTROLFILE
RC_PROXY_COPY_DETAILS
RC_PROXY_COPY_SUMMARY
RC_PROXY_DATAFILE
RC_REDO_LOG
RC_REDO_THREAD
RC_RESYNC
RC_RMAN_BACKUP_JOB_DETAILS
RC_RMAN_BACKUP_SUBJOB_DETAILS
RC_RMAN_BACKUP_TYPE
RC_RMAN_CONFIGURATION

RC_RMAN_OUTPUT
RC_RMAN_STATUS
RC_STORED_SCRIPT
RC_STORED_SCRIPT_LINE
RC_TABLESPACE
RC_TEMPFILE
RC_UNUSABLE_BACKUPFILE_DETAILS

> All of the recovery catalog views (except 4 of them) have their dynamic counterparts in the target database. The exceptions are understandably RC_CHECKPOINT, RC_RESYNC, RC_STORED_SCRIPT & RC_STORED_SCRIPT_LINE.

Please bear in mind any recovery catalog view will hold information about all the registered target databases unlike its single target database v$ equivalent.

Most of the recovery catalog views will include the columns DB_KEY and DBINC_KEY. This can facilitate joins between various recovery catalog views. RMAN identifies each registered target database uniquely by either the DB_KEY or the DBID. Each incarnation of the registered target database is uniquely recognized by DB_INC.

The primary keys of target database & recovery catalog views differ a little in structure. To illustrate the target database V$ARCHIVED_LOG view has the composite primary key made up of RECID and STAMP columns while the primary key of the recovery catalog RC_ARCHIVED_LOG view is AL_ KEY.

You can register multiple target databases in a single recovery catalog provided the DBIDs are unique. RMAN uses the DBID to uniquely identify each registered target database. Hence it is possible to register multiple target databases sharing the same database name!

However in duplicate dbid situations the DBA can register all the target databases in the same recovery catalog AFTER running the DBNEWID utility to change the dbid and/or db name.

Note: It is also possible a single target database is registered in multiple recovery catalogs for reasons of high availability.

```
$ nid

DBNEWID: Release 10.2.0.1.0—Production on Wed Aug 16 14:49:19 2006

Copyright (c) 1982, 2005, Oracle. All rights reserved.

Keyword         Description                     (Default)
--------------- ------------------------------- ------------
TARGET          Username/Password               (NONE)
DBNAME          New database name               (NONE)
LOGFILE         Output Log                      (NONE)
REVERT          Revert failed change            NO
SETNAME         Set a new database name only    NO
APPEND          Append to output log            NO
HELP            Displays these messages         NO

nid target=sys/<password> dbname=<newname> logfile=nid.log

Connected to database <dbname> (DBID=9999999999)

Changing database ID from <oldid> to <newid>
Changing database name from <oldname> to <newname>

    Datafile <filename> - dbid changed, wrote new name
    Control File <filename> - dbid changed, wrote new name

    Instance shut down

Database name changed to <newname>.
Modify parameter file and generate a new password file before restarting.
Database ID for database <newname> changed to 9999999999.
All previous backups and archived redo logs for this database are unusable.
Database has been shutdown, open database with RESETLOGS option.
Successfully changed database name and ID.
DBNEWID—Completed successfully.
```

3.2 RMAN Client

At the operating system prompt type rman. You will then see this:

$ rman

RMAN> connect target sys/r24rman@rmanelse;

connected to target database: RMANELSE (DBID=1826602558)

RMAN> connect catalog rman/rwoman@rman4all;

connected to recovery catalog database

RMAN connects to the target database as SYSDBA. To facilitate this you must either be the user who owns the oracle software or a member of the operating system DBA group.

Authentication can also be performed with a password file.
If the authentication fails RMAN exits with the ORA-01031 (insufficient privileges) error.

Most RMAN commands are terminated by a semicolon just like sqlplus.
An incomplete command without a semicolon terminator makes RMAN prompt for more lines with a line number.

RMAN> backup database
2> plus archivelog;

RMAN provides the useful command-line argument checksyntax to check syntactic correctness of various RMAN commands without executing them.

To leave the RMAN utility type exit to return to the OS.

RMAN> exit

$

$ rman checksyntax

RMAN> run (backup control file;)

RMAN-00558: error encountered while parsing input commands

RMAN-01006: error signalled during parse RMAN-02001: unrecognized punctuation symbol "("

RMAN> run { backup controlfile; }

The command has no syntax errors

From within RMAN you can execute sql statements also.

RMAN> sql 'alter system archive log current';

You can exit to the OS temporarily & return to RMAN by using host & exit command.

RMAN> host;

$ exit

exit
host command complete
RMAN>

You can redirect the screen output to a file by spooling it.

RMAN> spool log to 'bkup_incr_cum';

RMAN> backup incremental level 1 cumulative DATABASE format '+MY_DG1' tag 'incre_cum_bkup';

RMAN> spool log off

Spooling for log turned off

You can also direct the output to both the screen & a file using the 'tee' command.

$ rman | tee rman_oper.log

RMAN channels

A channel is a connection between RMAN and the database instance representing a stream of data for a device. Each connection spawns a dedicated server session on the target (or auxiliary) instance. This server session performs the actual work of backup, restore or recovery.

In this example we are allocating a channel to perform tape backup using the Tivoli media manager.

```
RMAN> run
{ allocate channel t1 type 'sbt_tape' parms
      'ENV=(TDPO_OPTFILE=/usr/tivoli/tsm/client/oracle/bin64/tdpo.opt)';
   backup database; }
```

For RMAN a disk channel is configured by default. After completing the job the channel is automatically released by RMAN. If the DBA configures or allocates multiple channels simultaneously for a single job RMAN can read from/write to multiple backup sets or image copies in parallel. Each such channel can perform work on a separate backup set or disk copy.

Tip: More the number of channels higher the degree of parallelism of job execution!

A similar concept is the PARALLELISM setting. This option allocates the number of automatic channels of the specified device type. In this example we indicate to RMAN to allocate as many channels as the number of devices for the tape storage system.

```
RMAN> configure device type sbt parallelism 5;
```

You can execute a file containing RMAN commands from the OS prompt by using the cmdfile clause. A logfile can also capture all the execution output.

```
$ rman cmdfile = <filename> log = <filename>
```

RMAN errors always start with RMAN-00569 at the top of the error stack.

```
RMAN-00571: ===========================================================

RMAN-00569: =========== ERROR MESSAGE STACK FOLLOWS =====

RMAN-00571: ===========================================================
```

3.3 Persistent Configuration Settings

The DBA can configure persistent RMAN settings which impact the backup, restore and maintenance operations. RMAN has several configuration settings with default values. Some of these may have to be modified to suit your particular environment. These configuration values persist until they are cleared or changed.

3.3.1 Displaying Current Settings

To display the current values simply do this:

RMAN> show all;

RMAN configuration parameters are:
CONFIGURE RETENTION POLICY TO REDUNDANCY 1; # default
CONFIGURE BACKUP OPTIMIZATION OFF; # default
CONFIGURE DEFAULT DEVICE TYPE TO DISK; # default
CONFIGURE CONTROLFILE AUTOBACKUP OFF; # default
CONFIGURE CONTROLFILE AUTOBACKUP FORMAT FOR DEVICE TYPE DISK TO '%F'; # default
CONFIGURE DEVICE TYPE DISK PARALLELISM 1 BACKUP TYPE TO BACKUPSET; # default
CONFIGURE DATAFILE BACKUP COPIES FOR DEVICE TYPE DISK TO 1; # default
CONFIGURE ARCHIVELOG BACKUP COPIES FOR DEVICE TYPE DISK TO 1; # default
CONFIGURE MAXSETSIZE TO UNLIMITED; # default
CONFIGURE ENCRYPTION FOR DATABASE OFF; # default
CONFIGURE ENCRYPTION ALGORITHM 'AES128'; # default
CONFIGURE ARCHIVELOG DELETION POLICY TO NONE; # default
CONFIGURE SNAPSHOT CONTROLFILE NAME TO
'/u01/app/oracle/product/10.2.0/dbs/snapcf_<dbname>.f'; # default

3.3.2 Configuring Various Settings

We will now configure a few common settings.

The following backs up database as compressed backup sets using tape storage media:

RMAN> configure device type sbt backup type to compressed backupset;

We can also enable automatic backup of the vital controlfile like this:

RMAN> configure controlfile autobackup on;
old RMAN configuration parameters:
CONFIGURE CONTROLFILE AUTOBACKUP OFF;
new RMAN configuration parameters:
CONFIGURE CONTROLFILE AUTOBACKUP ON;
new RMAN configuration parameters are successfully stored
starting full resync of recovery catalog
full resync complete

After every BACKUP command RMAN also backs up the control file and the server parameter file into its own backup set. The format string for this AUTOBACKUP must include ONLY the %F substitution variable.

The DBA can specify any location to hold this backup like an ASM disk group or the tape.

RMAN> configure controlfile autobackup for device type disk to '+MY_DG1';

RMAN> configure controlfile autobackup format for device type sbt to 'cfsp_auto_%F';

After the control file autobackup completes, the alert log of the target database will have an entry like this:

Sun June 4 08:30:15 2006

Starting control autobackup

Control autobackup written to SBT_TAPE device

     comment 'API Version 2.0, MMS Version 5.2.0.0',

     media 'TAPEPOOL2'

     handle 'c-288297259-20060528-04'

Any structual changes to the target database control file like adding a tablespace, renaming a datafile, dropping a logfile etc would trigger this autobackup.

SQL> ALTER DATABASE DROP LOGFILE GROUP 2;

Fri Jul 21 17:44:06 2006

Deleted Oracle managed file +MY_DG1/rmanelse/onlinelog/group_2.275.
593971735

Starting control autobackup

Control autobackup written to DISK device

> handle '/u01/app/oracle/admin/RMANELSE/aux_dest/c-1826602558-
> 20060721-01'

Completed: alter database drop logfile group 2

Fri Jul 21 17:51:04 2006

SQL> ALTER DATABASE ADD LOGFILE GROUP 2;

('/u01/app/oracle/admin/RMANELSE/aux_dest/onredo_1.log',

 '/u01/app/oracle/admin/RMANELSE/aux_dest/onredo_2.log') size 10M

Fri Jul 21 17:51:04 2006

Starting control autobackup

Control autobackup written to DISK device

> handle '/u01/app/oracle/admin/RMANELSE/aux_dest/c-1826602558-
> 20060721-02'

Completed: alter database add logfile group 2

('/u01/app/oracle/admin/RMANELSE/aux_dest/onredo_1.log',

 '/u01/app/oracle/admin/RMANELSE/aux_dest/onredo_2.log') size 10M

Fri Jul 21 17:52:03 2006

Note: Even when autobackup is off (default) any backup that includes datafile 1 (the system tablespace) automatically also includes the current control file.

> It is strongly recommended to enable the controlfile autobackup. This will also help in situations when the target database structural changes have not yet propagated to the recovery catalog.

We can also specify the backup format for both the disk & tape locations.

RMAN> configure channel device type sbt format 'orabkup_%U';

RMAN> configure channel device type disk format '+MY_DG1';

By default the default device type for RMAN is the DISK. When the BACKUP command is issued RMAN allocates channels only of the default device type. This can be overridden by manually allocating channels in a RUN block.

You can also direct RMAN to create all the backups on tape media like this.

RMAN> configure default device type to sbt;

The DBA can establish a channel to perform RMAN operations using Tivoli tape media.

RMAN> configure channel device type sbt parms
'ENV=(TDPO_OPTFILE=/usr/tivoli/tsm/client/oracle/bin64/tdpo.opt)';

You can configure the default backup type for disk or tape backups to one of BACKUPSET, COMPRESSED BACKUPSET or COPY. The default for DISK is BACKUPSET.

RMAN> configure backup type to copy;

Note: For sbt (tape) devices COPY is not a valid backup type.

By default the disk backups are created in the flash recovery area if configured. If no flash recovery area is available they would be stored in $ORACLE_HOME/dbs. The default format for backup filenames is the unique system generated %U.

Backup encryption for the entire target database is enabled by this:

RMAN> configure encryption for database on;

We can also turn on encryption on a tablespace basis.

RMAN> configure encryption for tablespace auxdata1, auxdata2 on;

Encryption algorithm is defined here.

RMAN> configure encryption alogorithm 'AES192';

The algorithm can be any one of **AES128, AES192 and AES256.**

By default RMAN creates the snapshot controlfile used to propagate the controlfile metadata into the recovery catalog under $ORACLE_HOME/dbs with the name snapcf_$ORACLE_SID.f. This can be altered as needed.

RMAN> configure snapshot controlfile name to
'/u01/app/oracle/admin/RMANELSE/snapcf.f';

The DBA can also exclude some tablespaces from being backed up using the BACKUP DATABASE command. Obviously the SYSTEM tablespace can NOT be excluded from the whole database backups.

RMAN> configure exclude for tablespace auxdata1, auxdata2;

What should be the retention policy for all the backups? You can specify a time window of recoverability (the earliest date to which the database needs to be reconstructed). This window is always in the form of (SYSDATE—past integer days).

RMAN> configure retention policy to recovery window of 30 days;

Above we are instructing RMAN to ensure all backups needed to recover the target database to any point in time in the last 30 days are retained.

Please be aware the smallest unit of retention for a backupset backup is the backup set and not a single backup piece.

The DBA can parallelize RMAN jobs by setting the PARALLELISM parameter. This will determine the number of automatic channels allocated of the specified device type.

You can change the parallelism for a device type to n as under:

RMAN> configure device type disk parallelism 2;

RMAN> configure device type sbt parallelism 5;

Note: This parallelism affects ONLY the automatic channels. Regardless of this setting manual channels can be allocated.

You can revert any configuration setting to its default value by using the clear clause:

RMAN> configure controlfile autobackup clear;

In the above example we have disabled the autobackup of the target database control file.

Note: CONFIGURE should NOT be used within a RUN block.

3.4 Stored Scripts

Like PL/SQL stored procedures we can also store RMAN commands (any command permissible within a run block) as scripts in the recovery catalog. While a global script can execute against any registered target database a local script is associated with just one registered target database.

Now let us create a stored script.

RMAN> connect target sys/r24rman@racdb;

connected to target database: RACDB (DBID=559768190)

RMAN> connect catalog rman/rwoman@rman4all;

connected to recovery catalog database

RMAN> create global script hot_incr_bkup from file 'open_script';

script commands will be loaded from file open_script
created global script hot_incr_bkup

How do you see what this script does?

RMAN> print script hot_incr_bkup;

printing stored global script: hot_incr_bkup
{
backup incremental level 0 DATABASE format 'db_%d_%U' tag
'Incremental_0';
backup archivelog all format 'arch_%d_%U' delete input;
}

The DBA can execute the script in a run block.

RMAN> run { execute script hot_incr_bkup; }

The DBA can modify an existing script also.

RMAN> replace global script hot_incr_bkup from file 'open_script';

You can delete the script like this.

RMAN> delete global script 'hot_incr_bkup';

You can obtain a listing of all the stored scripts also.

RMAN> list script names;

List of Stored Scripts in Recovery Catalog
    Global Scripts

        Script Name
        Description
        ----
        hot_incr_bkup

The DBA can also wipe out all the repository metadata from the recovery catalog. The command used is UNREGISTER DATABASE. All the stored scripts are also deleted.

Tip: Delete all the backups & copies of the target database before unregistering.

RMAN> connect target sys/r24rman@racdb;

connected to target database: RACDB (DBID=559768190)

RMAN> connect catalog rman/rwoman@rman4all;

connected to recovery catalog database

RMAN> unregister database;

database name is "RACDB" and DBID is 559768190

Do you really want to unregister the database (enter YES or NO)? yes
database unregistered from the recovery catalog

Recovery Catalog Resynchronization

RMAN automatically performs the resynchronization of the recovery catalog with the target database control file as needed. However some scenarios may demand a manual resynchronization. These include:

- Recovery Catalog Unavailability

- Infrequent Backups: This is relevant if numerous online redo logs get archived during the period between the target database backups. If the target database control file ages out the archived log records even before RMAN propagates this information into the recovery catalog we will have the undesirable situation of the recovery catalog being out of sync with the target database control file.

- Changes to the physical structures of the target database: Altering/ Creating/Dropping tablespaces and/or datafiles. Any changes to redo log archive parameters.

Tip: For the target database control file ensure CONTROL_FILE_RECORD_ KEEP_TIME is longer than the interval between backups or resynchronizations. Setting this to zero is dangerous as the control file backup records may be reused before RMAN recovery catalog resynchronization.

RMAN> resync catalog;

starting full resync of recovery catalog
full resync complete

3.5 Flash Recovery Area—Setup

Ideally the flash recovery area should be large enough to contain datafile copies, online redo logs, control files, archived redo logs (yet to be swept to tape) etc. For the scenario of scarce disk availablilty this area must have room to hold those archived logs not backed up to tape. Flashback logs used for rewinding the database are also maintained in this location.

Note:
In a RAC environment the flash recovery area must be located on a cluster file system, ASM or a shared NFS mounted directory. Also the location and disk quota must be the same across all instances.

Wokshop—Configure Flash Recovery Area

For the target database we specify the upper limit of this area first like this:

SQL> ALTER SYSTEM SET DB_RECOVERY_FILE_DEST_SIZE = 100G
SCOPE = BOTH SID = '*';

(For a RAC database this is set across all the instances by means of '*')

After assigning the quota now we define the physical location to hold this area.

SQL> ALTER SYSTEM SET DB_RECOVERY_FILE_DEST = '+dg1'
SCOPE = BOTH SID = '*';

In the above example an Automatic Storage Management (ASM) disk group named dg1 is defined as the Flash Recovery Area. The DBA has to ensure the ASM instance is up & running with the diskgroup mounted.

Note: Generally this recovery area is +dg1/<dbname>/flashback.

The dynamic V$RECOVERY_FILE_DEST view has information about the Flash Recovery Area location, space allocated, and space that can be reclaimed by deletion of obsolete files.

```
SQL>column name format a10 head Name
SQL>column space_limit format 999,999,999,999 head Space_max
SQL>column space_used format 999,999,999,999 head Space_used
SQL>column space_reclaimable format 999,999,999,999 head Space_reclaim
SQL>column number_of_files format 999 head Files

SQL> SELECT * FROM V$RECOVERY_FILE_DEST;
Name          Space_max        Space_used    Space_reclaim Files
----------    ----------------  ----------------  ---------------- -----
+MY_DG1   2,147,483,648   187,809,792             0    44
```

You are aware the database engine automatically manages the space in the Flash Recovery Area. The deletion of files is governed both by the retention policy defined (considered obsolete) and the sweeping of database files to tape (hence not needed to be retained on disk). Just like tablespaces a warning alert for reclaimable space less than 15% and a critical alert for reclaimable space less than 3% are written to both the DBA_OUTSTANDING_ALERTS table and alert log.

After the target database has been configured for the Flash Recovery Area it is imperative for the DBA to define the retention policy as well.

Chapter 3 Recapitulation

RMAN connects to target databases ONLY through a dedicated server process.

All of the recovery catalog views (except 4 of them) have their dynamic counterparts in the target database. The exceptions are understandably RC_CHECKPOINT, RC_RESYNC, RC_STORED_SCRIPT & RC_STORED_SCRIPT_LINE.

You can register multiple target databases in a single recovery catalog provided the DBIDs are unique.

RMAN provides the useful command-line argument 'checksyntax' to check syntactic correctness of various RMAN commands without executing them.

A channel is a connection between RMAN and the database instance representing a stream of data for a device. This server session performs the actual work of backup, restore or recovery.

RMAN errors always start with RMAN-00569 at the top of the error stack.

The DBA can configure persistent RMAN settings which impact the backup, restore and maintenance operations. These configuration values persist until they are cleared or changed.

After every BACKUP command RMAN also backs up the control file and the server parameter file into its own backup set if the controlfile autobackup is enabled.
It is strongly recommended to enable the controlfile autobackup. This will also help in situations when the target database structural changes have not yet propagated to the recovery catalog.

By default RMAN creates the snapshot controlfile used to propagate the controlfile metadata into the recovery catalog under $ORACLE_HOME/dbs with the name snapcf_$ORACLE_SID.f.

Like PL/SQL stored procedures we can also store RMAN commands (any command permissible within a run block) as scripts in the recovery catalog.

RMAN automatically performs the resynchronization of the recovery catalog with the target database control file as needed.

For the target database control file ensure CONTROL_FILE_RECORD_ KEEP_TIME is longer than the interval between backups or resynchronizations. Setting this to zero is dangerous as the control file backup records may be reused before RMAN recovery catalog resynchronization.

Ideally the flash recovery area should be large enough to contain datafile copies, online redo logs, control files, archived redo logs (yet to be swept to tape) etc.

To configure the flash recovery area 2 parameters need to be defined: DB_RECOVERY_FILE_DEST_SIZE first and then DB_RECOVERY_FILE_ DEST.

Chapter 4 Objectives

- TDP & RMAN Integration
- NetBackup & RMAN Integration
- Troubleshooting
- Secure Backup

Chapter 4
Media Management

In this chapter we will discuss the 2 most commonly employed Media Management systems in conjunction with RMAN. Conceptually this can be shown by the following diagram:

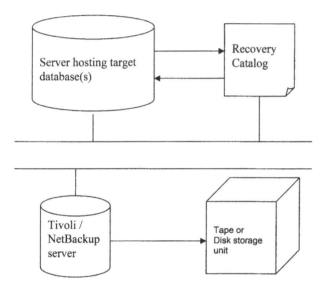

Figure 4-1 RMAN & media managers
Note: TCP/IP is the network communication layer between the NetBackup server and the NetBackup client(s).

4.1 Tivoli Storage Manager

This is a very popular media manager offered by IBM. RMAN can be directly linked with this media system through the database agent called **Tivoli Data Protection (TDP)** for Oracle.

4.1.1 Setup

Tivoli Storage Manager is a separately licensed product that provides storage management services in a multi-platform environment.

TDP for Oracle acts as the interface to the Tivoli Storage Manager server. TDP interfaces with RMAN and performs Oracle backups to the Tivoli Storage Manager server.

TDP also supports backup and restore operations in a LAN-free environment. Data moves over the storage area network (SAN) to a SAN-attached storage device via the Tivoli Storage Manager Storage Agent. In this scenario Network bottlenecks & overheads are greatly avoided. In fact this even enables the Tivoli Storage Manager server to accept a greater number of simultaneous client requests.

The pre-existing conditions for installing TDP are the configuration of Tivoli Storage Manager server version 5.1 (or later) & installation of Tivoli Storage Manager API version 5.1 (or later).

The Storage Administrator will have to execute the following tasks also after TDP is installed:

- Define the TDP options in the tdpo.opt file
- Register the TDP node with a Tivoli Storage Manager server
- Define the Tivoli Storage Manager options in the dsm.opt and dsm.sys files
- Specify the Tivoli Storage Manager policy requirements
- Initialize the password on a Tivoli Storage Manager server

The default folder of TDP for Oracle (64-bit) is /usr/tivoli/tsm/client/oracle/bin64. Tivoli Storage Manager API (64-bit) would be installed in /usr/tivoli/tsm/client/api/bin64. (On AIX this file is called libApiTSM64.a). We also have a command line backup/archive client named dsmc to perform certain administrative functions on the Tivoli Storage Manager server.

A Tivoli Storage Manager storage agent (dsmagent) will have to be running on the server hosting the target databases.

Some of the key options that can be set in the tdpo.opt file are:

- dsmi_log—this is the directory that contains the TDP error log (tdpoerror.log).

- tdpo_fs—specifies a file space name on the Tivoli Storage Manager server for the TDP backup, delete and restore operations. The default file space name is adsmorc. With multiple target databases this option can be used to back up each one of them to its own file space.

- tdpo_node—this is the TDP node name used during operations with the Tivoli Storage Manager server.

For 'redirected' restores (restore of data from one Oracle database server to another Oracle database server) the value of the tdpo_node option in the tdpo.opt file on the destination Oracle server must match the value on the source Oracle server. TDP, Command Line Backup/Archive Client Interface and the Tivoli Storage Manager API must be at the same levels on both the servers as well.

The Storage Administrator can define some options in the Tivoli Storage Manager client system options file (dsm.sys by default). The 2 key options are servername (Tivoli Storage Manager server) and nodename (host with TDP installation). This file would be found in the directory where the Tivoli Storage Manager API is installed.

4.1.2 RMAN Integration

Oracle must be linked into TDP to communicate with the Tivoli Storage Manager server. We can do this by creating symbolic links to the media manager library (**libobk**) file. This file is a shared library module used by RMAN.

Note: Contrary to the general misconception the target database(s) need NOT be shutdown before the linking.

This example assumes we are using 64-bit Oracle binaries.
cd $ORACLE_HOME/lib

Note: the name of this libobk file is dependent upon the platform.

```
AIX      : ln -s /usr/lib/libobk64.a libobk.a
HP-UX : ln -s /usr/lib/pa20_64/libobk.sl libobk.sl
Solaris  : ln -s /usr/lib/sparcv9/libobk.so libobk.so
Linux    : ln -s /usr/lib/libobk64 libobk
```

The file in /usr/lib/subfolder is in turn linked to its physical library counterpart under /usr/tivoli/tsm/client/oracle/bin64/.

The TDP options file tdpo.opt contains options that control its functioning. The ONLY environment variable of TDP in a RMAN script is the fully qualified path name to this option file.

```
run
{
allocate channel t1 type 'sbt_tape' parms
'ENV=(TDPO_OPTFILE =/usr/tivoli/tsm/client/oracle/bin64/tdpo.opt)';
allocate channel t2 type 'sbt_tape' parms
'ENV=(TDPO_OPTFILE =/usr/tivoli/tsm/client/oracle/bin64/tdpo.opt)';
backup
filesperset 10
format 'db_%d_%U'
(database);
}
```

$ cat tdpo.opt

```
DSMI_ORC_CONFIG      /usr/tivoli/tsm/client/ba/bin/dsm.opt
DSMI_LOG             /usr/tivoli/tsm/client/oracle/bin64
TDPO_NODE            < nodename >
TDPO_PSWDPATH        /usr/tivoli/tsm/client/oracle/bin64
TDPO_OWNER           oracle
```

Note: If the storage agent licence (agent.lic) file is not found in /usr/tivoli/tsm/client/oracle/bin64 ($install_dir) RMAN will not be able to initialize the media layer.

To help troubleshoot a TDP trace file can be generated. This can be done just by adding the following lines to your tdpo.opt file:
tdpo_trace_flags orclevel0 orclevel1 orclevel2

tdpo_trace_file /usr/tivoli/tsm/client/oracle/bin64/tdpo.out

4.1.3 Utilites

2 utilities are provided with TDP: **tdpoconf** and **tdposync**.

The tdpoconf utility is used for password maintenance and general setup.
Two arguments are available for tdpoconf:
PASSWord—this creates an encrypted password file TDPO.Nodename.
SHOWENVironment—this outputs information about the Tivoli Storage
Manager API and the Tivoli Storage Manager server.

$ tdpoconf

ANU0100E Incomplete command:
IBM Tivoli Storage Manager for Databases:
Data Protection for Oracle
Version 5, Release 2, Level 0.0
(C) Copyright IBM Corporation 1997, 2003. All rights reserved.

TDPOCONF SHOWENVironment
[-TDPO_OPTfile=filename] (default: $install_dir/tdpo.opt)
[-OUTFile=filename]

TDPOCONF PASSWord
[-TDPO_OPTfile=filename] (default: $install_dir/tdpo.opt)

TDPOCONF HELP

$ tdpoconf showenv

IBM Tivoli Storage Manager for Databases:
Data Protection for Oracle
Version 5, Release 2, Level 0.0
(C) Copyright IBM Corporation 1997, 2003. All rights reserved.

DATA PROTECTION FOR ORACLE INFORMATION
Version: 5
Release: 2
Level: 0

Sublevel: 0
Platform: 64bit TDP Oracle AIX

TSM SERVER INFORMATION
Server Name: < servername >
Server Address: < serveraddress >
Server Type: AIX-RS/6000
Server Port: 1500
Communication Method: TCP/IP

SESSION INFORMATION
Owner Name: oracle
Node Name: < nodename >
Node Type: TDP Oracle AIX
DSMI_DIR: /usr/tivoli/tsm/client/api/bin64
DSMI_ORC_CONFIG: /usr/tivoli/tsm/client/ba/bin/dsm.opt
TDPO_OPTFILE: /usr/tivoli/tsm/client/oracle/bin64/tdpo.opt
Password Directory: /usr/tivoli/tsm/client/oracle/bin64
Compression: FALSE

The tdposync utility is used to delete the Oracle backups on the Tivoli Storage Manager server which are not in the RMAN catalog. This allows you to repair any discrepancies between them by resynchronizing. Removing unwanted objects in the Tivoli Storage Manager storage reclaims space.

Note: syncdb is the only switch available to tdposync utility.

CAUTION! **The deletion process is irreversible.**

$ tdposync

ANU0100E Incomplete command:
IBM Tivoli Storage Manager for Databases:
Data Protection for Oracle
Version 5, Release 2, Level 0.0
(C) Copyright IBM Corporation 1997, 2003. All rights reserved.
TDPOSYNC SYNCdb
[-NUMCATalogs=number] (default: 1)
[-TDPO_OPTfile=filename] (default: $install_dir/tdpo.opt)

Now let us also look at what the command line backup/archive client interface **dsmc** can do for us.

$ dsmc
IBM Tivoli Storage Manager
Command Line Backup/Archive Client Interface
  Client Version 5, Release 3, Level 0.0
  Client date/time: 06/06/06 09:47:01
(c) Copyright by IBM Corporation and other(s) 1990, 2004. All Rights Reserved.
Node Name: < nodename >
Session established with server < >: AIX-RS/6000
  Server Version 5, Release 3, Level 2.0
  Server date/time: 06/06/06 09:47:01 Last access: 06/02/06 09:34:25

tsm>?
The following help topics are available.
Enter the number of the desired help topic or 'q' to quit,
'd' to scroll down, 'u' to scroll up.

      0—Summary of Changes for TSM Version 5.3
      1—Using Commands
      2—Select from the commands listed below:
      3—ARCHIVE
      4—BACKUP GROUP
      5—BACKUP IMAGE
      6—BACKUP NAS
      7—BACKUP WAS
      8—CANCEL PROCESS
      9—CANCEL RESTORE
      10—DELETE ACCESS
      11—DELETE ARCHIVE
      12—DELETE BACKUP
      13—DELETE FILESPACE
      14—DELETE GROUP
      15—EXPIRE
      16—HELP
      17—INCREMENTAL
      18—LOOP
      19—MACRO
      20—MONITOR PROCESS

21—PREVIEW
22—QUERY ACCESS
23—QUERY ARCHIVE
24—QUERY BACKUP
25—QUERY BACKUPSET
26—QUERY FILESPACE
27—QUERY GROUP
28—QUERY IMAGE
29—QUERY INCLEXCL
30—QUERY MGMTCLASS
31—QUERY NODE
32—QUERY OPTIONS
33—QUERY RESTORE
34—QUERY SCHEDULE
35—QUERY SESSION
36—QUERY SYSTEMINFO
37—QUERY WAS
38—RESTART RESTORE
39—RESTORE
40—RESTORE BACKUPSET
41—RESTORE GROUP
42—RESTORE IMAGE
43—RESTORE NAS
44—RESTORE WAS
45—RETRIEVE
46—SCHEDULE
47—SELECTIVE
48—SET ACCESS
49—SET PASSWORD
50—SET WASPASSWORD
51—Using Processing Options
52—Select from processing options below.
53—ARCHMC
54—ARCHSYMLINKASFILE
55—ASNODENAME
56—AUTOMOUNT
57—CHANGINGRETRIES
58—CLASS
59—CLUSTERNODE
60—COLLOCATEBYFILESPEC

61—COMMMETHOD
62—COMMRESTARTDURATION
63—COMMRESTARTINTERVAL
64—COMPRESSALWAYS
65—COMPRESSION
66—CONSOLE
67—DATEFORMAT
68—DEFAULTSERVER
69—DELETEFILES
70—DESCRIPTION
71—DETAIL
72—DIRMC
73—DIRSONLY
74—DISKBUFFSIZE
75—DOMAIN
76—DOMAIN.IMAGE
77—DOMAIN.NAS
78—EDITOR
79—ENABLELANFREE
80—ENCRYPTIONTYPE
81—ENCRYPTKEY
82—ERRORLOGMAX
83—ERRORLOGNAME
84—ERRORLOGRETENTION
85—EXCLUDE OPTIONS
86—FILELIST
87—FILENAME
88—FILESONLY
89—FOLLOWSYMBOLIC
90—FROMDATE
91—FROMNODE
92—FROMOWNER
93—FROMTIME
94—GROUPNAME
95—GROUPS
96—GUITREEVIEWAFTERBACKUP
97—HTTPPORT
98—IFNEWER
99—IMAGETOFILE
100—IMAGETYPE

101—INACTIVE
102—INCLEXCL
103—INCLUDE OPTIONS
104—INCRBYDATE
105—INCREMENTAL
106—LANFREECOMMMETHOD
107—LANFREESHMPORT
108—LANFREETCPPORT
109—LARGECOMMBUFFERS
110—LATEST
111—LOCALBACKUPSET
112—LOCATION
113—MAILPROG
114—MAKESPARSEFILE
115—MANAGEDSERVICES
116—MAXCMDRETRIES
117—MEMORYEFFICIENTBACKUP
118—MODE
119—MONITOR
120—NASNODENAME
121—NFSTIMEOUT
122—NODENAME
123—NOPROMPT
124—NUMBERFORMAT
125—OPTFILE
126—PASSWORD
127—PASSWORDACCESS
128—PASSWORDDIR
129—PICK
130—PITDATE
131—PITTIME
132—POSTSCHEDULECMD/POSTNSCHEDULECMD
133—PRESCHEDULECMD/PRENSCHEDULECMD
134—PRESERVELASTACCESSDATE
135—PRESERVEPATH
136—QUERYSCHEDPERIOD
137—QUIET
138—REMOVEOPERANDLIMIT
139—REPLACE
140—RESOURCEUTILIZATION

141—RETRYPERIOD
142—REVOKEREMOTEACCESS
143—SCHEDCMDDISABLED
144—SCHEDLOGMAX
145—SCHEDLOGNAME
146—SCHEDLOGRETENTION
147—SCHEDMODE
148—SCROLLLINES
149—SCROLLPROMPT
150—SERVERNAME
151—SESSIONINITIATION
152—SHMPORT
153—SHOWMEMBERS
154—SNAPSHOTCACHESIZE
155—SNAPSHOTROOT
156—SUBDIR
157—TAPEPROMPT
158—TCPADMINPORT
159—TCPBUFFSIZE
160—TCPCLIENTADDRESS
161—TCPCLIENTPORT
162—TCPNODELAY
163—TCPPORT
164—TCPSERVERADDRESS
165—TCPWINDOWSIZE
166—TIMEFORMAT
167—TOC
168—TODATE
169—TOTIME
170—TXNBYTELIMIT
171—TYPE
172—USERS
173—V2ARCHIVE
174—VERBOSE
175—VERIFYIMAGE
176—VIRTUALFSNAME
177—VIRTUALMOUNTPOINT
178—VIRTUALNODENAME
179—WASEXPHOME
180—WASHOME

181—WASNDHOME
182—WASNODE
183—WASTYPE
184—WASUSER
185—WEBPORTS
186—Glossary
187—Select from the messages listed below:
188—ANS200—ANS219
189—ANS220—ANS239
190—ANS240—ANS259
191—ANS260—ANS279
192—ANS280—ANS299
193—ANS300—ANS319
194—ANS320—ANS339
195—ANS340—ANS359
196—ANS400—ANS419
197—ANS420—ANS439
198—ANS1000—ANS1019
199—ANS1020—ANS1039
200—ANS1040—ANS1059
201—ANS1060—ANS1079
202—ANS1080—ANS1099
203—ANS1100—ANS1119
204—ANS1120—ANS1139
205—ANS1140—ANS1159
206—ANS1160—ANS1179
207—ANS1180—ANS1199
208—ANS1200—ANS1219
209—ANS1220—ANS1239
210—ANS1240—ANS1259
211—ANS1260—ANS1279
212—ANS1280—ANS1299
213—ANS1300—ANS1319
214—ANS1320—ANS1339
215—ANS1340—ANS1359
216—ANS1360—ANS1379
217—ANS1380—ANS1399
218—ANS1400—ANS1419
219—ANS1420—ANS1439
220—ANS1440—ANS1459

221—ANS1460—ANS1479
222—ANS1480—ANS1499
223—ANS1500—ANS1519
224—ANS1520—ANS1539
225—ANS1540—ANS1559
226—ANS1560—ANS1579
227—ANS1600—ANS1619
228—ANS1620—ANS1639
229—ANS1780—ANS1799
230—ANS1800—ANS1819
231—ANS1820—ANS1839
232—ANS1840—ANS1859
233—ANS1860—ANS1879
234—ANS1880—ANS1899
235—ANS1900—ANS1919
236—ANS1920—ANS1939
237—ANS1940—ANS1959
238—ANS1960—ANS1979
239—ANS1980—ANS1999
240—ANS2000—ANS2019
241—ANS2020—ANS2039
242—ANS2040—ANS2059
243—ANS2600—ANS2619
244—ANS2620—ANS2639
245—ANS2700—ANS2719
246—ANS2720—ANS2739
247—ANS2740—ANS2759
248—ANS2760—ANS2779
249—ANS2780—ANS2799
250—ANS2800—ANS2819
251—ANS2820—ANS2839
252—ANS3000—ANS3019
253—ANS3400—ANS3419
254—ANS4000—ANS4019
255—ANS4020—ANS4039
256—ANS4040—ANS4059
257—ANS4500—ANS4519
258—ANS4900—ANS4919
259—ANS4980—ANS4999
260—ANS5000—ANS5019

261—ANS5020—ANS5039
262—ANS5080—ANS5099
263—ANS5120—ANS5139
264—ANS5140—ANS5159
265—ANS5160—ANS5179
266—ANS5180—ANS5199
267—ANS5200—ANS5219
268—ANS5220—ANS5239
269—ANS6000—ANS6019
270—ANS7420—ANS7439
271—ANS7500—ANS7519
272—ANS7520—ANS7539
273—ANS7540—ANS7559
274—ANS7560—ANS7579
275—ANS7640—ANS7659
276—ANS7660—ANS7679
277—ANS7700—ANS7719
278—ANS8000—ANS8019
279—ANS8020—ANS8039
280—ANS8040—ANS8059
281—ANS8060—ANS8079
282—ANS8500—ANS8519
283—ANS8560—ANS8579
284—ANS8760—ANS8779
285—ANS8780—ANS8799
286—ANS8800—ANS8819
287—ANS8820—ANS8839
288—ANS8840—ANS8859
289—ANS8920—ANS8939
290—ANS8940—ANS8959
291—ANS9000—ANS9019
292—ANS9020—ANS9039
293—ANS9040—ANS9059
294—ANS9060—ANS9079
295—ANS9080—ANS9099
296—ANS9100—ANS9119
297—ANS9120—ANS9139
298—ANS9140—ANS9159
299—ANS9160—ANS9179
300—ANS9180—ANS9199

301—ANS9200—ANS9219
302—ANS9220—ANS9239
303—ANS9240—ANS9259
304—ANS9260—ANS9279
305—ANS9280—ANS9299
306—ANS9300—ANS9319
307—ANS9340—ANS9359
308—ANS9400—ANS9419
309—ANS9420—ANS9439
310—ANS9440—ANS9459
311—ANS9460—ANS9479
312—ANS9500—ANS9519
313—ANS9520—ANS9539
314—ANS9540—ANS9559
315—ANS9600—ANS9619
316—ANS9640—ANS9659
317—ANS9720—ANS9739
318—ANS9740—ANS9759
319—ANS9760—ANS9779
320—ANS9780—ANS9799
321—ANS9800—ANS9819
322—ANS9820—ANS9839
323—ANS9840—ANS9859
324—ANS9860—ANS9879
325—ANS9880—ANS9899
326—ANS9900—ANS9919
327—ANS9920—ANS9939
328—ANS9940—ANS9959
329—ANS9960—ANS9979
330—ANS9980—ANS9999
331—ANS10880—ANS10899
332—ANS11140—ANS11159
333—ANS11440—ANS11459
334—ANS11460—ANS11479
335—ANS13040—ANS13059
336—ANS16400—ANS16419

We also can use the administrative interface to check on our TDP traffic to the TSM server.

```
$ dsmadmc -se=sta -id=status -pa=statuspw "q se"
IBM Tivoli Storage Manager
Command Line Administrative Interface—Version 5, Release 3, Level 0.0
(c) Copyright by IBM Corporation and other(s) 1990, 2004. All Rights Reserved.

Session established with server < servername >: AIX-RS/6000
  Server Version 5, Release 3, Level 2.0
  Server date/time: 06/23/06 09:19:26 Last access: 00/00/00 00:00:00
ANS8000I Server command: 'q se'
```

Sess Number	Comm. Method	Sess State	Wait Time	Bytes Sent	Byte Recvd	Sess Type	Platform	Client Name
1	Tcp/Ip	Run	0 S	668	1.4 K	Server	AIX-RS/-	< ... > 6000
4	Tcp/Ip	IdleW	50 S	216.5 K	271.9 K	Server	AIX-RS/-	< ... > 6000
371	Tcp/Ip	SendW	0 S	15.3 G	845	Node	TDP Ora-< ... >	
1,089	Tcp/Ip	IdleW	0 S	1.5 M	3.9 M	Server	AIX-RS/-	< ... > 6000
13,001	Tcp/Ip	Run	0 S	132	158	Admin	AIX	STATUS

```
ANS8002I Highest return code was 0.
```

4.2 NetBackup

Many Oracle data centers also employ this product from Veritas (now Symantec Corporation).

4.2.1 Setup

NetBackup server, NetBackup client and NetBackup for Oracle database agent are the 3 components making up the NetBackup ecosystem.

NetBackup server is the master node that manages the entire array of backup & recovery operations. The server hosting the target Oracle database runs NetBackup client software. NetBackup for Oracle database agent (also on the database host) is the Media Management Layer that integrates with RMAN.

RMAN initiates a backup request and then the NetBackup media server connects to NetBackup for Oracle on the client and transfers the data to secondary media. For a restore the data flows in the opposite direction.

The latest Netbackup version for the server, client & database agent is 6.0. The Storage administrator must install the NetBackup v6.0 server or client software as appropriate (after this the/usr/openv/netbackup directory will come into being).

The following requirements have to be met for the NetBackup server and client software:

- The NetBackup server software is installed and functional on the NetBackup server.

- The NetBackup client software is installed on the client (host for the target database) where databases have to be backed up.

- Versions of the NetBackup client and NetBackup for Oracle database agent (also on the database host) should be identical.

Backup media is configured in a Media Manager or a disk storage system. A NetBackup policy & schedule need to be defined for Oracle backups.

A NetBackup policy defines the backup criteria for a specific group of one or more clients. These criteria include:

- Storage unit and media to use

- Policy attributes

- Backup schedules

- Clients to be backed up

- Backup templates or script files to be run on the clients

A full backup schedule must also be created to enable scheduled backup operations on the client. Each NetBackup policy has its own set of schedules. The schedule initiates automatic and user created backups.

An Oracle backup requires an Application Backup schedule, which is created automatically when an Oracle policy is set up. The schedule manages the backup operations. Also you have to set up one or more automatic backup schedules for NetBackup to perform automatic scheduled backups.

With the initial NetBackup for Oracle installation sample scripts are available in the install_path/netbackup/ext/db_ext/oracle/samples/rman location. Some of these include cold_database_backup.sh, hot_database_backup.sh, database_restore.sh, pit_database_restore.sh etc.

4.2.2 RMAN Integration

Now we must link Netbackup with Oracle.
The default location for the NetBackup API library is /usr/openv/netbackup/bin.

To link automatically (as the oracle user) execute /usr/openv/netbackup/bin/oracle_link.
The output of this operation is written to/tmp/make_trace.<pid>.

We can also manually link the media manager library file as under:
cd $ORACLE_HOME/lib

As the Oracle user create the link.

```
ln -s /usr/openv/netbackup/bin/libobk.a64 libobk.a       (AIX)
ln -s /usr/openv/netbackup/bin/libobk.sl64 libobk.sl     (HP-UX)
ln -s /usr/openv/netbackup/bin/libobk.so64.1 libobk.so   (Solaris)
ln -s /usr/openv/netbackup/bin/libobk.so libobk          (Linux)
```

Again we are using 64-bit Oracle binaries here.

After linking you can invoke RMAN to communicate to the NetBackup server. In this example we use the send command to specify the policy and server for a database backup. This is done after all channels are allocated and before the actual backup command.

```
run {
allocate channel t1 type 'SBT_TAPE';
allocate channel t2 type 'SBT_TAPE';
```

send 'NB_ORA_POLICY=<policy name>, NB_ORA_SERV=<server name>';
backup
(database format 'db_%d_%U');
}

These are the key environment variables used by NetBackup for Oracle:

NB_ORA_SERV   (name of the NetBackup server)
NB_ORA_POLICY   (name of the defined Oracle policy)
NB_ORA_CLIENT   (name of the NetBackup client hosting the target database)
NB_ORA_SCHED   (name of the defined Oracle schedule)

We can backup databases easily by setting up NetBackup schedules for automatic backups.

4.2.3 Utilities

Netbackup provides the bplist command to browse Oracle backups.
The command returns a list of backup file names.
You should be logged into either the master server or to the client as root to run bplist.
In this example bplist searches all the Oracle backups for a client named veritas:

/usr/openv/netbackup/bin/bplist -C veritas -t 4 -R/

While the -t 4 switch denotes the Oracle backups we use the -R argument to indicate the default number (999) of directory levels to search.

The DBA can also perform redirected restores. Only the user on the client receiving the backup image can initiate this kind of restore.

The NetBackup server must be configured to allow a redirected restore. The administrator can remove restrictions for all clients by creating the following file on the Netbackup master server:/usr/openv/netbackup/db/altnames/No.Restrictions.

Alternatively to restrict clients to restore only from certain other clients the file /usr/openv/netbackup/db/altnames/client_name can be created.

While accomplishing this ensure the NB_ORA_CLIENT environment variable is set to the hostname of the source client.

A NetBackup for Oracle user can create an Oracle client bp.conf file in the Oracle user's home directory on the NetBackup for Oracle client host. When a NetBackup for Oracle operation is started, the user's bp.conf file is searched before the master configuration file (/usr/openv/netbackup/bp.conf) on the client. Any option found at the user level overrides the same option's setting at the master level.

The following options can be set in the user's bp.conf file:
BPBACKUP_POLICY—specifies the name of the policy to use for the Oracle backup
BPBACKUP_SCHED—is the name of the Application Backup schedule to use
CLIENT_NAME—specifies the name of the Oracle client
CLIENT_READ_TIMEOUT—is the number of seconds that the Oracle client initially waits for a response from the NetBackup server. The default is 900.
SERVER—specifies the name of the NetBackup master server.
VERBOSE—is the level to control debugging information in the logs

A higher value is more suited for systematic troubleshooting. While the default value of 0 is sufficient you can also set the debugging level to 1, 2, 3, 4, or 5. At level 5 logging is the most detailed.

Here are some general tips to help troubleshoot NetBackup for Oracle errors:

The **bphdb** NetBackup for Oracle binary should exist in/usr/openv/netbackup/bin. (This resides on the client and is used by the NetBackup scheduler to start the backups.)
Check that both the NetBackup server and client software are working properly. The NetBackup client must be running the same version of software as the NetBackup server.
Also NetBackup for Oracle database agent should match NetBackup client version wise.

Check that the following NetBackup log directories exist with 777 permissions.

On the client: bpdbsbora, dbclient, bphdb and bpcd
(example:/usr/openv/netbackup/logs/bphdb)
On the NetBackup master server: bprd and bpdbm
On the host with the storage unit: bpbrm and bptm

If NetBackup and RMAN are able to communicate a log is created in /usr/openv/netbackup/logs/dbclient.

4.3 Media Manager Troubleshooting

This section applies to any media manager employed in general.

The DBA can look for a file named 'sbtio.log' which is the third party media management software log. This may be located in the directory specified in the USER_DUMP_DEST initialization parameter or $ORACLE_HOME/dbs. This contains vendor specific information written by the media management software. However this log will not contain any Oracle database or RMAN errors.

The following error implies problems with the libobk file of the media manager. Ensure the correct file exists and that you have linked it as illustrated in the previous sections.

```
RMAN-00571: ===========================================
RMAN-00569: ========= ERROR MESSAGE STACK FOLLOWS ======
RMAN-00571: ===========================================
RMAN-03009: failure of allocate command on c1 channel at 08/12/2006 17:16:54
ORA-19554: error allocating device, device type: SBT_TAPE, device name:
ORA-27211: Failed to load Media Management Library
```

In the event of a media manager error RMAN always signals the ORA-19511 error. RMAN will display the error passed back to it by the media manager. You may have to contact the media management vendor to resolve such issues. Look at the example below.

```
RMAN-00571: ===========================================
RMAN-00569: ========= ERROR MESSAGE STACK FOLLOWS ======
RMAN-00571: ===========================================
RMAN-03009: failure of backup command on t1 channel at 08/04/2006 13:18:19
ORA-19506: failed to create sequential file, name="07d36ecp_1_1", parms=""
ORA-27007: failed to open file
SVR4 Error: 2: No such file or directory
Additional information: 7005
Additional information: 1
ORA-19511: Error received from media manager layer, error text:
SBT error = 7005, errno = 2, sbtopen: system error
```

The simplest way to confirm the proper configuration of the media manager & RMAN integration is to allocate a channel. If RMAN does not report any error then we can determine the media manger is correctly configured to work with RMAN.

```
RMAN> run
{ allocate channel t1 type 'sbt_tape' parms
  'ENV=(TDPO_OPTFILE =/usr/tivoli/tsm/client/oracle/bin64/tdpo.opt)';
  release channel t1; }
```

```
RMAN> run
{ allocate channel t2 type 'SBT_TAPE';
  send 'NB_ORA_POLICY=<policyname>, NB_ORA_SERV=<servername>';
  release channel t2; }
```

4.4 Secure Backup

Oracle Secure Backup is a new solution that provides data protection through file system backup to tape. RMAN can work with the Oracle Secure Backup SBT interface for backing up Oracle databases. All major tape libraries are supported.

Oracle Secure Backup can back up all kinds of files on the file system including non-database files. The DBA can use the command-line interface called obtool to perform administration tasks.

To enable RMAN to perform backups using Oracle Secure Backup the SBT library must be located on the server running the target database.

This is the brief outline of RMAN operating with Oracle Secure Backup:

- Start RMAN, allocate a SBT channel and execute a BACKUP or RESTORE command.

- The channel allocation spawns a server session on the target database.

- This session submits the backup or restore job through the Oracle Secure Backup SBT library.

- Oracle Secure Backup creates the backup or restore job with a unique identifier.

- Oracle Secure Backup creates or restores the backup pieces.

The default Oracle Secure Backup home directory is /usr/local/oracle/backup for UNIX and Linux. The SBT library path is the lib subdirectory of this home which is linked to the library in /lib or /usr/lib directory. RMAN can locate the SBT library automatically once this home folder is specified.

Please be aware the Oracle Secure Backup maintains its own catalog independently of the RMAN recovery catalog for storing metadata about the RMAN backup pieces.

Chapter 4 Recapitulation

TDP interfaces with RMAN and performs Oracle backups to the Tivoli Storage Manager server.

The ONLY environment variable of TDP in a RMAN script is the fully qualified path name to this option file.

The tdposync utility is used to delete the Oracle backups on the Tivoli Storage Manager server which are not in the RMAN catalog.

NetBackup for Oracle database agent (also on the database host) is the Media Management Layer that integrates with RMAN.

These are the key environment variables used by NetBackup for Oracle:

NB_ORA_SERV   (name of the NetBackup server)
NB_ORA_POLICY   (name of the defined Oracle policy)
NB_ORA_CLIENT   (name of the NetBackup client hosting the target database)
NB_ORA_SCHED   (name of the defined Oracle schedule)

The simplest way to confirm the proper configuration of the media manager & RMAN integration is to allocate a channel. If RMAN does not report any error then we can determine the media manger is correctly configured to work with RMAN.

In the event of a media manager error RMAN always signals the ORA-19511 error.

Oracle Secure Backup is a new solution that provides data protection through file system backup to tape.

RMAN can work with the Oracle Secure Backup SBT interface for backing up Oracle databases.

Chapter 5 Objectives

- Backup Concepts
- Incremental Backups
- Basic Listing
- Backup Encryption
- Tuning Backup
- Implement Backup

Chapter 5
Backup

In this chapter we will dwell on various database backup concepts like formats, objects that can be backed up, full & incremental backups, reports etc. A detailed workshop at the end will reinforce all the concepts presented here.

RMAN backups differ from user-managed backups in a very fundamental manner in that the database is NOT placed in or out of hot backup modes using ALTER DATABASE/TABLESPACE BEGIN BACKUP or ALTER DATABASE/TABLESPACE END BACKUP.

For a database in noarchivelog mode a consistent backup can be performed ONLY after a normal shutdown. After the database has been shut down normally it can be mounted for RMAN to begin the backup. This backup can later be restored and the database opened without any need of media recovery.

5.1 Backup Sets

Unless otherwise specified RMAN always defaults to backup set as its internal file storage format. We know a backup set is maintained in a proprietary RMAN-specific format. The backup set is the smallest unit of RMAN backup. Only those backup sets completed successfully are recorded in the repository.

Please note datafiles and archivelogs are never lumped in the same backup set. Also a file cannot span backup sets.

If no location is designated RMAN stores the backup sets in the OS dependent default location. On Unix & Linux this is $ORACLE_HOME/dbs.

Tape backups are always stored as backup sets.

In the command below we instruct RMAN to backup the entire database to an ASM disk group as backup set.

RMAN> backup database format '+dgroup1';

5.2 Image Copies

Image copy files can only exist on disk. These are byte-for-byte duplicates which can be created by RMAN or any OS utility. Here %U denotes a unique name generated by RMAN for the backup.

RMAN> backup as copy database format '/orabkup/%U';

$ cp/oradata/cust_data_01.dbf/orabkup/cust_data_01.dbf

Now we can add metadata about this copied file to the RMAN repository.

RMAN> catalog datafilecopy '/orabkup/cust_data_01.dbf';

5.3 Backup Objects

RMAN can back up the following database objects or structures: database, tablespace, datafile, control file, spfile and archived redo log. Let us discuss each of these in a detailed manner. But let us briefly talk about the various common formats used to determine the location and/or names of the backups.

RMAN by default generates unique filenames. The format used is '%U' which holds different meanings for backup pieces and image copies.

For a backup piece %U is the combination of three sub formats: %u_%p_%c
%c is the copy number of the backup piece (value 1).
%p specifies the piece number in the backup set. Starts at 1 and is incremented by 1 as each backup piece gets created.
%u is an 8-character name made up of compressed notation of the backup set or image copy number and the time the backup set or image copy was created.

Some other formats include:

%d denotes the target database name.
%F is made up of the target database DBID, timestamp of backup creation and a hexadecimal sequence. This is the ONLY allowable representation for

controlfile autobackups. It is of the form c-DBID-YYYYMMDD-xx (xx ranges from 00 to 'FF').

5.3.1 Controlfile/spfile

The DBA can back up the control file with the database in mounted or open state. RMAN can obtain a read-consistent version of the control file by using a special structure called snapshot control file.

> If CONFIGURE CONTROLFILE AUTOBACKUP is ON then RMAN automatically backs up the control file and server parameter file after every backup and after database structural changes. Also the control file and server parameter file are stored together in a separate backup set/piece.

If the autobackup feature is not enabled (default behavior) then we can manually back up the control file in one of the following ways:

RMAN> backup current controlfile;

RMAN> backup datafile 1;

Note: The system tablespace file is always the crucial file# 1 in the Oracle database. Whenever system tablespace is backed up the control file is automatically backed up too.

RMAN> backup database;

The server parameter file (spfile) can be backed up but not the initialization parameter file.

RMAN> backup spfile;

TIP: For backing up the server parameter file ensure the database instance was started using spfile but not initialization parameter file.

5.3.2 Datafile

Now let us backup an individual datafile of any tablespace.

RMAN> backup datafile '/oradata/cust_data_01.dbf';

5.3.3. Tablespace

An entire tablespace can be backed up as under:

RMAN> backup tablespace users, tools;

Note: Though locally-managed temporary tablespaces can not be backed up RMAN will recreate them during database recovery.

5.3.4 Database

We have seen before how to back up an entire database.

RMAN> backup database;

5.3.5 Archived Redo Logs

If the target database is in archivelog mode the DBA can back up the archived redo logs like this:

RMAN> backup archivelog all delete input;

In the above command RMAN will first switch out of the current online redo log group and then perform the backup of all archived logs. After successfully backing up the input files the archive destination will be purged.

Note: Any log_archive _format defined should necessarily include the thread variable (%t) and the resetlogs variable(%r) besides the sequence variable(%s). This is true even for non RAC databases where the thread variable has no relevance!

The DBA can also specify an archived log or a range of archived logs to be backed up. While ALL indicates all the available archived logs you can restrict the scope by using any of these sub clauses. Broadly we can think along System Change Number (SCN), log sequence # and timestamp of archiving. For the RAC database archived logs generated by a particular instance can also be denoted by the thread variable.

FROM SCN =
UNTIL SCN =
FROM SEQUENCE =
SEQUENCE =

UNTIL SEQUENCE =
FROM TIME =
UNTIL TIME =
THREAD =

How do you also instruct RMAN to backup the entire target database AND the archived redo logs?

RMAN> connect target;

RMAN> connect catalog rman/rwoman@rman4all;

RMAN> backup database plus archivelog;

RMAN will archive the current redo log, backup all the archived logs, backup the database and then once again archive the current redo log and back up all the archived logs that may have been generated during this backup period.

This is better demonstrated by the following output.

RMAN> backup as copy database plus archivelog;

```
Starting backup at 19-JUN-06
current log archived
allocated channel: ORA_DISK_1
channel ORA_DISK_1: sid=149 instance=RACDB1 devtype=DISK
channel ORA_DISK_1: starting archive copy
input archive log thread=1 sequence=72 recid=14 stamp=593532289
output   filename=+MY_DG1/racdb/archivelog/2006_06_19/thread_1_seq_
72.275.593554777 recid=17 stamp=593554783
channel ORA_DISK_1: archivelog copy complete, elapsed time: 00:00:09
channel ORA_DISK_1: starting archive copy
input archive log thread=2 sequence=39 recid=16 stamp=593554769
output   filename=+MY_DG1/racdb/archivelog/2006_06_19/thread_2_seq_
39.276.593554785 recid=18 stamp=593554789
channel ORA_DISK_1: archivelog copy complete, elapsed time: 00:00:08
channel ORA_DISK_1: starting archive copy
input archive log thread=1 sequence=71 recid=11 stamp=593452827
output   filename=+MY_DG1/racdb/archivelog/2006_06_19/thread_1_seq_
71.277.593554795 recid=19 stamp=593554797
```

channel ORA_DISK_1: archivelog copy complete, elapsed time: 00:00:06
channel ORA_DISK_1: starting archive copy
input archive log thread=2 sequence=38 recid=13 stamp=593516106
output filename=+MY_DG1/racdb/archivelog/2006_06_19/thread_2_seq_
38.280.593554813 recid=22 stamp=593554815
channel ORA_DISK_1: archivelog copy complete, elapsed time: 00:00:05
Finished backup at 19-JUN-06

Starting backup at 19-JUN-06
using channel ORA_DISK_1
channel ORA_DISK_1: starting datafile copy
input datafile fno=00001 name=+MY_DG2/racdb/datafile/system.256.
562151237
output filename=+MY_DG1/racdb/datafile/system.281.593554819 tag=TAG
20060619T202017 recid=2 stamp=593554884
channel ORA_DISK_1: datafile copy complete, elapsed time: 00:01:08
channel ORA_DISK_1: starting datafile copy
input datafile fno=00003 name=+MY_DG2/racdb/datafile/sysaux.257.562151243
output filename=+MY_DG1/racdb/datafile/sysaux.282.593554887 tag=TAG
20060619T202017 recid=3 stamp=593554940
channel ORA_DISK_1: datafile copy complete, elapsed time: 00:00:56
channel ORA_DISK_1: starting datafile copy
input datafile fno=00005 name=+MY_DG2/racdb/datafile/example.265.
562151495
output filename=+MY_DG1/racdb/datafile/example.283.593554945 tag=
TAG20060619T202017 recid=4 stamp=593554956
channel ORA_DISK_1: datafile copy complete, elapsed time: 00:00:16
channel ORA_DISK_1: starting datafile copy
input datafile fno=00008 name=+MY_DG2/racdb/datafile/soe.272.562263577
output filename=+MY_DG1/racdb/datafile/soe.284.593554961 tag=TAG2006
0619T202017 recid=5 stamp=593554973
channel ORA_DISK_1: datafile copy complete, elapsed time: 00:00:16
channel ORA_DISK_1: starting datafile copy
input datafile fno=00002 name=+MY_DG2/racdb/datafile/undotbs1.258.
562151247
output filename=+MY_DG1/racdb/datafile/undotbs1.285.593554979 tag=TAG
20060619T202017 recid=6 stamp=593554992
channel ORA_DISK_1: datafile copy complete, elapsed time: 00:00:17
channel ORA_DISK_1: starting datafile copy
input datafile fno=00004 name=+MY_DG2/racdb/datafile/users.259.562151249

output filename=+MY_DG1/racdb/datafile/users.286.593554995 tag=TAG 20060619T202017 recid=7 stamp=593555005
channel ORA_DISK_1: datafile copy complete, elapsed time: 00:00:17
channel ORA_DISK_1: starting datafile copy
input datafile fno=00006 name=+MY_DG2/racdb/datafile/undotbs2.267. 562154137
output filename=+MY_DG1/racdb/datafile/undotbs2.287.593555013 tag=TAG 20060619T202017 recid=8 stamp=593555024
channel ORA_DISK_1: datafile copy complete, elapsed time: 00:00:17
channel ORA_DISK_1: starting datafile copy
copying current control file
output filename=+MY_DG1/racdb/controlfile/backup.288.593555029 tag=TAG 20060619T202017 recid=9 stamp=593555033
channel ORA_DISK_1: datafile copy complete, elapsed time: 00:00:09
channel ORA_DISK_1: starting datafile copy
input datafile fno=00007 name=+MY_DG2/racdb/datafile/flow_1.271.562196855
output filename=+MY_DG1/racdb/datafile/flow_1.289.593555037 tag=TAG 20060619T202017 recid=10 stamp=593555038
channel ORA_DISK_1: datafile copy complete, elapsed time: 00:00:03
channel ORA_DISK_1: starting full datafile backupset
channel ORA_DISK_1: specifying datafile(s) in backupset
including current SPFILE in backupset
channel ORA_DISK_1: starting piece 1 at 19-JUN-06
channel ORA_DISK_1: finished piece 1 at 19-JUN-06
piece handle=+MY_DG1/racdb/backupset/2006_06_19/nnsnf0_tag20060619t 202017_0.290.593555043 tag=TAG20060619T202017 comment=NONE
channel ORA_DISK_1: backup set complete, elapsed time: 00:00:04
Finished backup at 19-JUN-06

Starting backup at 19-JUN-06
current log archived
using channel ORA_DISK_1
channel ORA_DISK_1: starting archive copy
input archive log thread=1 sequence=73 recid=24 stamp=593555048
output filename=+MY_DG1/racdb/archivelog/2006_06_19/thread_1_seq_ 73.293.593555061 recid=25 stamp=593555063
channel ORA_DISK_1: archivelog copy complete, elapsed time: 00:00:04
channel ORA_DISK_1: starting archive copy
input archive log thread=2 sequence=40 recid=23 stamp=593555046

output   filename=+MY_DG1/racdb/archivelog/2006_06_19/thread_2_seq_
40.294.593555067 recid=26 stamp=593555066
channel ORA_DISK_1: archivelog copy complete, elapsed time: 00:00:01
Finished backup at 19-JUN-06

The DBA can also create a base level 0 backup (as backupset) of the database
specifying an ASM disk group for both the datafiles & the archived logs. Here
RMAN is directed to delete the archived logs after they are backed up. Remember
the incremental clause does not apply to archived logs.

RMAN> backup incremental level 0 database format '+MY_DG1' plus archivelog
format '+MY_DG1' delete input;

Note: Archived logs and datafiles are never placed together in any backup set.

5.3.6 Other Backup Features

You can also parallelize the backup operation as under:

RMAN> run
{ allocate channel t1 device type sbt;
  allocate channel t2 device type sbt;
  allocate channel t3 device type sbt;
  allocate channel t4 device type sbt;
  backup datafile 1,2,3,4; }

In the above example the 4 allocated channels simultaneously backup those 4
different datafiles (channel t1 backs up datafile 1, channel t2 backs up datafile 2
etc) to 4 distinct tape drives.

RMAN names the default disk channel as ORA_DISK_1. If parallelism is
enabled the channels are serially numbered from 1 to the PARALLELISM value.
If PARALLELISM is set to 3 then the disk channels are ORA_DISK_1,
ORA_DISK_2 and ORA_DISK_3.

Employing archived redo log failover RMAN can backup archived logs even
when some archived logs are not available on a few destinations or some
destinations have corrupted archived logs. RMAN needs just one good copy of
any archived log sequence for a given thread.

For backup sets RMAN can multiplex files meaning multiple files from disk are concurrently read and then written to one backup set.

RMAN> backup
  (datafile 1,2,3,4 channel ORA_DISK_1)
  (datafile 5,6,7,8 channel ORA_DISK_2);

Note: You can NOT multiplex image copies.

Can we backup the backupset? The answer is in the affirmative. You can backup any backup set created on disk. The DBA can copy backup sets between disks or copy them to tape with properly configured/allocated tape channel.

Note: Backup sets can NOT be backed up as image copies.

Using the BACKUP BACKUPSET command RMAN can perform some housekeeping to optimize disk space utilization. Disk backups older than a fortnight can be swept to tape.

RMAN> backup device type sbt backupset completed before 'sysdate -14' delete input;

You can back up existing image copies of database files as backup sets.

RMAN> backup as backupset copy of tablespace auxdata;

RMAN can assign a user-designated name better known as 'tag' to backup sets and image copies during the backup operation. The maximum allowable tag length is 30 bytes. Typically you will direct RMAN to restore backups specifying a tag.

Uniqueness of tags is not enforced by RMAN as multiple backup sets or image copies can share the same tag. If RMAN does have a conflict due to the same tag held by different backups while restoring datafiles it will restore the most recent backup of them all provided the specified requirements are met.

RMAN can generate long term backups for vaulting. If the LOGS option is used RMAN will also save all the archived logs needed for the recovery of this long term backup. For an online backup the LOGS clause is mandatory to perform recovery.

An end date or the FOREVER clause may be used to determine the length of retention. The backup is not considered obsolete until the end of such a period.

RMAN> backup database keep until time "to_date('15-AUG-2007', 'dd-mon-yyyy')" nologs;

Please be aware KEEP FOREVER can NOT be used in conjunction with the LOGS option as RMAN will have to retain all the archived redo logs indefinitely.

5.3.7 Block Corruption & Recovery

RMAN can check both physical(media) & logical corruption of datafiles. Any logical corruption reported by RMAN is logged in the database alert log file.

The backup operation will complete successfully only if RMAN finds the total number of physical and logical corruptions is less than the value dictated by the MAXCORRUPT parameter. RMAN populates the dynamic V$DATABASE_BLOCK_CORRUPTION view with the corrupt blocks information.
SQL> desc V$DATABASE_BLOCK_CORRUPTION

Name	Null?	Type
FILE#		NUMBER
BLOCK#		NUMBER
BLOCKS		NUMBER
CORRUPTION_CHANGE#		NUMBER
CORRUPTION_TYPE		VARCHAR2(9)

Though no actual backup is performed you can confirm all database files are eligible to be backed up by using the VALIDATE clause.

RMAN> backup validate check logical database;

RMAN> blockrecover corruption list;

The above operation will check all the datafiles for physical and logical corruption as also the presence of those files in the expected locations. Having updated V$DATABASE_BLOCK_CORRUPTION RMAN can recover all those corrupted blocks. You could also make RMAN include the archived logs.

RMAN> backup validate check logical database archivelog all;

Starting backup at 26-AUG-06
allocated channel: ORA_DISK_1
channel ORA_DISK_1: sid=26 devtype=DISK
channel ORA_DISK_1: starting full datafile backupset
channel ORA_DISK_1: specifying datafile(s) in backupset
input datafile fno=00001 name=+MY_DG1/rmanelse/datafile/system.279.596679619
input datafile fno=00003 name=+MY_DG1/rmanelse/datafile/sysaux.289.596679669
input datafile fno=00005 name=+MY_DG1/rmanelse/datafile/example.276.596679707
input datafile fno=00002 name=+MY_DG1/rmanelse/datafile/undotbs1.298.596679719
input datafile fno=00004 name=+MY_DG1/rmanelse/datafile/users.304.596679735
input datafile fno=00006 name=+MY_DG1/rmanelse/datafile/auxdata.281.596679751
channel ORA_DISK_1: backup set complete, elapsed time: 00:02:26
channel ORA_DISK_1: starting archive log backupset
channel ORA_DISK_1: specifying archive log(s) in backup set
input archive log thread=1 sequence=54 recid=132 stamp=599508457
channel ORA_DISK_1: backup set complete, elapsed time: 00:00:02
Finished backup at 26-AUG-06

Starting blockrecover at 26-AUG-06
allocated channel: ORA_SBT_TAPE_1
channel ORA_SBT_TAPE_1: sid=24 devtype=SBT_TAPE
channel ORA_SBT_TAPE_1: Oracle Secure Backup
allocated channel: ORA_SBT_TAPE_2
channel ORA_SBT_TAPE_2: sid=42 devtype=SBT_TAPE
channel ORA_SBT_TAPE_2: Oracle Secure Backup
allocated channel: ORA_SBT_TAPE_3
channel ORA_SBT_TAPE_3: sid=14 devtype=SBT_TAPE
channel ORA_SBT_TAPE_3: Oracle Secure Backup
using channel ORA_DISK_1

starting media recovery
media recovery complete, elapsed time: 00:00:01

Finished blockrecover at 26-AUG-06

5.3.8 Recovery Area

The occupants of the Recovery Area like full and incremental backup sets, control file autobackups, archived logs, datafile copies etc. can also be backed up by RMAN. However bear in mind flashback logs, the current control file and online redo logs are never backed up.

RMAN> backup db_recovery_file_dest;

(Recovery Area is synonymous with db_recovery_file_dest).

This area can be backed up ONLY to tape.

If no FORMAT option is specified for disk backups RMAN will create backup sets and image copies in the flash recovery area with Oracle Managed Files (OMF) names. The control file autobackups can also be placed here if no destination is configured for it. The recovery area is also the container for archived redo logs when the parameter LOG_ARCHIVE_DEST_n is set to 'LOCATION=USE_DB_RECOVERY_FILE_DEST'. While restoring archived logs with SET ARCHIVELOG DESTINATION not being used to supersede this location RMAN restores all of them to the flash recovery area.

When RMAN recovers the target database or performs FLASHBACK DATABASE the restored archived redo logs for media recovery are staged in the flash recovery area. After completing the recovery RMAN removes them from this location.

Note: The archived redo logs in the flash recovery area are named in OMF format independent of any the LOG_ARCHIVE_FORMAT initialization parameter setting.

5.4 Incremental Backups

The ability of RMAN to perform incremental backups is a very COMPELLING argument in its favor for employing RMAN based enterprise business continuity solutions. Incremental backups have several benefits to offer as under:

- Downsizing the backup window both in terms of time & space consumed
- Elimination of network bandwidth bottlenecks

- Recovering changes even after NOLOGGING database operations

TIP: Since archiving of redo logs will NOT capture nologging changes incremental backups can be pressed into database restore & recovery service by the DBA effectively under such conditions.

Incremental backups can be at only two levels: 0 or 1. A level 0 incremental backup is the ground zero framework for subsequent incremental backups. This is just like a full database backup but differs from it in that a full backup can NOT be used later for performing incremental updates.

> A level 1 incremental backup can be either **differential** (default) or **cumulative**. In a differential incremental backup all blocks changed after the last incremental backup at level 1 or 0 are backed up. In a cumulative incremental backup all blocks changed after the last incremental backup at level 0 are backed up.

Now let us perform the base backup of the entire target database which will back up all the data blocks.

RMAN> backup incremental level 0 database tag 'weekly_incrbase_bkup';

Note: You can associate a meaningful case insensitive name tag (upto 30 characters long) with a backup.

After level 0 we perform the level 1 differential incremental backup of the database:

RMAN> backup incremental level 1 database;

The DBA can also perform cumulative incremental backups which naturally consume more space & time but will enable faster database restore & recovery by decreasing the number of differential incremental backups that need to be applied.

RMAN> backup incremental level 1 cumulative database;

We can now browse through the detailed output of performing incremental backups.

$ export ORACLE_SID=RMANELSE

RMAN> connect target;

connected to target database: RMANELSE (DBID=1826602558)

RMAN> connect catalog rman/rwoman@rman4all;

connected to recovery catalog database

RMAN> set encryption identified by 'rman2secure' only;

executing command: SET encryption

RMAN> backup incremental level 0 DATABASE format '+MY_DG1' plus archivelog format '+MY_DG1' delete input;

Starting backup at 30-JUN-06
current log archived
allocated channel: ORA_DISK_1
channel ORA_DISK_1: sid=29 devtype=DISK
channel ORA_DISK_1: starting archive log backupset
channel ORA_DISK_1: specifying archive log(s) in backup set
input archive log thread=1 sequence=1 recid=1 stamp=594469675
input archive log thread=1 sequence=2 recid=3 stamp=594472768
input archive log thread=2 sequence=1 recid=2 stamp=594472766
channel ORA_DISK_1: starting piece 1 at 30-JUN-06
channel ORA_DISK_1: finished piece 1 at 30-JUN-06
piece handle=+MY_DG1/rmanelse/backupset/2006_06_30/annnf0_tag2006
0630t111932_0.287.594472775 tag=TAG20060630T111932 comment=NONE
channel ORA_DISK_1: backup set complete, elapsed time: 00:00:16
channel ORA_DISK_1: deleting archive log(s)
archive log filename=/u01/app/oracle/admin/RMANELSE/arch/1_1_593971715
.dbf recid=1 stamp=594469675
archive log filename=/u01/app/oracle/admin/RMANELSE/arch/1_2_593971715
.dbf recid=3 stamp=594472768
archive log filename=/u01/app/oracle/admin/RMANELSE/arch/2_1_593971715
.dbf recid=2 stamp=594472766
Finished backup at 30-JUN-06

Starting backup at 30-JUN-06
using channel ORA_DISK_1

channel ORA_DISK_1: starting incremental level 0 datafile backupset
channel ORA_DISK_1: specifying datafile(s) in backupset
input datafile fno=00001 name=+MY_DG1/rmanelse/datafile/system.304
.593971515
input datafile fno=00003 name=+MY_DG1/rmanelse/datafile/sysaux.281
.593971515
input datafile fno=00005 name=+MY_DG1/rmanelse/datafile/example.282
.593971515
input datafile fno=00002 name=+MY_DG1/rmanelse/datafile/undotbs1.286
.593971515
input datafile fno=00004 name=+MY_DG1/rmanelse/datafile/users.283
.593971515
channel ORA_DISK_1: starting piece 1 at 30-JUN-06
channel ORA_DISK_1: finished piece 1 at 30-JUN-06
piece handle=+MY_DG1/rmanelse/backupset/2006_06_30/nnndn0_tag2006
0630t111950_0.292.594472791 tag=TAG20060630T111950 comment=NONE
channel ORA_DISK_1: backup set complete, elapsed time: 00:03:45
channel ORA_DISK_1: starting incremental level 0 datafile backupset
channel ORA_DISK_1: specifying datafile(s) in backupset
including current control file in backupset
including current SPFILE in backupset
channel ORA_DISK_1: starting piece 1 at 30-JUN-06
channel ORA_DISK_1: finished piece 1 at 30-JUN-06
piece handle=+MY_DG1/rmanelse/backupset/2006_06_30/ncsnn0_tag2006
0630t111950_0.262.594473021 tag=TAG20060630T111950 comment=NONE
channel ORA_DISK_1: backup set complete, elapsed time: 00:00:08
Finished backup at 30-JUN-06

Starting backup at 30-JUN-06
current log archived
using channel ORA_DISK_1
channel ORA_DISK_1: starting archive log backupset
channel ORA_DISK_1: specifying archive log(s) in backup set
input archive log thread=1 sequence=3 recid=5 stamp=594473024
input archive log thread=2 sequence=2 recid=4 stamp=594473024
channel ORA_DISK_1: starting piece 1 at 30-JUN-06
channel ORA_DISK_1: finished piece 1 at 30-JUN-06
piece handle=+MY_DG1/rmanelse/backupset/2006_06_30/annnf0_tag2006
0630t112348_0.303.594473031 tag=TAG20060630T112348 comment=NONE
channel ORA_DISK_1: backup set complete, elapsed time: 00:00:02

channel ORA_DISK_1: deleting archive log(s)
archive log filename=/u01/app/oracle/admin/RMANELSE/arch/1_3_593971715
.dbf recid=5 stamp=594473024
archive log filename=/u01/app/oracle/admin/RMANELSE/arch/2_2_593971715
.dbf recid=4 stamp=594473024
Finished backup at 30-JUN-06

Starting Control File and SPFILE Autobackup at 30-JUN-06
piece handle=+MY_DG1/rmanelse/autobackup/2006_06_30/s_594480941
.273.594480945 comment=NONE
Finished Control File and SPFILE Autobackup at 30-JUN-06

RMAN> backup incremental level 1 DATABASE format '+MY_DG1' tag
'incre_diff_bkup';

Starting backup at 17-JUN-06
allocated channel: ORA_DISK_1
channel ORA_DISK_1: sid=128 instance=RACDB1 devtype=DISK
channel ORA_DISK_1: starting incremental level 1 datafile backupset
channel ORA_DISK_1: specifying datafile(s) in backupset
input datafile fno=00001 name=+MY_DG2/racdb/datafile/system.256.562151237
input datafile fno=00003 name=+MY_DG2/racdb/datafile/sysaux.257.562151243
input datafile fno=00005 name=+MY_DG2/racdb/datafile/example.265.562151495
input datafile fno=00008 name=+MY_DG2/racdb/datafile/soe.272.562263577
input datafile fno=00002 name=+MY_DG2/racdb/datafile/undotbs1.258.562151247
input datafile fno=00004 name=+MY_DG2/racdb/datafile/users.259.562151249
input datafile fno=00006 name=+MY_DG2/racdb/datafile/undotbs2.267
.562154137 input datafile fno=00007 name=+MY_DG2/racdb/datafile/flow_
1.271.562196855
channel ORA_DISK_1: starting piece 1 at 17-JUN-06
channel ORA_DISK_1: finished piece 1 at 17-JUN-06
piece handle=+MY_DG1/racdb/backupset/2006_06_18/nnndn1_incre_diff_
bkup_0.258.593458089 tag=INCRE_DIFF_BKUP comment=NONE
channel ORA_DISK_1: backup set complete, elapsed time: 00:01:37
channel ORA_DISK_1: starting incremental level 1 datafile backupset
channel ORA_DISK_1: specifying datafile(s) in backupset
including current control file in backupset
including current SPFILE in backupset
channel ORA_DISK_1: starting piece 1 at 17-JUN-06
channel ORA_DISK_1: finished piece 1 at 17-JUN-06

piece handle=+MY_DG1/racdb/backupset/2006_06_18/ncsnn1_incre_diff_
bkup_0.259.593458189 tag=INCRE_DIFF_BKUP comment=NONE
channel ORA_DISK_1: backup set complete, elapsed time: 00:00:05
Finished backup at 17-JUN-06

RMAN> backup incremental level 1 cumulative DATABASE format
'+MY_DG1' tag 'incre_cum_bkup';

Starting backup at 18-JUN-06
allocated channel: ORA_DISK_1
channel ORA_DISK_1: sid=148 instance=RACDB1 devtype=DISK
channel ORA_DISK_1: starting incremental level 1 datafile backupset
channel ORA_DISK_1: specifying datafile(s) in backupset
input datafile fno=00001 name=+MY_DG2/racdb/datafile/system.256
.562151237
input datafile fno=00003 name=+MY_DG2/racdb/datafile/sysaux.257
.562151243
input datafile fno=00005 name=+MY_DG2/racdb/datafile/example.265
.562151495
input datafile fno=00008 name=+MY_DG2/racdb/datafile/soe.272.562263577
input datafile fno=00002 name=+MY_DG2/racdb/datafile/undotbs1.258
.562151247
input datafile fno=00004 name=+MY_DG2/racdb/datafile/users.259
.562151249
input datafile fno=00006 name=+MY_DG2/racdb/datafile/undotbs2.267
.562154137
input datafile fno=00007 name=+MY_DG2/racdb/datafile/flow_1.271
.562196855
channel ORA_DISK_1: starting piece 1 at 18-JUN-06
channel ORA_DISK_1: finished piece 1 at 18-JUN-06
piece handle=+MY_DG1/racdb/backupset/2006_06_18/nnndn1_incre_cum_
bkup_0.260.593459329 tag=INCRE_CUM_BKUP comment=NONE
channel ORA_DISK_1: backup set complete, elapsed time: 00:01:35
channel ORA_DISK_1: starting incremental level 1 datafile backupset
channel ORA_DISK_1: specifying datafile(s) in backupset
including current control file in backupset
including current SPFILE in backupset
channel ORA_DISK_1: starting piece 1 at 18-JUN-06
channel ORA_DISK_1: finished piece 1 at 18-JUN-06

piece handle=+MY_DG1/racdb/backupset/2006_06_18/ncsnn1_incre_cum_
bkup_0.261.593459429 tag=INCRE_CUM_BKUP comment=NONE
channel ORA_DISK_1: backup set complete, elapsed time: 00:00:07
Finished backup at 18-JUN-06

> The performance of incremental backups can be dramatically enhanced by
> implementing the **change tracking file**. This file records all the changed
> blocks in each datafile. RMAN uses this file to isolate the changed blocks
> eligible for incremental backup. This obviates the need to scan all blocks in
> the database which could be an expensive overhead especially for relatively
> large static databases.

The author has personally realized a downsized time window for daily incremental
backups. Before enabling change tracking the incremental backups used to take
about 30 minutes but after this enablement the backup duration nosedived to
about 5 minutes! Such is the tangible gain of employing the change tracking file!!

SQL> ALTER DATABASE ENABLE BLOCK CHANGE TRACKING
USING FILE '/u01/app/oracle/admin/RACDB/blkchgtrk.dbf';

The dynamic view V$BLOCK_CHANGE_TRACKING can be queried to
obtain the status of this functionality. To begin with a 10M file is created for this
purpose by the database.

You can also incrementally backup individual tablespaces.

RMAN> backup incremental level 1 tablespace example format '+MY_DG1';

Starting backup at 30-JUN-06
allocated channel: ORA_DISK_1
channel ORA_DISK_1: sid=30 devtype=DISK
channel ORA_DISK_1: starting incremental level 1 datafile backupset
channel ORA_DISK_1: specifying datafile(s) in backupset
input datafile fno=00005 name=+MY_DG1/rmanelse/datafile/example.282.
593971515
channel ORA_DISK_1: starting piece 1 at 30-JUN-06
channel ORA_DISK_1: finished piece 1 at 30-JUN-06
piece handle=+MY_DG1/rmanelse/backupset/2006_06_30/nnndn1_tag2006
0630t132349_0.302.594480231 tag=TAG20060630T132349 comment=NONE

channel ORA_DISK_1: backup set complete, elapsed time: 00:00:15
Finished backup at 30-JUN-06

RMAN> backup incremental level 1 cumulative tablespace example format '+MY_DG1' tag 'incre_cum_bkup';

Starting backup at 30-JUN-06
allocated channel: ORA_DISK_1
channel ORA_DISK_1: sid=45 devtype=DISK
channel ORA_DISK_1: starting incremental level 1 datafile backupset
channel ORA_DISK_1: specifying datafile(s) in backupset
input datafile fno=00005 name=+MY_DG1/rmanelse/datafile/example.282
.593971515
channel ORA_DISK_1: starting piece 1 at 30-JUN-06
channel ORA_DISK_1: finished piece 1 at 30-JUN-06
piece handle=+MY_DG1/rmanelse/backupset/2006_06_30/nnndn1_incre_
cum_bkup_0.285.594480609 tag=INCRE_CUM_BKUP comment=NONE
channel ORA_DISK_1: backup set complete, elapsed time: 00:00:15
Finished backup at 30-JUN-06

The DBA can also deploy the strategy of making incremental backups to disk (as image copies) which can then be copied to tape with the BACKUP AS BACKUPSET command.

The DBA can use the novel feature of incrementally updated backups. This will reduce the recovery window for the media recovery of the target database.

To begin with RMAN creates an image copy backup of the datafile. Incremental backups are regularly taken and applied to the image copy backup to roll it forward.

Consider the code below to understand this strategy.

RMAN> run
   { recover copy of database with tag 'incr_upd_dly';
     backup incremental level 1 for recover of copy with tag 'incr_upd_dly' database; }

If no level 0 image copy backup of a datafile is available RMAN creates an image copy backup of the datafile in lieu of level 1. Further executions of this command generate the level 1 incremental backups of the datafile. RMAN then applies any available incremental level 1 backups to the datafile copies.

For the first run RMAN will have no datafile copy or level 1 incremental backup to work with. During the second run a datafile copy will exist but no incremental level 1 backup. Starting with the third run both datafile copy and level 1 incremental backup will be available. Now RMAN will apply the level 1 incremental backup to the datafile copy.

To restore and recover the target database the DBA can restore the incrementally updated datafile copies and then apply the most recent incremental level 1 backup and the archived redo logs. This ensures you will have not more than 24 hours of archived logs to apply to recover the database at any point in time if this strategy is implemented on a daily basis.

RMAN> connect target;

connected to target database: RMANELSE (DBID=1826602558)

RMAN> connect catalog rman/rwoman@rman4all;

connected to recovery catalog database

This is the first run.

RMAN> run
   { recover copy of database with tag 'incr_upd_dly';
     backup incremental level 1 for recover of copy with tag 'incr_upd_dly' database; }

Starting recover at 26-AUG-06
allocated channel: ORA_SBT_TAPE_1
channel ORA_SBT_TAPE_1: sid=21 devtype=SBT_TAPE
channel ORA_SBT_TAPE_1: Oracle Secure Backup
allocated channel: ORA_SBT_TAPE_2
channel ORA_SBT_TAPE_2: sid=23 devtype=SBT_TAPE
channel ORA_SBT_TAPE_2: Oracle Secure Backup
allocated channel: ORA_SBT_TAPE_3
channel ORA_SBT_TAPE_3: sid=30 devtype=SBT_TAPE
channel ORA_SBT_TAPE_3: Oracle Secure Backup
using channel ORA_DISK_1
no copy of datafile 1 found to recover
no copy of datafile 2 found to recover
no copy of datafile 3 found to recover

no copy of datafile 4 found to recover
no copy of datafile 5 found to recover
no copy of datafile 6 found to recover
Finished recover at 26-AUG-06

Starting backup at 26-AUG-06
released channel: ORA_SBT_TAPE_1
released channel: ORA_SBT_TAPE_2
released channel: ORA_SBT_TAPE_3
using channel ORA_DISK_1
ignoring encryption for proxy or image copies
no parent backup or copy of datafile 1 found
no parent backup or copy of datafile 3 found
no parent backup or copy of datafile 5 found
no parent backup or copy of datafile 2 found
no parent backup or copy of datafile 4 found
no parent backup or copy of datafile 6 found
channel ORA_DISK_1: starting datafile copy
input datafile fno=00001 name=+MY_DG1/rmanelse/datafile/system.279
.596679619
output filename=/u01/app/oracle/admin/RMANELSE/aux_dest/RMANELSE/
datafile/o1_mf_system_2h1czcb5_.dbf tag=INCR_UPD_DLY recid=51 stamp=
599502817
channel ORA_DISK_1: datafile copy complete, elapsed time: 00:01:06
channel ORA_DISK_1: starting datafile copy
input datafile fno=00003 name=+MY_DG1/rmanelse/datafile/sysaux.289
.596679669
output filename=/u01/app/oracle/admin/RMANELSE/aux_dest/RMANELSE/
datafile/o1_mf_sysaux_2h1d1dsv_.dbf tag=INCR_UPD_DLY recid=52 stamp=
599502870
channel ORA_DISK_1: datafile copy complete, elapsed time: 00:00:45
channel ORA_DISK_1: starting datafile copy
input datafile fno=00005 name=+MY_DG1/rmanelse/datafile/example.276
.596679707
output filename=/u01/app/oracle/admin/RMANELSE/aux_dest/RMANELSE/
datafile/o1_mf_example_2h1d2tdm_.dbf tag=INCR_UPD_DLY recid=53
stamp=599502884
channel ORA_DISK_1: datafile copy complete, elapsed time: 00:00:15
channel ORA_DISK_1: starting datafile copy

input datafile fno=00002 name=+MY_DG1/rmanelse/datafile/undotbs1.298
.596679719
output filename=/u01/app/oracle/admin/RMANELSE/aux_dest/RMANELSE/
datafile/o1_mf_undotbs1_2h1d39vx_.dbf tag=INCR_UPD_DLY recid=54
stamp=599502898
channel ORA_DISK_1: datafile copy complete, elapsed time: 00:00:15
channel ORA_DISK_1: starting datafile copy
input datafile fno=00004 name=+MY_DG1/rmanelse/datafile/users.304
.596679735
output filename=/u01/app/oracle/admin/RMANELSE/aux_dest/RMANELSE/
datafile/o1_mf_users_2h1d3s6h_.dbf tag=INCR_UPD_DLY recid=55 stamp=
599502914
channel ORA_DISK_1: datafile copy complete, elapsed time: 00:00:15
channel ORA_DISK_1: starting datafile copy
input datafile fno=00006 name=+MY_DG1/rmanelse/datafile/auxdata.281
.596679751
output filename=/u01/app/oracle/admin/RMANELSE/aux_dest/RMANELSE/
datafile/o1_mf_auxdata_2h1d48dq_.dbf tag=INCR_UPD_DLY recid=56 stamp=
599502921
channel ORA_DISK_1: datafile copy complete, elapsed time: 00:00:03
Finished backup at 26-AUG-06

Starting Control File and SPFILE Autobackup at 26-AUG-06
piece handle=+MY_DG1/rmanelse/autobackup/2006_08_26/s_599502925
.286.599502929 comment=NONE
Finished Control File and SPFILE Autobackup at 26-AUG-06

This is the second run.

Starting recover at 27-AUG-06
allocated channel: ORA_SBT_TAPE_1
channel ORA_SBT_TAPE_1: sid=26 devtype=SBT_TAPE
channel ORA_SBT_TAPE_1: Oracle Secure Backup
allocated channel: ORA_SBT_TAPE_2
channel ORA_SBT_TAPE_2: sid=30 devtype=SBT_TAPE
channel ORA_SBT_TAPE_2: Oracle Secure Backup
allocated channel: ORA_SBT_TAPE_3
channel ORA_SBT_TAPE_3: sid=42 devtype=SBT_TAPE
channel ORA_SBT_TAPE_3: Oracle Secure Backup
allocated channel: ORA_DISK_1

channel ORA_DISK_1: sid=38 devtype=DISK
no copy of datafile 1 found to recover
no copy of datafile 2 found to recover
no copy of datafile 3 found to recover
no copy of datafile 4 found to recover
no copy of datafile 5 found to recover
no copy of datafile 6 found to recover
Finished recover at 27-AUG-06

Starting backup at 27-AUG-06
released channel: ORA_SBT_TAPE_1
released channel: ORA_SBT_TAPE_2
released channel: ORA_SBT_TAPE_3
using channel ORA_DISK_1
channel ORA_DISK_1: starting incremental level 1 datafile backupset
channel ORA_DISK_1: specifying datafile(s) in backupset
input datafile fno=00001 name=+MY_DG1/rmanelse/datafile/system.279
.596679619
input datafile fno=00003 name=+MY_DG1/rmanelse/datafile/sysaux.289
.596679669
input datafile fno=00005 name=+MY_DG1/rmanelse/datafile/example.276
.596679707
input datafile fno=00002 name=+MY_DG1/rmanelse/datafile/undotbs1.298
.596679719
input datafile fno=00004 name=+MY_DG1/rmanelse/datafile/users.304
.596679735
input datafile fno=00006 name=+MY_DG1/rmanelse/datafile/auxdata.281
.596679751
channel ORA_DISK_1: starting piece 1 at 27-AUG-06
channel ORA_DISK_1: finished piece 1 at 27-AUG-06
piece handle=/u01/app/oracle/admin/RMANELSE/aux_dest/RMANELSE/
backupset/2006_08_27/o1_mf_nnnd1_TAG20060827T164859_2h1dxwt3_.b
kp tag=TAG20060826T164859 comment=NONE
channel ORA_DISK_1: backup set complete, elapsed time: 00:00:03
Finished backup at 27-AUG-06

Starting Control File and SPFILE Autobackup at 27-AUG-06
piece handle=+MY_DG1/rmanelse/autobackup/2006_08_27/s_599503745
.296.599503749 comment=NONE
Finished Control File and SPFILE Autobackup at 27-AUG-06

This is the third run.

Starting recover at 28-AUG-06
allocated channel: ORA_SBT_TAPE_1
channel ORA_SBT_TAPE_1: sid=30 devtype=SBT_TAPE
channel ORA_SBT_TAPE_1: Oracle Secure Backup
allocated channel: ORA_SBT_TAPE_2
channel ORA_SBT_TAPE_2: sid=42 devtype=SBT_TAPE
channel ORA_SBT_TAPE_2: Oracle Secure Backup
allocated channel: ORA_SBT_TAPE_3
channel ORA_SBT_TAPE_3: sid=21 devtype=SBT_TAPE
channel ORA_SBT_TAPE_3: Oracle Secure Backup
allocated channel: ORA_DISK_1
channel ORA_DISK_1: sid=23 devtype=DISK
channel ORA_DISK_1: starting incremental datafile backupset restore
channel ORA_DISK_1: specifying datafile copies to recover
recovering datafile copy fno=00001 name=/u01/app/oracle/admin/RMANELSE/
aux_dest/RMANELSE/datafile/o1_mf_system_2h1czcb5_.dbf
recovering datafile copy fno=00002 name=/u01/app/oracle/admin/RMANELSE/
aux_dest/RMANELSE/datafile/o1_mf_undotbs1_2h1d39vx_.dbf
recovering datafile copy fno=00003 name=/u01/app/oracle/admin/RMANELSE/
aux_dest/RMANELSE/datafile/o1_mf_sysaux_2h1d1dsv_.dbf
recovering datafile copy fno=00004 name=/u01/app/oracle/admin/RMANELSE/
aux_dest/RMANELSE/datafile/o1_mf_users_2h1d3s6h_.dbf
recovering datafile copy fno=00005 name=/u01/app/oracle/admin/RMANELSE/
aux_dest/RMANELSE/datafile/o1_mf_example_2h1d2tdm_.dbf
recovering datafile copy fno=00006 name=/u01/app/oracle/admin/RMANELSE/
aux_dest/RMANELSE/datafile/o1_mf_auxdata_2h1d48dq_.dbf
channel ORA_DISK_1: reading from backup piece/u01/app/oracle/admin/
RMANELSE/aux_dest/RMANELSE/backupset/2006_08_27/o1_mf_nnnd1_T
AG20060827T164859_2h1dxwt3_.bkp
channel ORA_DISK_1: restored backup piece 1
piece   handle=/u01/app/oracle/admin/RMANELSE/aux_dest/RMANELSE/
backupset/2006_08_27/o1_mf_nnnd1_TAG20060827T164859_2h1dxwt3_.b
kp tag=TAG20060827T164859
channel ORA_DISK_1: restore complete, elapsed time: 00:00:04
Finished recover at 28-AUG-06

Starting backup at 28-AUG-06
released channel: ORA_SBT_TAPE_1

released channel: ORA_SBT_TAPE_2
released channel: ORA_SBT_TAPE_3
using channel ORA_DISK_1
channel ORA_DISK_1: starting incremental level 1 datafile backupset
channel ORA_DISK_1: specifying datafile(s) in backupset
input datafile fno=00001 name=+MY_DG1/rmanelse/datafile/system.279
.596679619
input datafile fno=00003 name=+MY_DG1/rmanelse/datafile/sysaux.289
.596679669
input datafile fno=00005 name=+MY_DG1/rmanelse/datafile/example.276
.596679707
input datafile fno=00002 name=+MY_DG1/rmanelse/datafile/undotbs1.298
.596679719
input datafile fno=00004 name=+MY_DG1/rmanelse/datafile/users.304
.596679735
input datafile fno=00006 name=+MY_DG1/rmanelse/datafile/auxdata.281
.596679751
channel ORA_DISK_1: starting piece 1 at 28-AUG-06
channel ORA_DISK_1: finished piece 1 at 28-AUG-06
piece handle=/u01/app/oracle/admin/RMANELSE/aux_dest/RMANELSE/
backupset/2006_08_28/o1_mf_nnnd1_TAG20060828T165320_2h1f6121_.b
kp tag=TAG20060828T165320 comment=NONE
channel ORA_DISK_1: backup set complete, elapsed time: 00:00:03
Finished backup at 28-AUG-06

Starting Control File and SPFILE Autobackup at 28-AUG-06
piece handle=+MY_DG1/rmanelse/autobackup/2006_08_28/s_599504005
.262.599504009 comment=NONE
Finished Control File and SPFILE Autobackup at 28-AUG-06

RMAN> list backup;

List of Backup Sets
===================

BS Key	Type	LV	Size	Device Type	Elapsed Time	Completion Time
4402	Full		14.95M	DISK	00:00:06	26-AUG-06

    BP Key: 4403 Status: AVAILABLE Compressed: NO Tag: TAG20060826
T163525

Piece Name: +MY_DG1/rmanelse/autobackup/2006_08_26/s_599502925
.286.599502929

Control File Included: Ckp SCN: 4520949   Ckp time: 26-AUG-06

SPFILE Included: Modification time: 26-AUG-06

BS Key Type LV Size   Device Type Elapsed Time Completion Time
------- ---- -- ---------- ------------ ------------- ---------------

4433   Incr 1 1.17M   DISK   00:00:02   26-AUG-06

BP Key: 4436 Status: AVAILABLE Compressed: NO Tag: TAG20060826
T164859

Piece Name: /u01/app/oracle/admin/RMANELSE/aux_dest/RMANELSE/
backupset/2006_08_26/o1_mf_nnnd1_TAG20060826T164859_2h1dxwt3_
.bkp

List of Datafiles in backup set 4433

File LV Type Ckp SCN   Ckp Time Name
---- -- ---- ---------- --------- ----

1 1   Incr 4522231 26-AUG-06 +MY_DG1/rmanelse/datafile/system.279
.596679619

2 1   Incr 4522231 26-AUG-06 +MY_DG1/rmanelse/datafile/undotbs1.298
.596679719

3 1   Incr 4522231 26-AUG-06 +MY_DG1/rmanelse/datafile/sysaux.289
.596679669

4 1   Incr 4522231 26-AUG-06   +MY_DG1/rmanelse/datafile/users.304
.596679735

5 1   Incr 4522231 26-AUG-06 +MY_DG1/rmanelse/datafile/example.276
.596679707

6 1   Incr 4522231 26-AUG-06 +MY_DG1/rmanelse/datafile/auxdata.281
.596679751

BS Key Type LV Size   Device Type Elapsed Time Completion Time
------- ---- -- ---------- ------------ ------------- ---------------

4448   Full   14.95M   DISK   00:00:05   27-AUG-06

BP Key: 4455 Status: AVAILABLE Compressed: NO Tag: TAG20060827
T164905

Piece Name: +MY_DG1/rmanelse/autobackup/2006_08_27/s_599503745
.296.599503749

Control File Included: Ckp SCN: 4522242   Ckp time: 27-AUG-06

SPFILE Included: Modification time: 27-AUG-06

```
BS Key  Type LV Size      Device Type Elapsed Time Completion Time
------- ---- -- ---------- ----------- ------------- ----------------
4486    Incr 1 632.00K  DISK       00:00:02   27-AUG-06
```
     BP Key: 4489 Status: AVAILABLE Compressed: NO Tag: TAG20060827
T165320
     Piece Name: /u01/app/oracle/admin/RMANELSE/aux_dest/RMANELSE/
backupset/2006_08_27/o1_mf_nnnd1_TAG20060827T165320_2h1f6121_
.bkp
  List of Datafiles in backup set 4486
  File LV Type Ckp SCN   Ckp Time Name
```
  ---- -- ---- ---------- --------- ----
   1  1   Incr 4522571  27-AUG-06  +MY_DG1/rmanelse/datafile/system.279
.596679619
   2  1   Incr 4522571  27-AUG-06 +MY_DG1/rmanelse/datafile/undotbs1.298
.596679719
   3  1   Incr 4522571  27-AUG-06  +MY_DG1/rmanelse/datafile/sysaux.289
.596679669
   4  1   Incr 4522571  27-AUG-06   +MY_DG1/rmanelse/datafile/users.304
.596679735
   5  1   Incr 4522571  27-AUG-06  +MY_DG1/rmanelse/datafile/example.276
.596679707
   6  1   Incr 4522571  27-AUG-06  +MY_DG1/rmanelse/datafile/auxdata.281
.596679751
```

```
BS Key  Type LV Size      Device Type Elapsed Time Completion Time
------- ---- -- ---------- ----------- ------------- ----------------
4503    Full   14.95M   DISK       00:00:05   28-AUG-06
```
     BP Key: 4510 Status: AVAILABLE Compressed: NO Tag: TAG20060828
T165325
     Piece Name: +MY_DG1/rmanelse/autobackup/2006_08_28/s_599504005
.262.599504009
  Control File Included: Ckp SCN: 4522582   Ckp time: 28-AUG-06
  SPFILE Included: Modification time: 28-AUG-06

RMAN> list copy;

specification does not match any archive log in the recovery catalog

List of Datafile Copies
Key   File S Completion Time Ckp SCN   Ckp Time   Name

```
------- ---- - ---------------- ---------- ---------------- ----
4477    1    A 26-AUG-06    4522231    26-AUG-06
/u01/app/oracle/admin/RMANELSE/aux_dest/RMANELSE/datafile/o1_mf_
system_2h1czcb5_.dbf
4476    2    A 26-AUG-06    4522231    26-AUG-06
/u01/app/oracle/admin/RMANELSE/aux_dest/RMANELSE/datafile/o1_mf_
undotbs1_2h1d39vx_.dbf
4478    3    A 26-AUG-06    4522231    26-AUG-06
/u01/app/oracle/admin/RMANELSE/aux_dest/RMANELSE/datafile/o1_mf_
sysaux_2h1d1dsv_.dbf
4475    4    A 26-AUG-06    4522231    26-AUG-06
/u01/app/oracle/admin/RMANELSE/aux_dest/RMANELSE/datafile/o1_mf_
users_2h1d3s6h_.dbf
4473    5    A 26-AUG-06    4522231    26-AUG-06
/u01/app/oracle/admin/RMANELSE/aux_dest/RMANELSE/datafile/o1_mf_
example_2h1d2tdm_.dbf
4474    6    A 26-AUG-06    4522231    26-AUG-06
/u01/app/oracle/admin/RMANELSE/aux_dest/RMANELSE/datafile/o1_mf_
auxdata_2h1d48dq_.dbf
```

How often do we have to perform base level 0 backups? You can work with this number to determine: If one-fourths of the data blocks (25%) or more are being backed up as indicated by this query we conclude level 0 backups are needed.

```
SQL> SELECT FILE#, BLOCKS, DATAFILE_BLOCKS FROM V$BACKUP_
DATAFILE
WHERE INCREMENTAL_LEVEL = 1
AND BLOCKS/DATAFILE_BLOCKS > .25
ORDER BY FILE#;
```

The target database session id is displayed for each allocated RMAN channel in the output as under:

```
channel t1: sid=15 devtype=SBT_TAPE
```

The serial# can be queried from the dynamic V$SESSION view using this session id. If warranted the session can be killed using the ALTER SYSTEM command supplying the sid and serial#.

One common backup failure is due to the wait for control file enqueue. You may see the error ORA-00230: operation disallowed: snapshot control file enqueue unavailable. You can identify the offending RMAN session to be killed if needed.

To illustrate this could be caused by an online backup job & archived log sweep job starting off at the same time. The backup job starts creating a snapshot controlfile while the sweep job also tries to create a new snapshot control file. This results in the controlfile enqueue contention.

```
SQL> SELECT s.SID, USERNAME, PROGRAM, ACTION, LOGON_TIME
FROM V$SESSION s, V$ENQUEUE_LOCK el
WHERE el.SID = s.SID
AND el.TYPE = 'CF'
AND el.ID1 = 0
AND el.ID2 = 2;
```

This could also happen due to some media manager issues like tape resources being unavailable. The DBA can have the TSM or the NetBackup agent recycled on the target host to resolve it.

The DBA can obtain the server process id from this query.

```
SQL> SELECT s.SID, p.SPID, s.CLIENT_INFO
FROM V$PROCESS p, V$SESSION s
WHERE p.ADDR = s.PADDR
AND CLIENT_INFO LIKE 'rman%';
```

For the RMAN backup to tape we can obtain the wait information from this query.

```
SQL> SELECT p.SPID, EVENT, SECONDS_IN_WAIT, STATE, CLIENT_
INFO
FROM V$SESSION_WAIT sw, V$SESSION s, V$PROCESS p
WHERE sw.EVENT LIKE 'sbt%'
AND s.SID=sw.SID AND s.PADDR=p.ADDR;
```

How do you determine the progress of your RMAN backup operation?

```
SQL> SELECT SID, SERIAL#, CONTEXT, SOFAR, TOTALWORK,
ROUND(SOFAR/TOTALWORK*100,2) "%_COMPLETE"
```

```
FROM V$SESSION_LONGOPS
WHERE OPNAME LIKE 'RMAN%'
AND OPNAME NOT LIKE '%aggregate%'
AND TOTALWORK!= 0
AND SOFAR <> TOTALWORK;
```

5.5 Basic Listing

In the target database the dynamic view V$RMAN_STATUS holds information about all the RMAN jobs.

```
SQL> desc v$rman_status
Name                            Null?    Type
------------------------------- -------- ---------------------------
SID                                      NUMBER
RECID                                    NUMBER
STAMP                                    NUMBER
PARENT_RECID                             NUMBER
PARENT_STAMP                             NUMBER
SESSION_RECID                            NUMBER
SESSION_STAMP                            NUMBER
ROW_LEVEL                                NUMBER
ROW_TYPE                                 VARCHAR2(19)
COMMAND_ID                               VARCHAR2(33)
OPERATION                                VARCHAR2(33)
STATUS                                   VARCHAR2(23)
MBYTES_PROCESSED                         NUMBER
START_TIME                               DATE
END_TIME                                 DATE
INPUT_BYTES                              NUMBER
OUTPUT_BYTES                             NUMBER
OPTIMIZED                                VARCHAR2(3)
OBJECT_TYPE                              VARCHAR2(13)
OUTPUT_DEVICE_TYPE                       VARCHAR2(17)
```

The columns of particular interest to us are the operation, status, start_time and end_time. For example one of the operations is: CONTROL FILE AND SPFILE AUTOBACK.

The DBA can obtain useful reporting from the RMAN repository by using list & report commands.

Now we list the target database backups (as backupsets).

RMAN> list backup;

List of Backup Sets
===================

BS Key Type LV Size   Device Type Elapsed Time Completion Time
------- ---- -- ---------- ----------- ------------ ---------------
298   Incr 0 1.06G   DISK   00:03:17   16-JUN-06
    BP Key: 301 Status: AVAILABLE Compressed: NO Tag: TAG20060616T
125312
    Piece Name: +MY_DG1/racdb/backupset/2006_06_16/nnndn0_tag200606
16t125312_0.256.593268795
  List of Datafiles in backup set 298
  File LV Type Ckp SCN   Ckp Time Name
  ---- -- ---- ---------- --------- ----
  1   0 Incr 3065015   16-JUN-06
+MY_DG2/racdb/datafile/system.256.562151237
  2   0 Incr 3065015   16-JUN-06
+MY_DG2/racdb/datafile/undotbs1.258.562151247
  3   0 Incr 3065015   16-JUN-06
+MY_DG2/racdb/datafile/sysaux.257.562151243
  4   0 Incr 3065015   16-JUN-06
+MY_DG2/racdb/datafile/users.259.562151249
  5   0 Incr 3065015   16-JUN-06
+MY_DG2/racdb/datafile/example.265.562151495
  6   0 Incr 3065015   16-JUN-06
+MY_DG2/racdb/datafile/undotbs2.267.562154137
  7   0 Incr 3065015   16-JUN-06
+MY_DG2/racdb/datafile/flow_1.271.562196855
  8   0 Incr 3065015   16-JUN-06
+MY_DG2/racdb/datafile/soe.272.562263577

BS Key Size   Device Type Elapsed Time Completion Time
------- ---------- ----------- ------------ ---------------
323   78.46M   DISK   00:00:14   16-JUN-06
    BP Key: 332 Status: AVAILABLE Compressed: NO Tag: TAG20060616
T125639

Piece Name: +MY_DG1/racdb/backupset/2006_06_16/annnf0_tag200606
16t125639_0.257.593269003

List of Archived Logs in backup set 323

Thrd	Seq	Low SCN	Low Time	Next SCN	Next Time
1	67	2905884	14-JUN-06	2946974	15-JUN-06
1	68	2946974	15-JUN-06	3015250	15-JUN-06
2	35	3015253	15-JUN-06	3037298	16-JUN-06
2	36	3037298	16-JUN-06	3065391	16-JUN-06

BS Key	Type	LV	Size	Device Type	Elapsed Time	Completion Time
419	Incr	1	59.48M	DISK	00:01:34	17-JUN-06

BP Key: 423 Status: AVAILABLE Compressed: NO Tag: INCRE_DIFF_
BKUP

Piece Name: +MY_DG1/racdb/backupset/2006_06_18/nnndn1_incre_diff_
bkup_0.258.593458089

List of Datafiles in backup set 419

File	LV	Type	Ckp SCN	Ckp Time	Name
1	1	Incr	3177658	18-JUN-06	
+MY_DG2/racdb/datafile/system.256.562151237					
2	1	Incr	3177658	18-JUN-06	
+MY_DG2/racdb/datafile/undotbs1.258.562151247					
3	1	Incr	3177658	18-JUN-06	
+MY_DG2/racdb/datafile/sysaux.257.562151243					
4	1	Incr	3177658	18-JUN-06	
+MY_DG2/racdb/datafile/users.259.562151249					
5	1	Incr	3177658	18-JUN-06	
+MY_DG2/racdb/datafile/example.265.562151495					
6	1	Incr	3177658	18-JUN-06	
+MY_DG2/racdb/datafile/undotbs2.267.562154137					
7	1	Incr	3177658	18-JUN-06	
+MY_DG2/racdb/datafile/flow_1.271.562196855					
8	1	Incr	3177658	18-JUN-06	
+MY_DG2/racdb/datafile/soe.272.562263577					

BS Key	Type	LV	Size	Device Type	Elapsed Time	Completion Time
441	Incr	1	59.87M	DISK	00:01:32	18-JUN-06

BP Key: 445 Status: AVAILABLE Compressed: NO Tag: INCRE_CUM_
BKUP
    Piece Name: +MY_DG1/racdb/backupset/2006_06_18/nnndn1_incre_cum_
bkup_0.260.593459329
  List of Datafiles in backup set 441
  File LV Type Ckp SCN   Ckp Time Name
  ---- -- ---- ---------- --------- ----
  1   1 Incr 3180284   18-JUN-06
+MY_DG2/racdb/datafile/system.256.562151237
  2   1 Incr 3180284   18-JUN-06
+MY_DG2/racdb/datafile/undotbs1.258.562151247
  3   1 Incr 3180284   18-JUN-06
+MY_DG2/racdb/datafile/sysaux.257.562151243
  4   1 Incr 3180284   18-JUN-06
+MY_DG2/racdb/datafile/users.259.562151249
  5   1 Incr 3180284   18-JUN-06
+MY_DG2/racdb/datafile/example.265.562151495
  6   1 Incr 3180284   18-JUN-06
+MY_DG2/racdb/datafile/undotbs2.267.562154137
  7   1 Incr 3180284   18-JUN-06
+MY_DG2/racdb/datafile/flow_1.271.562196855
  8   1 Incr 3180284   18-JUN-06
+MY_DG2/racdb/datafile/soe.272.562263577

BS Key Type LV Size   Device Type Elapsed Time Completion Time
------- ---- -- ---------- ----------- ------------ ---------------
521   Full   14.64M   DISK   00:00:05   18-JUN-06
    BP Key: 530 Status: AVAILABLE Compressed: NO Tag: TAG20060619T
095918
    Piece Name: +MY_DG1/racdb/autobackup/2006_06_19/s_593517558.263
.593517563
  Control File Included: Ckp SCN: 3224675   Ckp time: 18-JUN-06
  SPFILE Included: Modification time: 18-JUN-06

Below you will find the listing of backup (as image copies).

RMAN> list copy;
List of Datafile Copies
Key   File S Completion Time Ckp SCN   Ckp Time   Name
------- ---- - --------------- ---------- --------------- ----

611   1   A 19-JUN-06   3314303   19-JUN-06
+MY_DG1/racdb/datafile/system.281.593554819
615   2   A 19-JUN-06   3314530   19-JUN-06
+MY_DG1/racdb/datafile/undotbs1.285.593554979
612   3   A 19-JUN-06   3314414   19-JUN-06
+MY_DG1/racdb/datafile/sysaux.282.593554887
616   4   A 19-JUN-06   3314586   19-JUN-06
+MY_DG1/racdb/datafile/users.286.593554995
613   5   A 19-JUN-06   3314504   19-JUN-06
+MY_DG1/racdb/datafile/example.283.593554945
617   6   A 19-JUN-06   3314613   19-JUN-06
+MY_DG1/racdb/datafile/undotbs2.287.593555013
619   7   A 19-JUN-06   3314640   19-JUN-06
+MY_DG1/racdb/datafile/flow_1.289.593555037
614   8   A 19-JUN-06   3314520   19-JUN-06
+MY_DG1/racdb/datafile/soe.284.593554961

List of Control File Copies
Key   S Completion Time Ckp SCN   Ckp Time   Name
------- - ---------------- ---------- ---------------- ----
618   A 19-JUN-06   3314636   19-JUN-06
+MY_DG1/racdb/controlfile/backup.288.593555029

List of Archived Log Copies
Key   Thrd Seq   S Low Time Name
------- ---- ------- - --------- ----
600   1   71   A 16-JUN-06
+MY_DG1/racdb/archivelog/2006_06_19/thread_1_seq_71.277.593554795
598   1   72   A 18-JUN-06
+MY_DG1/racdb/archivelog/2006_06_19/thread_1_seq_72.275.593554777
601   2   37   A 16-JUN-06
+MY_DG1/racdb/archivelog/2006_06_19/thread_2_seq_37.278.593554799
603   2   38   A 18-JUN-06
+MY_DG1/racdb/archivelog/2006_06_19/thread_2_seq_38.280.593554813

Whenever the target database is opened with the RESETLOGS clause after recovery a new incarnation of the database gets created in the repository. If a recovery catalog is employed as the repository of several target databases we can query the incarnation of any database as under:

RMAN> list incarnation of database <dbname>;

starting full resync of recovery catalog
full resync complete

List of Database Incarnations

DB Key	Inc Key	DB Name	DB ID	STATUS	Reset SCN	Reset Time
1072	2619	RMANELSE	1826602558	PARENT	4092628	21-JUL-06
1072	3304	RMANELSE	1826602558	CURRENT	4134506	25-JUL-06

Before we ask RMAN to output reports about target database recoverability it is safe to perform maintenance first. This will update the status of the backup to its current condition.

RMAN> crosscheck backup;

allocated channel: ORA_DISK_1
channel ORA_DISK_1: sid=128 instance=RACDB2 devtype=DISK

crosschecked backup piece: found to be 'AVAILABLE'
backup piece handle=+MY_DG1/racdb/backupset/2006_06_16/nnndn0_tag 20060616t125312_0.256.593268795 recid=8 stamp=593268793
crosschecked backup piece: found to be 'AVAILABLE'
backup piece handle=+MY_DG1/racdb/backupset/2006_06_16/annnf0_tag 20060616t125639_0.257.593269003 recid=9 stamp=593269000
crosschecked backup piece: found to be 'AVAILABLE'
backup piece handle=/u01/app/oracle/product/10.2.0/db_1/dbs/c-559768190-20060616-00 recid=10 stamp=593269023
Crosschecked 3 objects

RMAN> crosscheck copy;

allocated channel: ORA_DISK_1
channel ORA_DISK_1: sid=148 instance=RACDB2 devtype=DISK
validation succeeded for datafile copy
datafile copy filename=+MY_DG1/racdb/datafile/system.281.593554819 recid=2 stamp=593554884
validation succeeded for datafile copy

datafile copy filename=+MY_DG1/racdb/datafile/undotbs1.285.593554979 recid=6 stamp=593554992
validation succeeded for datafile copy
datafile copy filename=+MY_DG1/racdb/datafile/sysaux.282.593554887 recid=3 stamp=593554940
validation succeeded for datafile copy
datafile copy filename=+MY_DG1/racdb/datafile/users.286.593554995 recid=7 stamp=593555005
validation succeeded for datafile copy
datafile copy filename=+MY_DG1/racdb/datafile/example.283.593554945 recid=4 stamp=593554956
validation succeeded for datafile copy
datafile copy filename=+MY_DG1/racdb/datafile/undotbs2.287.593555013 recid=8 stamp=593555024
validation succeeded for datafile copy
datafile copy filename=+MY_DG1/racdb/datafile/flow_1.289.593555037 recid=10 stamp=593555038
validation succeeded for datafile copy
datafile copy filename=+MY_DG1/racdb/datafile/soe.284.593554961 recid=5 stamp=593554973
validation succeeded for control file copy
control file copy filename=+MY_DG1/racdb/controlfile/backup.288.593555029 recid=9 stamp=593555033
validation succeeded for archived log
archive log filename=+MY_DG1/racdb/archivelog/2006_06_19/thread_1_seq_71.277.593554795 recid=19 stamp=593554797
validation succeeded for archived log
archive log filename=+MY_DG1/racdb/archivelog/2006_06_19/thread_1_seq_72.275.593554777 recid=17 stamp=593554783
validation succeeded for archived log
archive log filename=+MY_DG1/racdb/archivelog/2006_06_19/thread_2_seq_37.278.593554799 recid=20 stamp=593554803
validation succeeded for archived log
archive log filename=+MY_DG1/racdb/archivelog/2006_06_19/thread_2_seq_38.280.593554813 recid=22 stamp=593554815
Crosschecked 13 objects

This will show all files needing recovery applying more than n incremental backups.

RMAN> report need backup incremental n;

Below we can see the backups not needed to recover the target database to a point in time within the last month.

RMAN> report obsolete recovery window of 30 days;

RMAN> connect target;

connected to target database: RMANELSE (DBID=1826602558)

RMAN> connect catalog rman/rwoman@rman4all;

connected to recovery catalog database

RMAN> report obsolete recovery window of 2 days;

Report of obsolete backups and copies
Type   Key   Completion Time   Filename/Handle
-------------------- ------ ------------------------ -------------------------
Backup Set   1117   30-JUN-06
  Backup Piece   1120   30-JUN-06
+MY_DG1/rmanelse/backupset/2006_06_30/annnf0_tag20060630t111932_0.
287.594472775
Backup Set   1119   30-JUN-06
  Backup Piece   1122   30-JUN-06
+MY_DG1/rmanelse/backupset/2006_06_30/ncsnn0_tag20060630t111950_0.
262.594473021
Backup Set   1155   30-JUN-06
  Backup Piece   1158   30-JUN-06
+MY_DG1/rmanelse/backupset/2006_06_30/nnndn1_tag20060630t132349_
0.302.594480231
Backup Set   1196   30-JUN-06
  Backup Piece   1199   30-JUN-06
+MY_DG1/rmanelse/autobackup/2006_06_30/s_594480941.273.594480945

This shows the datafiles whose recovery requires more than two days' worth of archived redo logs.

RMAN> report need backup days 2 database;

Report of files whose recovery needs more than 2 days of archived logs
File Days Name
---- ----- --
1   3   +MY_DG1/rmanelse/datafile/system.283.594828005
2   3   +MY_DG1/rmanelse/datafile/undotbs1.281.594828007
3   3   +MY_DG1/rmanelse/datafile/sysaux.286.594828007
4   3   +MY_DG1/rmanelse/datafile/users.304.594828007
5   3   +MY_DG1/rmanelse/datafile/example.282.594828007

Datafiles that require the application of five or more incremental backups to be recovered to their current state:

RMAN> report need backup incremental 5 database;

5.6 Recovery Catalog Backup

It is imperative for the DBA to back up the Recovery Catalog (database) should a disaster strike. Normally this database would have a small footprint in terms of size. Daily full database/catalog schema exports should be performed. Oracle Corporation strongly recommends this database be run in archivelog mode as well. Online backups should be performed using the NOCATALOG option. Also if feasible a closed consistent (cold) backup of this database and the day's worth of archived logs can be swept to tape on a nightly basis.

Tip: Since we will be using the recovery catalog database controlfile itself as the RMAN repository for backup ensure you set the CONTROLFILE_RECORD_KEEP_TIME to a high value to prevent the loss of repository metadata.

Additionally the DBA should enable the control file autobackup and configure the appropriate retention policy. For increased protection you can back up the catalog database using both disk & tape.

RMAN> backup database plus archivelog;

5.7 Backup Encryption

For enhanced security RMAN can encrypt any backup created as backup sets. However image copy backups can NOT be encrypted.

We have three encryption modes that can be used:

- transparent

- password

- dual

Both the transparent and dual mode call for the Oracle Encryption Wallet infrastructure. If the required key management framework is configured for Transparent Data Encryption (TDE) RMAN can backup with no further DBA intervention. If the wallet is lost RMAN will be unable to restore any transparently encrypted backups.

Note: RMAN defaults to Transparent encryption.

For the password encryption you can provide a password when creating backup sets. Please be aware the password encryption is NOT persistently configurable.
If you forget the password RMAN will be unable to restore any password encrypted backups.

In this example the password is set to the quoted string and the keyword only indicates to RMAN not to check any TDE wallet.

RMAN > set encryption on identified by 'rman2secure' only;

Dual mode encrypted backups can use either TDE wallet or password.

RMAN> set encryption on identified by 'rman2secure';

> Dual-mode encrypted backup can be restored by either the Oracle Encryption Wallet (transparent) or a password (decryption). If you forget the encryption password AND lose your wallet RMAN will be unable to restore dual mode encrypted backups.

Note: Even if the database master key is reset RMAN can always restore all the encrypted backups.

If the DBA wishes to encrypt all the RMAN backups across the board the TDE wallet has to be configured first.

RMAN> configure encryption for database on;

This persistent configuration can be overridden explicitly if needed.

RMAN> set encryption off;

Tip: Allocate or configure more channels to improve performance of RMAN encrypted backups.

You can also enable encryption for specific tablespaces.

RMAN> configure encryption for tablespace auxdata1, auxdata2 on;

Let us configure Transparent Data Encryption for use with our RMAN backups. Typically the wallet folder is $ORACLE_BASE/admin/<SID>/wallet which should pre-exist.

SQL> ALTER SYSTEM SET ENCRYPTION KEY AUTHENTICATED BY "DB4secure";

System altered.

After every database recycle ensure you open the wallet.

SQL> ALTER SYSTEM SET ENCRYPTION WALLET OPEN IDENTIFIED BY "DB4secure";

SQL> CREATE TABLE EMP(NAME VARCHAR2(10), SSN NUMBER(9) ENCRYPT) TABLESPACE AUXDATA;

Table created.

```
SQL> desc emp
 Name                              Null?    Type
 ----------------------------------- -------- ----------------------------
 NAME                                        VARCHAR2(10)
 SSN                                         NUMBER(9) ENCRYPT
```

5.8 Backup Performance

The performance of RMAN backup operations can be significantly improved by tuning the environment. We will briefly dwell on some areas to focus for achieving better results.

RMAN can multiplex the backup process by reading a number of target database files simultaneously from different inputs and then write them out to one backup piece. This multiplexing is driven primarily by the number of channels available for RMAN to perform the backup.

For tape writes the tape block size is an important factor that can influence the performance of the backup operation.

RMAN> configure channel device type sbt_tape parms="blksize=524288";

RMAN uses the buffers of the large pool (if configured) for its I/O operations. The size of this pool as defined by the LARGE_POOL_SIZE initialization parameter is another key variable impacting the backup operations. To eliminate shared pool contention you must define this pool adequately sized. Oracle recommends the following formula to calculate its size:

LARGE_POOL_SIZE = number of allocated channels * (16Mb + (4 * tape buffer size))

RMAN's I/O can be done either synchronously or asynchronously. In synchronous I/O a server process can perform tasks serially completing one at a time. This could become a bottleneck when the host system is under heavy loads. But in an asynchronous mode a server process can perform tasks in parallel.
On the operating systems that do not provide native asynchronous I/O Oracle can emulate synchronous I/O by forking special slave processes. This is achieved by setting the DBWR_IO_SLAVES parameter to a nonzero value. For every dbwr slave four backup disk I/O slaves are automatically spawned which can be used for backup.

How do we isolate the backup performance bottleneck issues to either disk or tape? RMAN provides a simple solution in the backup validation. You can do a comparison of the elapsed time for a full database backup to tape vs. BACKUP VALIDATE DATABASE. Here the backup validation causes only disk reads like in a physical backup but no actual tape I/O. If we observe the validation is markedly faster than a real tape backup we can infer tape is the culprit.

The DBA can also use the incremental backup strategy to enhance backup performance.

Media managers can offer their own tuning solutions also. IBM's TSM/TDP provides a faster backup & restore mechanism called 'LANFREE' to avoid slowdown caused by network constraints.

You can query the dynamic V$BACKUP_ASYNC_IO view for values of the column EFFECTIVE_BYTES_PER_SECOND. This gives a better handle on the actual data transfer rate for tape I/O. This view also contains two other columns of interest to us. For each datafile we can see the LONG_WAITS and the IO_COUNT. The ratio of LONG_WAITS to IO_COUNT is a good indicator of asynchronous I/O performance.

SQL> SELECT DEVICE_TYPE DEVICE, TYPE, FILENAME, TO_CHAR(OPEN_TIME,'DD-MM-YYYY HH24:MI:SS') OPEN, TO_CHAR(CLOSE_TIME,'DD-MM-YYYY HH24:MI:SS') CLOSE, ELAPSED_TIME ET, EFFECTIVE_BYTES_PER_SECOND EBPS FROM V$BACKUP_ASYNC_IO WHERE CLOSE_TIME > SYSDATE -14 ORDER BY CLOSE_TIME DESC;

One obvious indicator of I/O degradation is the population of the dynamic view V$BACKUP_SYNC_IO. If we observe database writing to this view then we can conclude our I/O is not asynchronous.

Generally the more channels are configured/allocated the better the performance of RMAN. The degree of device parallelism is another factor affecting throughput by determining the allocation of automatic channels.

RMAN> configure device type sbt_tape parallelism 5;

5.9 Workshop—Implement A Complete Backup Solution

We will now backup the entire target database to secondary storage (tape media).

```
#!/bin/ksh

# =====================================
# Online Incremental Backup of Database
# Parameters: SID of target
# =====================================

targetdb=$1
export ORACLE_SID=$1
```

```
PATH=$ORACLE_HOME/bin:/usr/sbin:/usr/bin:/usr/local/bin:/bin
export PATH

# read input parameter

if [[ "$1" = "" ]]
then
echo "online_incr_bkup.sh: missing parameter"
echo "Use: online_incr_bkup.sh <targetdb>"
exit 1
fi

# email DBAs

admins="jdoe@oracle.com raghav@us.ibm.com"
email_admin()
{
mailx -s "$subject" $admins < $logfile
exit 1;
}

log_timestamp=`date '+%d%m%y%:%H%M'`
logfile=/u01/app/oracle/admin/rmanlogs/"targetdb"_"online_incr_bkup"_"$
{log_timestamp}".log

# define incremental type
# perform cumulative only on Wednesdays

if [[ `date +%u` = "3" ]]; then
     lvl_type="1 CUMULATIVE";
elif [[ `date +%u` = "1" || `date +%u` = "2" || `date +%u` = "4" || `date +%u` =
"5" `date +%u` = "6" ]]; then
     lvl_type="1";
else lvl_type="0";
fi

# assign name tag

tag_timestamp=`date '+%d%m%y'`
bkuptag="Daily Incremental"_"${lvl_type}"_"${tag_timestamp}"
```

```
#===============================================================
# We want RMAN to ensure all backups needed to recover the target database to
any point in time in the last 30 days are retained.
# We are configuring RMAN to back up the control file and the server parameter
file into its own backup set.
# We would like to secure our backup to prevent misuse of vital data resulting
from lost/stolen tape media.
# Our media manager of choice here is Tivoli. Oracle RMAN linked with TDP
backs up our data to Tivoli Storage Manager.
# The database & archivelog backups are formatted to include db name (%d) and
a unique system generated identifier (%U).
#===============================================================

rman <<++EOF >> $logfile
connect target;
connect catalog rman/rwoman@RMAN4ALL;

CONFIGURE RETENTION POLICY TO RECOVERY WINDOW OF 30
DAYS;
CONFIGURE CONTROLFILE AUTOBACKUP ON;

set encryption on identified by 'rman2secure' only;

run
{
allocate channel t1 type 'sbt_tape' parms
     'ENV=(TDPO_OPTFILE=/usr/tivoli/tsm/client/oracle/bin64/tdpo.opt)';
allocate channel t2 type 'sbt_tape' parms
     'ENV=(TDPO_OPTFILE=/usr/tivoli/tsm/client/oracle/bin64/tdpo.opt)';

backup incremental level ${lvl_type} DATABASE format 'db_%d_%U' tag
$bkuptag';
backup archivelog all format 'arch_%d_%U' delete input;

release channel t1;
release channel t2;
}

quit
++EOF
```

```
# error handler and notification

rc=`egrep -i "ORA-|RMAN-" $logfile|wc -l`
  if [ $rc -ne 0 ]
    then
      subject="Attn: Error while performing $targetdb online incremental backup"
      email_admin;
    else
      close_time=`date '+%d%m%y:%H%M'`
      subject="Online incremental backup level ${lvl_type} of $targetdb successfully
completed at ${close_time}"
      email_admin;
  fi
exit 0
```

The DBA needs to backup the archived logs on a regular basis as well. The following script may be used to perform sweep of target database archived logs to tape.

```
#!/bin/ksh

# ===========================
# Backup of archived logs
# Parameter: SID of target
# ===========================

targetdb=$1
export ORACLE_SID=$1
PATH=$ORACLE_HOME/bin:/usr/sbin:/usr/bin:/usr/local/bin:/bin
export PATH

# read input parameter

if [[ "$1" = ' ' ]]
then
echo "archivelogs_sweep.sh: missing parameter"
echo "Use: archivelogs_sweep.sh <targetdb>"
exit 1
fi
```

```
# email DBAs

admins="jdoe@oracle.com raghav@us.ibm.com"
email_admin()
{
mailx -s "$subject" $admins < $logfile
exit 1;
}

log_timestamp=`date '+%d%m%y%:%H%M'`
logfile=/u01/app/oracle/admin/rmanlogs/"$targetdb"_"archivelogs_sweep"_"${log_timestamp}".log

rman <<++EOF >> $logfile
connect target;
connect catalog rman/rwoman@RMAN4ALL;

run
{
allocate channel t1 type 'sbt_tape' parms
    'ENV=(TDPO_OPTFILE=/usr/tivoli/tsm/client/oracle/bin64/tdpo.opt)';
backup archivelog all format 'arch_%d_%U' delete input;
release channel t1;
}

quit
++EOF

# error handler and notification

rc=`egrep -i "ORA-|RMAN-" $logfile|wc -l`
  if [ $rc -ne 0 ]
   then
    subject="Attn: Error while performing sweep of $targetdb archived logs"
    email_admin;
   else
    subject="$targetdb archived logs have been swept to tape"
    email_admin;
  fi
exit 0
```

Chapter 5 Recapitulation

RMAN backups differ from user-managed backups in a very fundamental manner in that the database is NOT placed in or out of hot backup modes using ALTER DATABASE/TABLESPACE BEGIN BACKUP or ALTER DATABASE/ TABLESPACE END BACKUP.

A backup set is maintained in a proprietary RMAN-specific format.

Tape backups are always stored as backup sets.

Backup copies are byte-for-byte duplicates which can be created by RMAN or any OS utility.

RMAN by default generates unique filenames. The format used is '%U' which holds different meanings for backup pieces and image copies.

RMAN can back up the following database objects or structures: database, tablespace, datafile, control file, spfile and archived redo log.

If CONFIGURE CONTROLFILE AUTOBACKUP is ON then RMAN automatically backs up the control file and server parameter file after every backup and after database structural changes. Also the control file and server parameter file are stored together in a separate backup set/piece.

Archived logs and datafiles are never placed together in any backup set.

For backup sets RMAN can multiplex files meaning multiple files from disk are concurrently read and then written to one backup set.

RMAN can generate long term backups for vaulting.

RMAN can check both physical (media) & logical corruption of datafiles.

The flash recovery area can be backed up ONLY to tape.

A level 1 incremental backup can be either differential (default) or cumulative.

In a differential incremental backup all blocks changed after the last incremental backup at level 1 or 0 are backed up. In a cumulative incremental backup all blocks changed after the last incremental backup at level 0 are backed up.

The performance of incremental backups can be dramatically enhanced by implementing the change tracking file. This file records all the changed blocks in each datafile. This obviates the need to scan all blocks in the database which could be an expensive overhead especially for relatively large static databases.

For long term backups please be aware the KEEP FOREVER clause can NOT be used in conjunction with the LOGS option as RMAN will have to retain all the archived redo logs indefinitely.

The recovery catalog database must be run in archivelog mode for performing online backups. Use the NOCATALOG option to back it up.

For backing up the recovery catalog database ensure you set the CONTROLFILE_RECORD_KEEP_TIME to a high value to prevent the loss of repository metadata as we will be using the recovery catalog database controlfile itself as the RMAN repository.

One common backup failure is due to the wait for control file enqueue. This results in the error ORA-00230: operation disallowed: snapshot control file enqueue unavailable. You can identify the offending RMAN session to be killed if needed.

For enhanced security RMAN can encrypt any backup created as backup sets. However image copy backups can NOT be encrypted.

We have three encryption modes that can be used: Transparent, Password & Dual. Both the transparent and dual mode call for the Oracle Encryption Wallet infrastructure.

Dual-mode encrypted backup can be restored by either the Oracle Encryption Wallet (transparent) or a password (decryption). If you forget the encryption password AND lose your wallet RMAN will be unable to restore dual mode encrypted backups.

RMAN can multiplex the backup process by reading a number of target database files simultaneously from different inputs and then write them out to one backup piece. This multiplexing is driven primarily by the number of channels available for RMAN to perform the backup.

For tape writes the tape block size is an important factor that can influence the performance of the backup operation.

RMAN uses the buffers of the large pool (if configured) for its I/O operations. The size of this pool as defined by the LARGE_POOL_SIZE initialization parameter is another key variable impacting the backup operations. To eliminate shared pool contention you must define this pool adequately sized.

You can query the dynamic V$BACKUP_ASYNC_IO view for values of the column EFFECTIVE_BYTES_PER_SECOND. This gives a better handle on the actual data transfer rate for tape I/O.

Generally the more channels are configured/allocated the better the performance of RMAN.

Chapter 6 Objectives

- Restoring spfile, controlfile
- Recovering datafile, tablespace, database
- Restoring Encrypted Backups
- Previewing Restore
- Validating Restore
- Tuning Restore/Recovery
- Recovery Scenarios

Chapter 6
Restore & Recovery

In this chapter we will cover one of the most important challenges of the DBA function: restore & recovery of mission critical production enterprise databases.

Using our backups we can reconstruct the database that had been wiped out by some unforeseen disaster. Just as we backed up several database structures we can restore & recover all those.

6.1 Spfile

This procedure restores the server parameter file from the controlfile autobackup.

$ export ORACLE_SID=RMANELSE

RMAN> connect target;

connected to target database (not started)

RMAN> connect catalog rman/rwoman@rman4all;

connected to recovery catalog database

RMAN> startup force nomount;

startup failed: ORA-01078: failure in processing system parameters
LRM-00109: could not open parameter file '/u01/app/oracle/product/10.2.0/db_1/dbs/initRMANELSE.ora'

starting Oracle instance without parameter file for retrieval of spfile
Oracle instance started

Total System Global Area   159383552 bytes

Fixed Size	1218268 bytes
Variable Size	58722596 bytes
Database Buffers	96468992 bytes
Redo Buffers	2973696 bytes

RMAN> restore spfile;

Starting restore at 30-JUN-06
allocated channel: ORA_DISK_1
channel ORA_DISK_1: sid=34 devtype=DISK

channel ORA_DISK_1: starting datafile backupset restore
channel ORA_DISK_1: restoring SPFILE
output filename=/u01/app/oracle/product/10.2.0/db_1/dbs/spfileRMANELSE.ora
channel ORA_DISK_1: reading from backup piece +MY_DG1/rmanelse/
autobackup/2006_06_30/s_594480941.273.594480945
channel ORA_DISK_1: restored backup piece 1
piece handle=+MY_DG1/rmanelse/autobackup/2006_06_30/s_594480941
.273.594480945 tag=TAG20060630T133541
channel ORA_DISK_1: restore complete, elapsed time: 00:00:08
Finished restore at 30-JUN-06

RMAN> startup force nomount;

Oracle instance started

Total System Global Area   100663296 bytes

Fixed Size	1217932 bytes
Variable Size	79694452 bytes
Database Buffers	16777216 bytes
Redo Buffers	2973696 bytes

6.2 Controlfile

Now we restore the vital control files in this section.
Note: The target database instance should be running in the unmounted state.

RMAN> connect target;

connected to target database: RMANELSE (not mounted)

RMAN> connect catalog rman/rwoman@rman4all;

connected to recovery catalog database

RMAN> restore controlfile;

Starting restore at 30-JUN-06
allocated channel: ORA_DISK_1
channel ORA_DISK_1: sid=44 devtype=DISK

channel ORA_DISK_1: starting datafile backupset restore
channel ORA_DISK_1: restoring control file
channel ORA_DISK_1: reading from backup piece +MY_DG1/rmanelse/
autobackup/2006_06_30/s_594480941.273.594480945
channel ORA_DISK_1: restored backup piece 1
piece handle=+MY_DG1/rmanelse/autobackup/2006_06_30/s_594480941
.273.594480945 tag=TAG20060630T133541
channel ORA_DISK_1: restore complete, elapsed time: 00:00:10
output filename=+MY_DG1/rmanelse/controlfile/current.289.594483525
Finished restore at 30-JUN-06

6.3 Datafile

We can restore & recover individual datafiles of the target database.
The target database instance could be running in the mounted or opened state.
However for restore & recovery of the datafile(s) of system tablespace the target
database will have to be in mounted state ONLY.

Tip: Datafile 1 is always the system tablespace datafile.

RMAN> connect target;

connected to target database: RMANELSE (DBID=1826602558, not open)

RMAN> connect catalog rman/rwoman@rman4all;

connected to recovery catalog database

RMAN> restore datafile 1;

RMAN> recover datafile 1;

Below we will restore & recover a datafile of a non-system tablespace.

RMAN> connect target;

connected to target database: RMANELSE (DBID=1826602558)

RMAN> connect catalog rman/rwoman@rman4all;

connected to recovery catalog database

RMAN> restore datafile 7;

Starting restore at 17-SEP-06
allocated channel: ORA_DISK_1
channel ORA_DISK_1: sid=20 devtype=DISK

channel ORA_DISK_1: starting datafile backupset restore
channel ORA_DISK_1: specifying datafile(s) to restore from backup set
restoring datafile 00007 to +MY_DG1/rmanelse/datafile/auxdata.262.601407821
channel   ORA_DISK_1:   reading   from   backup   piece/u01/app/oracle/
admin/RMANELSE/aux_dest/RMANELSE/backupset/2006_09_17/o1_mf_n
nnd0_TAG20060917T182532_2jvlty98_.bkpchannel ORA_DISK_1: restored
backup piece 1
piece   handle=/u01/app/oracle/admin/RMANELSE/aux_dest/RMANELSE/
backupset/2006_09_17/o1_mf_nnnd0_TAG20060917T182532_2jvlty98_
.bkp tag=TAG20060917T182532
channel ORA_DISK_1: restore complete, elapsed time: 00:00:08
Finished restore at 17-SEP-06
starting full resync of recovery catalog
full resync complete

RMAN> recover datafile 7;

Starting recover at 17-SEP-06
using channel ORA_DISK_1

starting media recovery
media recovery complete, elapsed time: 00:00:04

Finished recover at 17-SEP-06

You must then bring the datafile online for normal use.

6.4 Tablespace

You can restore one or more tablespaces of the target database.
The target database instance could be running in the mounted or opened state.

Again for restore & recovery of system tablespace the target database will have to be in mounted state ONLY.

RMAN> connect target;

connected to target database: RMANELSE (DBID=1826602558)

RMAN> connect catalog rman/rwoman@rman4all;

connected to recovery catalog database

RMAN> restore tablespace auxdata;

Starting restore at 17-SEP-06
starting full resync of recovery catalog
full resync complete
allocated channel: ORA_DISK_1
channel ORA_DISK_1: sid=36 devtype=DISK

channel ORA_DISK_1: starting datafile backupset restore
channel ORA_DISK_1: specifying datafile(s) to restore from backup set
restoring datafile 00006 to +MY_DG1/rmanelse/datafile/auxdata.281.596679751
restoring datafile 00007 to +MY_DG1/rmanelse/datafile/auxdata.262.601413469
channel ORA_DISK_1: reading from backup piece/u01/app/oracle/admin/
RMANELSE/aux_dest/RMANELSE/backupset/2006_09_17/o1_mf_nnnd0_
TAG20060917T182532_2jvlty98_.bkpchannel ORA_DISK_1: restored backup
piece 1

piece handle=/u01/app/oracle/admin/RMANELSE/aux_dest/RMANELSE/
backupset/2006_09_17/o1_mf_nnnd0_TAG20060917T182532_2jvlty98_
.bkp tag=TAG20060917T182532
channel ORA_DISK_1: restore complete, elapsed time: 00:00:08
Finished restore at 17-SEP-06
starting full resync of recovery catalog
full resync complete

RMAN> recover tablespace auxdata;

Starting recover at 17-SEP-06
using channel ORA_DISK_1

starting media recovery
media recovery complete, elapsed time: 00:00:04

Finished recover at 17-SEP-06

Now you can place the tablespace auxdata online.

The DBA can also 'redirect' the target database files to a different location for restore.

You can query the dynamic views v$datafile_header or v$recover_file to ascertain the status of various datafiles.

SQL> SELECT FILE#, STATUS, ERROR, RECOVER, TABLESPACE_NAME, NAME FROM V$DATAFILE_HEADER
WHERE RECOVER = 'YES' OR (RECOVER IS NULL AND ERROR IS NOT NULL);

While the RECOVER column shows if any datafile needs media recovery the ERROR column is indicative of an error condition while validating the datafile header.

SQL> SELECT FILE#, ERROR, ONLINE_STATUS, CHANGE#, TIME FROM V$RECOVER_FILE;

6.5 Database

Finally let us look at the big picture: restore & recovery of the entire target database. Understandably the target database must be in mounted state ONLY.

RMAN> restore database;

Note: Any read only tablespace will not be restored by default. To alter this RMAN behavior use restore database with the 'check readonly' clause.

```
$ export ORACLE_SID=+ASM1
$ asmcmd
ASMCMD> ls
MY_DG1/
MY_DG2/
ASMCMD> cd my_dg1
ASMCMD> ls
RMANELSE/
ASMCMD> cd rmanelse
ASMCMD> cd datafile
ASMCMD> ls
EXAMPLE.282.594484287
SYSAUX.281.593971515
SYSTEM.304.593971515
UNDOTBS1.286.593971515
USERS.283.593971515
```

To simulate the loss of all the datafiles we will delete them from the ASM based storage.

```
ASMCMD> rm *
You may delete multiple files and/or directories.
Are you sure? (y/n) y
ASMCMD> ls
asmcmd: entry 'datafile' does not exist in directory '+my_dg1/rmanelse/'
```

Note: ASM is intelligent to prevent deletion of any datafile presently being used by the target database. This is another compelling reason to employ ASM based database storage. Any attempt to remove is greeted with the ORA-15028 error. For non-ASM regular OS files we have no such smart protection.

$ export ORACLE_SID=RMANELSE

RMAN> connect target;

connected to target database: RMANELSE (DBID=1826602558, not open)

RMAN> connect catalog rman/rwoman@rman4all;

connected to recovery catalog database

RMAN> restore database;

```
Starting restore at 03-JUL-06
allocated channel: ORA_DISK_1
channel ORA_DISK_1: sid=40 devtype=DISK

channel ORA_DISK_1: starting datafile backupset restore
channel ORA_DISK_1: specifying datafile(s) to restore from backup set
restoring datafile 00001 to +MY_DG1/rmanelse/datafile/system.304.593971515
restoring datafile 00002 to +MY_DG1/rmanelse/datafile/undotbs1.286.593971515
restoring datafile 00003 to +MY_DG1/rmanelse/datafile/sysaux.281.593971515
restoring datafile 00004 to +MY_DG1/rmanelse/datafile/users.283.593971515
restoring datafile 00005 to +MY_DG1/rmanelse/datafile/example.282.594484287
channel ORA_DISK_1: reading from backup piece +MY_DG1/rmanelse/
backupset/2006_06_30/nnndn0_tag20060630t111950_0.292.594472791
RMAN-00571: ===========================================================
RMAN-00569: =========== ERROR MESSAGE STACK FOLLOWS ======
RMAN-00571: ===========================================================
RMAN-03002: failure of restore command at 07/03/2006 13:58:10
ORA-19870: error reading backup piece +MY_DG1/rmanelse/backupset/
2006_06_30/nnndn0_tag20060630t111950_0.292.594472791
ORA-19913: unable to decrypt backup
ORA-28365: wallet is not open
```

Dual mode encrypted backups can be restored using either the TDE wallet or a password.

SQL> ALTER SYSTEM SET ENCRYPTION WALLET OPEN IDENTIFIED BY "DB4secure";

RMAN> set decryption identified by 'rman2secure';

executing command: SET decryption

RMAN> restore database;

Starting restore at 03-JUL-06
using channel ORA_DISK_1

channel ORA_DISK_1: starting datafile backupset restore
channel ORA_DISK_1: specifying datafile(s) to restore from backup set
restoring datafile 00001 to +MY_DG1/rmanelse/datafile/system.304.593971515
restoring datafile 00002 to +MY_DG1/rmanelse/datafile/undotbs1.286.593971515
restoring datafile 00003 to +MY_DG1/rmanelse/datafile/sysaux.281.593971515
restoring datafile 00004 to +MY_DG1/rmanelse/datafile/users.283.593971515
restoring datafile 00005 to +MY_DG1/rmanelse/datafile/example.282.594484287
channel ORA_DISK_1: reading from backup piece +MY_DG1/rmanelse/backupset/2006_06_30/nnndn0_tag20060630t111950_0.292.594472791
channel ORA_DISK_1: restored backup piece 1
piece handle=+MY_DG1/rmanelse/backupset/2006_06_30/nnndn0_tag2006
0630t111950_0.292.594472791 tag=TAG20060630T111950
channel ORA_DISK_1: restore complete, elapsed time: 00:03:05
Finished restore at 03-JUL-06
starting full resync of recovery catalog
full resync complete

RMAN> recover database;

Starting recover at 03-JUL-06
using channel ORA_DISK_1
channel ORA_DISK_1: starting incremental datafile backupset restore
channel ORA_DISK_1: specifying datafile(s) to restore from backup set
destination for restore of datafile 00005: +MY_DG1/rmanelse/datafile/example
.282.594828007

channel ORA_DISK_1: reading from backup piece +MY_DG1/rmanelse/
backupset/2006_06_30/nnndn1_incre_cum_bkup_0.285.594480609
channel ORA_DISK_1: restored backup piece 1
piece handle=+MY_DG1/rmanelse/backupset/2006_06_30/nnndn1_incre_
cum_bkup_0.285.594480609 tag=INCRE_CUM_BKUP
channel ORA_DISK_1: restore complete, elapsed time: 00:00:01

starting media recovery

/u01/app/oracle/admin/RMANELSE/arch/1_5_593971715.dbf
archive log thread 2 sequence 3 is already on disk as file/u01/app/oracle/admin/
RMANELSE/arch/2_3_593971715.dbf
archive log thread 2 sequence 4 is already on disk as file
channel ORA_DISK_1: starting archive log restore to default destination
channel ORA_DISK_1: restoring archive log
channel ORA_DISK_1: reading from backup piece +MY_DG1/rmanelse/
backupset/2006_06_30/annnf0_tag20060630t112348_0.303.594473031
channel ORA_DISK_1: restored backup piece 1
piece handle=+MY_DG1/rmanelse/backupset/2006_06_30/annnf0_tag2006
0630t112348_0.303.594473031 tag=TAG20060630T112348
channel ORA_DISK_1: restore complete, elapsed time: 00:00:01
archive log filename=/u01/app/oracle/admin/RMANELSE/arch/2_2_593971715
.dbf thread=2 sequence=2
archive log filename=/u01/app/oracle/admin/RMANELSE/arch/1_4_593971715
.dbf thread=1 sequence=4
media recovery complete, elapsed time: 00:00:47
Finished recover at 03-JUL-06

For incomplete recovery or backup controlfile based recovery we need to reset the logs while opening the target database. Else we will encounter the ORA-01589 error.

RMAN> alter database open resetlogs;

database opened
new incarnation of database registered in recovery catalog
starting full resync of recovery catalog
full resync complete

> It is the best practice to issue this command from within RMAN itself as it in turn issues an implicit RESET DATABASE registering a new incarnation of the target database in the recovery catalog.

For situations involving limited disk space the DBA can specify the upper limit for the retention of restored archived logs by directing RMAN to recover the target database and in the process keep deleting the applied archived logs. In this example RMAN will not retain more than 100M of the archived logs on disk at any given time.

RMAN> recover database delete archivelog maxsize 100M;

We can also set multiple archivelog destinations for restoring archived logs.

RMAN> run
{ set archivelog destination to '/u01/app/oracle/admin/rmanelse/arch_1';
  restore archivelog sequence between 10000 and 11000;
  set archivelog destination to '/u02/app/oracle/admin/rmanelse/arch_2';
  restore archivelog sequence between 11001 and 11999;
  set archivelog destination to '/u03/app/oracle/admin/rmanelse/arch_3';
  restore archivelog sequence between 12000 and 12999; }

Note:
RMAN will automatically recreate temporary tablespaces while the target database is being opened after restore and recovery.

6.6 Restore of Encrypted Backups

The DBA can restore both transparent & dual mode RMAN encrypted backups just like a regular non-encrypted backup provided the TDE Wallet is correctly configured. Even if the current database master key is reset RMAN can successfully restore all the encrypted backups. Evidently if the Encryption Wallet is lost then you will NOT be able to restore any transparently encrypted backups.

If you are required to restore a password encrypted backup then supply the same password used at the time of encrypting that backup. Please be aware the password encryption is NOT persistently configurable. Hence if you forget the password RMAN can not restore that backup.

Dual mode encrypted backups can be restored using either the TDE wallet or a password.

Caution: If you forget the encryption password AND lose your wallet RMAN will be unable to restore dual mode encrypted backups.

SQL> ALTER SYSTEM SET ENCRYPTION WALLET OPEN IDENTIFIED BY "DB4secure";

RMAN> set decryption identified by 'rman2secure';

6.7 Restore Preview

The DBA can also use the PREVIEW clause with the restore. This will also help us to isolate some instances for directing RMAN to avail or avoid particular backups.

Tip: Use this in conjunction with the CHANGE ... AVAILABLE | UNAVAILABLE command that we will cover in the next chapter.

RMAN> restore database preview;

Starting restore at 02-JUL-06
allocated channel: ORA_DISK_1 channel ORA_DISK_1: sid=26 devtype=DISK

List of Backup Sets
===================

BS Key Type LV Size   Device Type Elapsed Time Completion Time
------- ---- -- ---------- ----------- ------------ ---------------
1118   Incr 0 1003.66M DISK   00:03:44   30-JUN-06
     BP Key: 1121 Status: AVAILABLE Compressed: NO Tag: TAG20060630
T111950
     Piece Name; +MY_DG1/rmanelse/backupset/2006_06_30/nnndn0_tag2006
0630t111950_0.292.594472791
  List of Datafiles in backup set 1118
  File LV Type Ckp SCN   Ckp Time Name
  ---- -- ---- ---------- ---------- ----
  1   0 Incr 3718782   30-JUN-06
+MY_DG1/rmanelse/datafile/system.304.593971515
  2   0 Incr 3718782   30-JUN-06

+MY_DG1/rmanelse/datafile/undotbs1.286.593971515
  3 0 Incr 3718782   30-JUN-06
+MY_DG1/rmanelse/datafile/sysaux.281.593971515
  4 0 Incr 3718782   30-JUN-06
+MY_DG1/rmanelse/datafile/users.283.593971515
  5 0 Incr 3718782   30-JUN-06
+MY_DG1/rmanelse/datafile/example.282.594484287

```
BS Key  Type LV Size      Device Type Elapsed Time Completion Time
------- ---- -- ---------- ----------- ------------- ---------------
1166    Incr 1  48.00K     DISK        00:00:12      30-JUN-06
    BP Key: 1168  Status: AVAILABLE  Compressed: NO  Tag: INCRE_CUM
_BKUP
    Piece Name: +MY_DG1/rmanelse/backupset/2006_06_30/nnndn1_incre_
cum_bkup_0.285.594480609
  List of Datafiles in backup set 1166
  File LV Type Ckp SCN    Ckp Time  Name
  ---- -- ---- ---------- --------- ----
   5   1  Incr 3728884    30-JUN-06
+MY_DG1/rmanelse/datafile/example.282.594484287
using channel ORA_DISK_1
```

```
BS Key  Size      Device Type Elapsed Time Completion Time
------- ---------- ----------- ------------- ----------------
1138    89.50K     DISK        00:00:02      30-JUN-06
    BP Key: 1141  Status: AVAILABLE  Compressed: NO  Tag: TAG20060630
T112348
    Piece Name: +MY_DG1/rmanelse/backupset/2006_06_30/annnf0_tag2006
0630t112348_0.303.594473031

  List of Archived Logs in backup set 1138
  Thrd Seq    Low SCN    Low Time  Next SCN   Next Time
  ---- ------- ---------- --------- ---------- ---------
   2   2       3718742    30-JUN-06 3718959    30-JUN-06
```

```
List of Archived Log Copies
Key    Thrd Seq    S Low Time  Name
------- ---- ------- - --------- ----
1367   1    3       A 30-JUN-06
/u01/app/oracle/admin/RMANELSE/arch/1_3_593971715.dbf
```

1368   1   4   A 30-JUN-06
/u01/app/oracle/admin/RMANELSE/arch/1_4_593971715.dbf
1366   1   5   A 30-JUN-06
/u01/app/oracle/admin/RMANELSE/arch/1_5_593971715.dbf
1369   2   3   A 30-JUN-06
/u01/app/oracle/admin/RMANELSE/arch/2_3_593971715.dbf
1370   2   4   A 30-JUN-06
/u01/app/oracle/admin/RMANELSE/arch/2_4_593971715.dbf
Media recovery start SCN is 3718782
Recovery must be done beyond SCN 3728884 to clear data files fuzziness
Finished restore at 02-JUL-06

Can you preview the restore of just one tablespace or even a few archived logs?

RMAN> restore tablespace example preview;

RMAN> restore archivelog from time 'sysdate-14' preview;

The DBA can avail of the RESTORE ... PREVIEW RECALL command to press into service the remotely stored backups needed.

RMAN> restore archivelog all preview;

List of remote backup files
============================
...
...

RMAN> restore archivelog all preview recall;

Initiated recall for the following list of remote backup files
==
...
...

You can repeat the RESTORE ... PREVIEW command until no backups needed for the restore are reported as remote.

6.8 Restore Validation

A very useful tool is the RESTORE … VALIDATE functionality. The backups are fully validated for restore eligibility.

RMAN> restore database validate;
Starting restore at 02-JUL-06
allocated channel: ORA_DISK_1
channel ORA_DISK_1: sid=27 devtype=DISK

channel ORA_DISK_1: starting validation of datafile backupset
channel ORA_DISK_1: reading from backup piece +MY_DG1/rmanelse/
backupset/2006_06_30/nnndn0_tag20060630t111950_0.292.594472791
channel ORA_DISK_1: restored backup piece 1
piece handle=+MY_DG1/rmanelse/backupset/2006_06_30/nnndn0_tag2006
0630t111950_0.292.594472791 tag=TAG20060630T111950
channel ORA_DISK_1: validation complete, elapsed time: 00:01:36
Finished restore at 02-JUL-06

Note: RMAN will need to decrypt the encrypted backup even for this validation.

We can also validate the restore of various database structures as under:

RMAN> restore controlfile validate;

RMAN> restore tablespace auxdata validate;

RMAN> restore archivelog all validate;

Please be aware the live datafiles need NOT go offline while validating the backup restore.

6.9 Restore/Recovery Performance

The performance of RMAN restore/recovery operations can be significantly improved by tuning the environment. We will briefly dwell on some areas to focus for achieving better results.

For tape reads the tape block size is an important factor that can influence the performance of the restore operation.

RMAN> configure channel device type sbt_tape parms="blksize=524288";

RMAN uses the buffers of the large pool (if configured) for its I/O operations. The size of this pool as defined by the LARGE_POOL_SIZE initialization parameter is another key variable impacting the restore operations. To eliminate shared pool contention you must define this pool adequately sized. Oracle recommends the following formula to calculate its size:

LARGE_POOL_SIZE = number of allocated channels * (16Mb + (4 * tape buffer size))

RMAN's I/O can be done either synchronously or asynchronously. In synchronous I/O a server process can perform tasks serially completing one at a time. This could become a bottleneck when the host system is under heavy loads. But in an asynchronous mode a server process can perform tasks in parallel.

On the operating systems that do not provide native asynchronous I/O Oracle can emulate synchronous I/O by forking special slave processes. This is achieved by setting the DBWR_IO_SLAVES parameter to a nonzero value. For every dbwr slave four backup disk I/O slaves are automatically spawned which can be used for restore.

Media managers can offer their own tuning solutions also. IBM's TSM/TDP provides a faster backup & restore mechanism called 'LANFREE' to avoid slowdown caused by network constraints.

You can query the dynamic V$BACKUP_ASYNC_IO view for values of the column EFFECTIVE_BYTES_PER_SECOND. This gives a better handle on the actual data transfer rate for tape I/O. This view also contains two other columns of interest to us. For each datafile we can see the LONG_WAITS and the IO_COUNT. The ratio of LONG_WAITS to IO_COUNT is a good indicator of asynchronous I/O performance.

SQL> SELECT DEVICE_TYPE DEVICE, TYPE, FILENAME, TO_ CHAR(OPEN_TIME,'DD-MM-YYYY HH24:MI:SS') OPEN, TO_ CHAR(CLOSE_TIME,'DD-MM-YYYY HH24:MI:SS') CLOSE, ELAPSED_ TIME ET, EFFECTIVE_BYTES_PER_SECOND EBPS FROM V$BACKUP_ ASYNC_IO WHERE CLOSE_TIME > SYSDATE -14 ORDER BY CLOSE_ TIME DESC;

One obvious indicator of I/O degradation is the population of the dynamic view V$BACKUP_SYNC_IO. If we observe database writing to this view then we can conclude our I/O is not asynchronous.

Generally the more channels are configured/allocated the better the performance of RMAN. The degree of device parallelism is another factor affecting throughput by determining the allocation of automatic channels.

RMAN> configure device type sbt_tape parallelism 5;

You can use this query to find out the database server session & the corresponding OS process for the RMAN job.

```
SQL> SELECT s.SID, p.SPID, s.CLIENT_INFO
FROM V$PROCESS p, V$SESSION s
WHERE p.ADDR = s.PADDR
AND CLIENT_INFO LIKE 'rman%';
```

How can a DBA determine the progress of the RMAN restore/recovery process?

```
SQL> SELECT SID, SERIAL#, CONTEXT, SOFAR, TOTALWORK,
ROUND(SOFAR/TOTALWORK*100,2) "%_COMPLETE"
FROM V$SESSION_LONGOPS
WHERE OPNAME LIKE 'RMAN%'
AND OPNAME NOT LIKE '%aggregate%'
AND TOTALWORK!= 0
AND SOFAR <> TOTALWORK;
```

6.10 Recovery Across Resetlogs

The DBA can perform target database restore & recovery spanning resetlogs operations.
Archived redo logs from previous incarnations may be used to perform media recovery.

Step 1 Connect to both the target & catalog databases.

RMAN> list incarnation;
You will see output similar to this.

List of Database Incarnations

DB Key	Inc Key	DB Name	DB ID	STATU	Reset SCN	Reset Time
4078	4089	RMANELSE	1826602558	PARENT	3729933	30-JUN-06
4078	4090	RMANELSE	1826602558	PARENT	4092628	21-JUL-06
4078	4079	RMANELSE	1826602558	CURRENT	4134506	25-JUL-06

Step 2 Update the recovery catalog by making any previous (parent) incarnation of the target database as its current incarnation.

RMAN> reset database to incarnation <parent_inckey>;

RMAN> shutdown immediate;

Step 3 Bring up the target instance for restoring an old backup of the controlfile (belonging to that prior incarnation).

RMAN> startup nomount;

RMAN> run
{ set until time "to_date('2006-07-13:08:10:00', 'YYYY-MM-DD:HH24:MI:SS')";
  restore controlfile;
  alter database mount; }

Step 4 Restore & Recover using the database files from that prior incarnation.

RMAN> run
{ set until time "to_date('2006-07-13:08:10:00', 'YYYY-MM-DD:HH24:MI:SS')";
  restore database;
  recover database; }

Step 5 After this recovery using backup controlfile open the target database initializing the online logs.

RMAN> alter database open resetlogs;

6.11 Workshop—Recreate Lost Datafiles

Can the DBA resort to RMAN for recreating missing datafiles? Absolutely. This is a very comforting thought indeed! Regardless of the availability of backups of the controlfile and/or the missing datafile we can recreate the datafile just by applying the necessary archived logs. During recovery RMAN will create the new datafile and apply the required archived logs.

We first take the tablespace with the missing datafile offline.

SQL> ALTER TABLESPACE AUXDATA OFFLINE IMMEDIATE;

$ export ORACLE_SID=RMANELSE

RMAN> connect target;

connected to target database: RMANELSE (DBID=1826602558)

RMAN> connect catalog rman/rwoman@rman4all;

connected to recovery catalog database

RMAN> restore tablespace auxdata;

Starting restore at 21-SEP-06
starting full resync of recovery catalog
full resync complete
allocated channel: ORA_SBT_TAPE_1
channel ORA_SBT_TAPE_1: sid=26 devtype=SBT_TAPE
channel ORA_SBT_TAPE_1: Oracle Secure Backup
allocated channel: ORA_SBT_TAPE_2
channel ORA_SBT_TAPE_2: sid=19 devtype=SBT_TAPE
channel ORA_SBT_TAPE_2: Oracle Secure Backup
allocated channel: ORA_SBT_TAPE_3
channel ORA_SBT_TAPE_3: sid=17 devtype=SBT_TAPE
channel ORA_SBT_TAPE_3: Oracle Secure Backup
allocated channel: ORA_DISK_1
channel ORA_DISK_1: sid=42 devtype=DISK

creating datafile fno=8 name=+MY_DG1/rmanelse/datafile/auxdata.302.601753655
channel ORA_DISK_1: starting datafile backupset restore
channel ORA_DISK_1: specifying datafile(s) to restore from backup set

restoring datafile 00006 to +MY_DG1/rmanelse/datafile/auxdata.262 .601419705

restoring datafile 00007 to +MY_DG1/rmanelse/datafile/auxdata.281.601419707

channel ORA_DISK_1: reading from backup piece/u01/app/oracle/admin/ RMANELSE/aux_dest/RMANELSE/backupset/2006_09_17/o1_mf_nnnd0_ TAG20060917T182532_2jvlty98_.bkpchannel ORA_DISK_1: restored backup piece 1

piece handle=/u01/app/oracle/admin/RMANELSE/aux_dest/RMANELSE/ backupset/2006_09_17/o1_mf_nnnd0_TAG20060917T182532_2jvlty98_ .bkp tag=TAG20060917T182532

channel ORA_DISK_1: restore complete, elapsed time: 00:00:08

Finished restore at 21-SEP-06

RMAN> recover tablespace auxdata;

Starting recover at 21-SEP-06

using channel ORA_SBT_TAPE_1

using channel ORA_SBT_TAPE_2

using channel ORA_SBT_TAPE_3

using channel ORA_DISK_1

starting media recovery

archive log thread 1 sequence 65 is already on disk as file/u01/app/oracle/admin/ RMANELSE/aux_dest/RMANELSE/archivelog/2006_09_17/o1_mf_1_65_ 2jvzf67k_.arc

archive log thread 1 sequence 66 is already on disk as file/u01/app/oracle/admin/ RMANELSE/aux_dest/RMANELSE/archivelog/2006_09_18/o1_mf_1_66_ 2jyfbcv5_.arc

archive log thread 1 sequence 67 is already on disk as file/u01/app/oracle/admin/ RMANELSE/aux_dest/RMANELSE/archivelog/2006_09_18/o1_mf_1_67_ 2jymzj5l_.arc

archive log thread 1 sequence 68 is already on disk as file/u01/app/oracle/admin/ RMANELSE/aux_dest/RMANELSE/archivelog/2006_09_18/o1_mf_1_68_ 2jyn39px_.arc

archive log thread 1 sequence 69 is already on disk as file/u01/app/oracle/admin/ RMANELSE/aux_dest/RMANELSE/archivelog/2006_09_19/o1_mf_1_69_ 2k17bf7k_.arc archive log thread 1 sequence 70 is already on disk as file/u01/app/oracle/admin/ RMANELSE/aux_dest/RMANELSE/archivelog/2006_09_21/o1_mf_1_70_ 2k61ovnc_.arc

channel ORA_DISK_1: starting archive log restore to default destination

channel ORA_DISK_1: restoring archive log

archive log thread=1 sequence=64

channel ORA_DISK_1: reading from backup piece/u01/app/oracle/admin/ RMANELSE/aux_dest/RMANELSE/backupset/2006_09_17/o1_mf_annnn_ TAG20060917T182902_2jvm1hrv_.bkpchannel ORA_DISK_1: restored backup piece 1

piece handle=/u01/app/oracle/admin/RMANELSE/aux_dest/RMANELSE/ backupset/2006_09_17/o1_mf_annnn_TAG20060917T182902_2jvm1hrv_ .bkp tag=TAG20060917T182902

channel ORA_DISK_1: restore complete, elapsed time: 00:00:01

archive log filename=/u01/app/oracle/admin/RMANELSE/aux_dest/RMANELSE/ archivelog/2006_09_21/o1_mf_1_64_2k6289yk_.arc thread=1 sequence=64

channel default: deleting archive log(s)

archive log filename=/u01/app/oracle/admin/RMANELSE/aux_dest/RMANELSE/ archivelog/2006_09_21/o1_mf_1_64_2k6289yk_.arc recid=149 stamp=601753802

archive log filename=/u01/app/oracle/admin/RMANELSE/aux_dest/RMANELSE/ archivelog/2006_09_17/o1_mf_1_65_2jvzf67k_.arc thread=1 sequence=65

archive log filename=/u01/app/oracle/admin/RMANELSE/aux_dest/RMANELSE/ archivelog/2006_09_18/o1_mf_1_66_2jyfbcv5_.arc thread=1 sequence=66

archive log filename=/u01/app/oracle/admin/RMANELSE/aux_dest/RMANELSE/ archivelog/2006_09_18/o1_mf_1_67_2jymzj5l_.arc thread=1 sequence=67

archive log filename=/u01/app/oracle/admin/RMANELSE/aux_dest/RMANELSE/ archivelog/2006_09_18/o1_mf_1_68_2jyn39px_.arc thread=1 sequence=68

media recovery complete, elapsed time: 00:00:05

Finished recover at 21-SEP-06

SQL> ALTER TABLESPACE AUXDATA ONLINE;

6.12 Restore & Recovery on a Different Host

The DBA can restore the database on a server different from the original host. After the restore of all the relevant database structures media recovery can be performed as needed.

Step 1 Connect to both the target & catalog databases.

Step 2 Set the dbid & startup the target instance without mounting the database.

RMAN> set dbid <integer>;
RMAN> startup force nomount;

Since RMAN will not find the actual server parameter file a dummy file will be used for the instance startup. You will see the output as under:

startup failed: ORA-01078: failure in processing system parameters
LRM-00109: could not open parameter file <'$ORACLE_HOME/dbs/initSID.ora'>
starting Oracle instance without parameter file for retrieval of spfile
Oracle instance started

Step 3 Restore the server parameter file as a client-side parameter file.

RMAN> run
{ allocate channel t1 type 'sbt_tape' parms
'ENV=(TDPO_OPTFILE =/usr/tivoli/tsm/client/oracle/bin64/tdpo.opt)';
 restore spfile to pfile '<filename>' from autobackup; }

Step 4 Now you may edit the pfile as needed & then bounce the instance for those edited values to take effect.

RMAN> startup force nomount pfile='<filename>';

Step 5 Restore the control file before mounting the target database.

RMAN> run
{ allocate channel t1 type 'sbt_tape' parms
'ENV=(TDPO_OPTFILE =/usr/tivoli/tsm/client/oracle/bin64/tdpo.opt)';
 restore controlfile from autobackup;
 alter database mount; }

Step 6 Rename the target database datafiles & online redo logs.

RMAN> run
{ set newname for datafile 1 to '<newfilename>';
 set newname for datafile 2 to '<newfilename>';
 ...
 ...

```
sql "alter database rename file "<oldlogfilename>"
to "<newlogfilename>" ";
...
```

Step 7 Perform an incomplete recovery of the target database with all the file names switched.

```
RMAN> run
set until time "to_date('2006-07-13:08:10:00', 'YYYY-MM-DD:HH24:MI:SS')";
allocate channel t1 type 'sbt_tape' parms
'ENV=(TDPO_OPTFILE =/usr/tivoli/tsm/client/oracle/bin64/tdpo.opt)';
 restore database;
 switch datafile all;
 recover database; }
```

Step 8 Having performed incomplete database recovery open the target database initializing the online logs.

```
RMAN> alter database open resetlogs;
```

Caution: If this exercise is being done just to validate disaster recovery readiness then do NOT connect to the recovery catalog while issuing the above statement. Else this new target database incarnation will get registered with the modified filenames thus jeopardizing the production database.

Chapter 6 Recapitulation

RMAN can start an Oracle instance without parameter file for retrieval of spfile.

For restore & recovery of the datafile(s) of system tablespace the target database will have to be in mounted state ONLY.

Any attempt to remove an ASM file presently being used by the target database is greeted with the ORA-15028 error. For non-ASM regular OS files we have no such smart protection.

Dual mode encrypted backups can be restored using either the TDE wallet or a password.
SQL> ALTER SYSTEM SET ENCRYPTION WALLET OPEN IDENTIFIED BY "DB4secure";
RMAN> set decryption identified by 'rman2secure';
If the TDE wallet is not open or a password is not provided while restore & recovery RMAN will throw ORA-19913: unable to decrypt backup & ORA-28365: wallet is not open errors.

For incomplete recovery or backup controlfile based recovery we need to reset the logs while opening the target database. Else we will encounter the ORA-01589 error.

The command 'alter database open resetlogs' is best issued from within RMAN itself as it in turn issues an implicit RESET DATABASE registering a new incarnation of the target database in the recovery catalog.

RMAN will automatically recreate temporary tablespaces while the target database is being opened after restore and recovery.

The DBA can also use the PREVIEW clause with the restore. This will help us to isolate some instances for directing RMAN to avail or avoid particular backups.

The target database backups can be fully validated for restore eligibility using the RESTORE … VALIDATE functionality. Please be aware the live datafiles need NOT go offline while validating the backup restore.

The DBA can determine the progress of the RMAN restore/recovery process by querying the dynamic V$SESSION_LONGOPS view.

For tape reads the tape block size is an important factor that can influence the performance of the restore operation.

RMAN uses the buffers of the large pool (if configured) for its I/O operations. The size of this pool as defined by the LARGE_POOL_SIZE initialization parameter is another key variable impacting the restore operations. To eliminate shared pool contention you must define this pool adequately sized.
You can query the dynamic V$BACKUP_ASYNC_IO view for values of the column EFFECTIVE_BYTES_PER_SECOND.

Generally the more channels are configured/allocated the better the performance of RMAN.

The DBA can perform target database restore & recovery spanning resetlogs operations. Archived redo logs from previous incarnations may be used to perform media recovery.

Regardless of the availability of backups of the controlfile and/or the datafile we can recreate any lost datafile just by applying the necessary archived logs. During recovery RMAN will create the new datafile and apply the required archived logs.

The DBA can restore the database on a server different from the original host. The caveat is NOT to connect to the recovery catalog while issuing the 'alter database open resetlogs' statement if this exercise is being done just to validate disaster recovery readiness. This is to prevent the new target database incarnation getting registered with the modified filenames thus jeopardizing the production database.

Chapter 7 Objectives

- Crosscheck
- Delete
- Change
- Catalog
- Resync
- Retrieval

Chapter 7
Maintenance

Regardless of the kind of RMAN repository we may use (target database control file or the recovery catalog) we have to maintain the metadata & manage the media files in an organized manner. Let us delve into those areas we need to focus on now.

Primarily we will learn 2 mechanisms of repository maintenance: Crosscheck & Delete. We will touch upon another 2 items later in this chapter.

7.1 Crosschecking

How do you ensure metadata about backups in the recovery catalog or control file truly reflect the actual physical state of the media files? Crosscheck performs exactly this synchronization.

A classic example is the deletion of archived logs from disk with an operating system command. The repository metadata may not reflect this at all.

Note: Only for the disk backups RMAN can evaluate the file headers to ascertain their validity. However for backups on tape crosscheck can only checks their presence.

> After crosscheck the status of backups can be any one of AVAILABLE, UNAVAILABLE and EXPIRED.

Below we wish to perform a crosscheck of the entire backup.

RMAN> connect target sys/r24rman@rmanelse;

connected to target database: RMANELSE (DBID=1826602558)

RMAN> connect catalog rman/rwoman@rman4all;

connected to recovery catalog database

RMAN> crosscheck backup;

using channel ORA_DISK_1
crosschecked backup piece: found to be 'AVAILABLE'
backup piece handle=+MY_DG1/rmanelse/backupset/2006_06_30/annnf0_
tag20060630t111932_0.287.594472775 recid=1 stamp=594472774
crosschecked backup piece: found to be 'AVAILABLE'
backup piece handle=+MY_DG1/rmanelse/backupset/2006_06_30/nnndn0_
tag20060630t111950_0.292.594472791 recid=2 stamp=594472791
crosschecked backup piccc: found to be 'AVAILABLE'
backup piece handle=+MY_DG1/rmanelse/backupset/2006_06_30/ncsnn0_
tag20060630t111950_0.262.594473021 recid=3 stamp=594473021
crosschecked backup piece: found to be 'AVAILABLE'
backup piece handle=+MY_DG1/rmanelse/backupset/2006_06_30/annnf0_
tag20060630t112348_0.303.594473031 recid=4 stamp=594473029
crosschecked backup piece: found to be 'AVAILABLE'
backup piece handle=+MY_DG1/rmanelse/backupset/2006_06_30/nnndn1_
tag20060630t132349_0.302.594480231 recid=5 stamp=594480230
crosschecked backup piece: found to be 'AVAILABLE'
backup piece handle=+MY_DG1/rmanelse/backupset/2006_06_30/nnndn1_
incre_cum_bkup_0.285.594480609 recid=6 stamp=594480609
crosschecked backup piece: found to be 'AVAILABLE'
backup piece handle=+MY_DG1/rmanelse/backupset/2006_06_30/annnf0_
tag20060630t133537_0.300.594480939 recid=7 stamp=594480938
crosschecked backup piece: found to be 'AVAILABLE'
backup piece handle=+MY_DG1/rmanelse/autobackup/2006_06_30/s_
594480941.273.594480945 recid=8 stamp=594480944
crosschecked backup piece: found to be 'AVAILABLE'
backup piece handle=+MY_DG1/rmanelse/autobackup/2006_06_30/s_
594484711.293.594484721 recid=8 stamp=594484720
Crosschecked 9 objects

We can now conclude we have the backup pieces available (in an ASM disk group) for RMAN.

However if RMAN was not able to locate the backup pieces those would have been marked 'EXPIRED'.

Further you can perform the crosscheck operation on a subset of the backup as under:

RMAN> crosscheck backupset 1118, 1155;

RMAN> crosscheck backup tag = 'incr_cum_bkup';

RMAN> crosscheck backup of archivelog all;
The DBA can also allocate a maintenance channel for tape.

RMAN> run
{ allocate channel for maintenance type 'sbt_tape'
 parms 'ENV=(TDPO_OPTFILE=/opt/tivoli/tsm/client/oracle/bin64/tdpo.opt)';
 crosscheck backup; }

Note: For disk based backups an explicit maintenance channel allocation is not needed.

Now let us see the output of performing a crosscheck operation on image copies.

$ export ORACLE_SID=RACDB

RMAN> connect target;

connected to target database: RACDB (DBID=559768190)

RMAN> connect catalog rman/rwoman@rman4all;

connected to recovery catalog database

RMAN> crosscheck copy;

allocated channel: ORA_DISK_1 channel ORA_DISK_1: sid=148 instance= RACDB2 devtype=DISK
validation succeeded for datafile copy
datafile copy filename=+MY_DG1/racdb/datafile/system.281.593554819 recid=2 stamp=593554884
validation succeeded for datafile copy
datafile copy filename=+MY_DG1/racdb/datafile/undotbs1.285.593554979 recid =6 stamp=593554992

validation succeeded for datafile copy
datafile copy filename=+MY_DG1/racdb/datafile/sysaux.282.593554887 recid=3 stamp=593554940
validation succeeded for datafile copy
datafile copy filename=+MY_DG1/racdb/datafile/users.286.593554995 recid=7 stamp=593555005
validation succeeded for datafile copy
datafile copy filename=+MY_DG1/racdb/datafile/example.283.593554945 recid=4 stamp=593554956
validation succeeded for datafile copy
datafile copy filename=+MY_DG1/racdb/datafile/undotbs2.287.593555013 rccid=8 stamp-593555024
validation succeeded for datafile copy
datafile copy filename=+MY_DG1/racdb/datafile/flow_1.289.593555037 recid=10 stamp=593555038
validation succeeded for datafile copy
datafile copy filename=+MY_DG1/racdb/datafile/soe.284.593554961 recid=5 stamp=593554973
validation succeeded for control file copy
control file copy filename=+MY_DG1/racdb/controlfile/backup.288.593555029 recid=9 stamp=593555033
validation succeeded for archived log
archive log filename=+MY_DG1/racdb/archivelog/2006_06_19/thread_1_seq_71.277.593554795 recid=19 stamp=593554797
validation succeeded for archived log
archive log filename=+MY_DG1/racdb/archivelog/2006_06_19/thread_1_seq_72.275.593554777 recid=17 stamp=593554783
validation succeeded for archived log
archive log filename=+MY_DG1/racdb/archivelog/2006_06_19/thread_2_seq_37.278.593554799 recid=20 stamp=593554803
validation succeeded for archived log
archive log filename=+MY_DG1/racdb/archivelog/2006_06_19/thread_2_seq_38.280.593554813 recid=22 stamp=593554815
Crosschecked 13 objects

As you can see we have configured the flash recovery area for the target database in an ASM disk group. The archived logs are placed (from both the threads of our RAC database) in this location.

The DBA can also perform crosscheck of backups using a date range as under:

RMAN> crosscheck backup completed between 'sysdate-30' and 'sysdate';

7.2 Deleting

What do we do with the unwanted backups or copies of our target database? Even tape storage can become expensive if allowed to grow unchecked. For removing the disk or tape backups we can use the DELETE command. This removes the physical files from the backup media, deletes the relevant repository metadata from the recovery catalog (if applicable) and updates the backup records in the target database control file.

Tip: Run crosscheck BEFORE any delete operation!

$ export ORACLE_SID=RACDB

RMAN> connect target;

connected to target database: RACDB (DBID=559768190)

RMAN> connect catalog rman/rwoman@rman4all;

connected to recovery catalog database

RMAN> delete expired backup;

allocated channel: ORA_DISK_1
channel ORA_DISK_1: sid=142 instance=RACDB1 devtype=DISK

List of Backup Pieces
BP Key BS Key Pc# Cp# Status   Device Type Piece Name
-------- ------- --- --- ----------- ----------- -----------
136   135   1 1   EXPIRED   DISK
/u01/app/oracle/product/10.2.0/db_1/dbs/db_RACDB_01hlkl44_1_1
167   158   1 1   EXPIRED   DISK
/u01/app/oracle/product/10.2.0/db_1/dbs/arch_RACDB_02hlklam_1_1
178   175   1 1   EXPIRED   DISK
/u01/app/oracle/product/10.2.0/db_1/dbs/c-559768190-20060614-00

Do you really want to delete the above objects (enter YES or NO)? YES
deleted backup piece
backup piece handle=/u01/app/oracle/product/10.2.0/db_1/dbs/db_RACDB_01hlkl44_1_1 recid=1 stamp=593122437
deleted backup piece
backup piece handle=/u01/app/oracle/product/10.2.0/db_1/dbs/arch_RACDB_02hlklam_1_1 recid=2 stamp=593122646
deleted backup piece
backup piece handle=/u01/app/oracle/product/10.2.0/db_1/dbs/c-559768190-20060615-00 recid=5 stamp=593199770
Deleted 3 EXPIRED objects

We can also delete specific backup objects.

RMAN> delete backupset 346;

using channel ORA_DISK_1

List of Backup Pieces
BP Key BS Key Pc# Cp# Status   Device Type Piece Name
------- ------- --- --- ------------ ------------ -----------
355   346   1   1   AVAILABLE   DISK
/u01/app/oracle/product/10.2.0/db_1/dbs/c-559768190-20060616-00

Do you really want to delete the above objects (enter YES or NO)? YES
deleted backup piece
backup piece handle=/u01/app/oracle/product/10.2.0/db_1/dbs/c-559768190-20060616-00 recid=10 stamp=593269023
Deleted 1 objects

RMAN> delete backup tag = 'incr_cum_bkup';

using channel ORA_DISK_1

List of Backup Pieces
BP Key BS Key Pc# Cp# Status   Device Type Piece Name
------- ------- --- --- ------------ ------------ -----------
508   505   1   1   AVAILABLE   DISK
+MY_DG1/racdb/backupset/2006_06_19/nnndn1_incr_cum_bkup_0.262
.593517541

Do you really want to delete the above objects (enter YES or NO)? YES
deleted backup piece backup piece handle=+MY_DG1/racdb/backupset/2006_
06_19/nnndn1_bkupfor_del_0.262.593517541 recid=15 stamp=593517540
Deleted 1 objects

You can delete backups that are obsolete (considered as no longer needed to
satisfy the defined recoverability objectives) as under:

RMAN> delete obsolete recovery window of 30 days;

Caution: the following 2 commands will wipe out all the cataloged backupsets &
copies!

Remove all the backupsets of the target database.

RMAN> delete backup;

starting full resync of recovery catalog
full resync complete
allocated channel: ORA_DISK_1
channel ORA_DISK_1: sid=141 instance=RACDB1 devtype=DISK

List of Backup Pieces
BP Key BS Key Pc# Cp# Status   Device Type Piece Name
------- ------- --- --- ----------- ----------- ----------
301   298   1 1   AVAILABLE   DISK
+MY_DG1/racdb/backupset/2006_06_16/nnndn0_tag20060616t125312_
0.256.593268795
332   323   1 1   AVAILABLE   DISK
+MY_DG1/racdb/backupset/2006_06_16/annnf0_tag20060616t125639_
0.257.593269003
423   419   1 1   AVAILABLE   DISK
+MY_DG1/racdb/backupset/2006_06_18/nnndn1_incre_diff_bkup_
0.258.593458089
424   420   1 1   AVAILABLE   DISK
+MY_DG1/racdb/backupset/2006_06_18/ncsnn1_incre_diff_bkup_0.259
.593458189
445   441   1 1   AVAILABLE   DISK
+MY_DG1/racdb/backupset/2006_06_18/nnndn1_incre_cum_bkup_0.260
.593459329

446   442   1 1 AVAILABLE DISK
+MY_DG1/racdb/backupset/2006_06_18/ncsnn1_incre_cum_bkup_0.261
.593459429
530   521   1 1 AVAILABLE DISK
+MY_DG1/racdb/autobackup/2006_06_19/s_593517558.263.593517563

Do you really want to delete the above objects (enter YES or NO)? YES
deleted backup piece
backup piece handle=+MY_DG1/racdb/backupset/2006_06_16/nnndn0_tag
20060616t125312_0.256.593268795 recid=8 stamp=593268793
deleted backup piece
backup piece handle=+MY_DG1/racdb/backupset/2006_06_16/annnf0_tag
20060616t125639_0.257.593269003 recid=9 stamp=593269000
deleted backup piece
backup piece handle=+MY_DG1/racdb/backupset/2006_06_18/nnndn1_
incre_diff_bkup_0.258.593458089 recid=11 stamp=593458089
deleted backup piece
backup piece handle=+MY_DG1/racdb/backupset/2006_06_18/ncsnn1_incre_
diff_bkup_0.259.593458189 recid=12 stamp=593458189
deleted backup piece
backup piece handle=+MY_DG1/racdb/backupset/2006_06_18/nnndn1_
incre_cum_bkup_0.260.593459329 recid=13 stamp=593459329
deleted backup piece
backup piece handle=+MY_DG1/racdb/backupset/2006_06_18/ncsnn1_incre_
cum_bkup_0.261.593459429 recid=14 stamp=593459428
deleted backup piece
backup piece handle=+MY_DG1/racdb/autobackup/2006_06_19/s_593517558
.263.593517563 recid=16 stamp=593517561
Deleted 7 objects

Now let us do likewise for the image copies.

RMAN> delete copy;

allocated channel: ORA_DISK_1
channel ORA_DISK_1: sid=132 instance=RACDB1 devtype=DISK

List of Datafile Copies

Key	File	S	Completion Time	Ckp SCN	Ckp Time	Name
611	1	A	19-JUN-06	3314303	19-JUN-06	
+MY_DG1/racdb/datafile/system.281.593554819						
615	2	A	19-JUN-06	3314530	19-JUN-06	
+MY_DG1/racdb/datafile/undotbs1.285.593554979						
612	3	A	19-JUN-06	3314414	19-JUN-06	
+MY_DG1/racdb/datafile/sysaux.282.593554887						
616	4	A	19-JUN-06	3314586	19-JUN-06	
+MY_DG1/racdb/datafile/users.286.593554995						
613	5	A	19-JUN-06	3314504	19-JUN-06	
+MY_DG1/racdb/datafile/example.283.593554945						
617	6	A	19-JUN-06	3314613	19-JUN-06	
+MY_DG1/racdb/datafile/undotbs2.287.593555013						
619	7	A	19-JUN-06	3314640	19-JUN-06	
+MY_DG1/racdb/datafile/flow_1.289.593555037						
614	8	A	19-JUN-06	3314520	19-JUN-06	
+MY_DG1/racdb/datafile/soe.284.593554961						

List of Control File Copies

Key	S	Completion Time	Ckp SCN	Ckp Time	Name
618	A	19-JUN-06	3314636	19-JUN-06	
+MY_DG1/racdb/controlfile/backup.288.593555029					

List of Archived Log Copies

Key	Thrd	Seq	S	Low Time	Name
600	1	71	A	16-JUN-06	
+MY_DG1/racdb/archivelog/2006_06_19/thread_1_seq_71.277.593554795					
598	1	72	A	18-JUN-06	
+MY_DG1/racdb/archivelog/2006_06_19/thread_1_seq_72.275.593554777					
601	2	37	A	16-JUN-06	
+MY_DG1/racdb/archivelog/2006_06_19/thread_2_seq_37.278.593554799					
603	2	38	A	18-JUN-06	
+MY_DG1/racdb/archivelog/2006_06_19/thread_2_seq_38.280.593554813					

Do you really want to delete the above objects (enter YES or NO)? YES
deleted datafile copy

datafile copy filename=+MY_DG1/racdb/datafile/system.281.593554819 recid=2 stamp=593554884
deleted datafile copy
datafile copy filename=+MY_DG1/racdb/datafile/undotbs1.285.593554979 recid=6 stamp=593554992
deleted datafile copy
datafile copy filename=+MY_DG1/racdb/datafile/sysaux.282.593554887 recid=3 stamp=593554940
deleted datafile copy
datafile copy filename=+MY_DG1/racdb/datafile/users.286.593554995 recid=7 stamp=593555005
deleted datafile copy
datafile copy filename=+MY_DG1/racdb/datafile/example.283.593554945 recid=4 stamp=593554956
deleted datafile copy
datafile copy filename=+MY_DG1/racdb/datafile/undotbs2.287.593555013 recid=8 stamp=593555024
deleted datafile copy
datafile copy filename=+MY_DG1/racdb/datafile/flow_1.289.593555037 recid=10 stamp=593555038
deleted datafile copy
datafile copy filename=+MY_DG1/racdb/datafile/soe.284.593554961 recid=5 stamp=593554973
deleted control file copy
control file copy filename=+MY_DG1/racdb/controlfile/backup.288.593555029 recid=9 stamp=593555033
deleted archive log
archive log filename=+MY_DG1/racdb/archivelog/2006_06_19/thread_1_seq_71.277.593554795 recid=19 stamp=593554797
deleted archive log
archive log filename=+MY_DG1/racdb/archivelog/2006_06_19/thread_1_seq_72.275.593554777 recid=17 stamp=593554783
deleted archive log
archive log filename=+MY_DG1/racdb/archivelog/2006_06_19/thread_2_seq_37.278.593554799 recid=20 stamp=593554803
deleted archive log
archive log filename=+MY_DG1/racdb/archivelog/2006_06_19/thread_2_seq_38.280.593554813 recid=22 stamp=593554815
Deleted 13 objects

Tip: Use the noprompt clause for non-interactive mode to avoid any confirmation prompting.

RMAN> delete noprompt backup;

You may run into the issue indicated below if crosscheck is not performed before actually deleting backups or copies.

RMAN-06207: WARNING: 1 objects could not be deleted for DISK channel(s) due
RMAN-06208:   to mismatched status. Use CROSSCHECK command to
fix statusRMAN-06210: List of Mismatched objects
RMAN-06211: ==========================
RMAN-06212:   Object Type   Filename/Handle
RMAN-06213: -------------- --
RMAN-06214: Datafile Copy /orabkup/cust_data_01_dbf.cp

7.3 Available/Unavailable

For the backup that cannot be located you can use the change … unavailable command. This instructs RMAN not to look for such media files when performing a restore or recovery. But if such unavailable backup files are found we can always mark them available later!

RMAN> change copy of archivelog sequence between 1000 and 1100 unavailable;

RMAN> change backupset 12 unavailable;

It is not uncommon for the DBA to face some dire situations when some archived logs are found to be missing. They may have been removed from disk before sweeping to tape. Subsequent sweeps will fail as RMAN will try to locate those missing archived logs for backing up. Unable to find them RMAN will just terminate the backup job with an error condition. The ONLY fix is then to run a crosscheck of archived logs to update the repository metadata.

RMAN> connect target sys/r24rman@rmanelse;

connected to target database: RMANELSE (DBID=1826602558)

RMAN> connect catalog rman/rwoman@rman4all;

connected to recovery catalog database

RMAN> change archivelog all crosscheck;

released channel: ORA_DISK_1
allocated channel: ORA_DISK_1
channel ORA_DISK_1: sid=37 devtype=DISK
validation succeeded for archived log
archive log filename=/u01/app/oracle/admin/RMANELSE/arch/1_3_593971715
.dbf recid=19 stamp=594484678
validation succeeded for archived log
archive log filename=/u01/app/oracle/admin/RMANELSE/arch/1_4_593971715
.dbf recid=20 stamp=594484679
validation succeeded for archived log
archive log filename=/u01/app/oracle/admin/RMANELSE/arch/2_2_593971715
.dbf recid=24 stamp=594828398
validation succeeded for archived log
archive log filename=/u01/app/oracle/admin/RMANELSE/arch/2_3_593971715
.dbf recid=21 stamp=594484679
Crosschecked 4 objects

> You can also change the retention period of any backupset. A regular backup may be converted to a long term backup for archiving. This is possible ONLY when employing a recovery catalog.

RMAN> change backup tag 'db_full_bkup' keep forever nologs;

This will apply an exemption to the current retention policy. We are also directing RMAN to preserve this backup. You can always reverse this exemption with the NOKEEP clause.

Note: For incremental backups we will not be able to execute this command. If attempted this error will be thrown: RMAN-06531: CHANGE ... KEEP not supported for incremental BACKUPSET.

Suppose the currently defined retention policy requires all backups be kept for a period of just one month. However we need to retain one particular backup for half the year.

RMAN> change backup tag 'incr_base_bkup' keep until 'sysdate+180';

Even after 30 days this backup will NOT be considered obsolete.

Can we undo the keep operation? Yes—use the CHANGE … NOKEEP clause to (re)apply the configured retention policy to the backup.

RMAN> change backup tag 'db_full_bkup' nokeep;

7.4 Cataloging

We know user-managed file copies need to be cataloged into the RMAN repository. This ensures the repository metadata is updated accordingly to enable RMAN to utilize these files later for any restore and/or recovery.

RMAN> catalog datafilecopy '/orabkup/cust_data_01.dbf';

```
starting full resync of recovery catalog
full resync complete
cataloged datafile copy
datafile copy filename=/orabkup/cust_data_01.dbf recid=11 stamp=594137448
```

Note: You can also catalog backup pieces on disk.

Once cataloged query the dynamic view v$backup_piece of the target database to confirm the operation.

SQL> SELECT HANDLE FROM V$BACKUP_PIECE;

Let us now catalog all the files in an ASM disk group:

RMAN> catalog start with '+MY_DG1';

Well you can catalog—but then can you uncatalog? Yes—just look at this example.

RMAN> change copy of datafile 10 uncatalog;

```
uncataloged datafile copy
datafile copy filename=/orabkup/cust_data_01_dbf.cp recid=12 stamp=594154413
Uncataloged 1 objects
```

7.5 Resynchronizing the Recovery Catalog

Generally RMAN performs implicit resynchronizations whenever needed. However a manual resynchronization may be in order under some situations like:

- Recovery Catalog Unavailability

- Generation of numerous archived logs during the period between any two successive target database backups

- Structural changes to the target database like adding or dropping tablespaces, renaming logfiles etc.

The DBA has to ensure the recovery catalog is resynchronized BEFORE the target database control file records are reused. The parameter CONTROL_FILE_RECORD_KEEP_TIME should be longer than the interval between successive resynchronizations.

Whenever the target database is opened with the RESETLOGS clause a new incarnation of the database is born. This is recorded in the dynamic V$DATABASE_INCARNATION view of the target database.

If the SQL statement ALTER DATABASE OPEN RESETLOGS is executed from within RMAN a new incarnation record is automatically inserted into the recovery catalog & an implicit RESET DATABASE command is automatically issued. This new incarnation of the target database is made its current incarnation and all the backups performed after this reset of the target database is tied to the new incarnation.

RMAN> resync catalog;

7.6 Retrieving Repository Data

List & Report are very useful commands to query the RMAN repository & obtain the necessary information about our backup and recovery operations.

7.6.1 List

The LIST command is used to obtain data about:

- Backup sets and image copies

- Specified structures contained within the backup files like archived logs, datafiles, control files, server parameter file etc.

- Various incarnations of target database(s) in the recovery catalog

Note: CROSSCHECK and DELETE commands can operate on the backup output files retrieved by LIST.

7.6.2 Report

Detailed RMAN reports for analysis can be generated by the REPORT command. You can run this command to obtain information about:

- Datafiles needing backup

- Obsolete backups

- Unrecoverable operations on any datafiles

- Current physical schema of the target database

To list all the datafiles needing more than a fortnight's worth of archived redo log files for complete recovery use this:

RMAN> report need backup days 14 database;

The DBA can get a listing of backups of datafiles, control files and archived redo logs considered obsolete (and hence can be deleted) using the OBSOLETE clause. This output is relative to the retention policy specified.

RMAN> report obsolete recovery window of 30 days;

We can know if unrecoverable operations (caused by NOLOGGING) have been executed against any datafiles. If any objects in a datafile have been subjected to such an operation (since the last backup of the datafile) this command will help us identify such datafiles.

RMAN> report unrecoverable database;

The DBA can also list all the datafiles and tablespaces of the target database as of a point in time.

RMAN> report schema at time 'sysdate—30';

Note: The recovery catalog is essential for reporting schema with the AT TIME switch.

Chapter 7 Recapitulation

Crosscheck performs the synchronization of repository metadata and the actual physical state of the backup files on media.

After crosscheck the status of backups can be any one of AVAILABLE, UNAVAILABLE and EXPIRED.

Delete command removes the physical files from the backup media, deletes the relevant repository metadata from the recovery catalog (if applicable) and updates the backup records in the target database control file.

The DBA can use the CHANGE … UNAVAILABLE command to instruct RMAN not to look for the specified media files when performing restore or recovery.

You can also change the retention period of any backupset. A regular backup may be converted to a long term backup for archiving. This is possible ONLY when employing a recovery catalog.

We know user-managed file copies need to be cataloged into the RMAN repository. This ensures the repository metadata is updated accordingly to enable RMAN to utilize these files later for any restore and/or recovery.

The DBA has to ensure the recovery catalog is resynchronized BEFORE the target database control file records are reused. The parameter CONTROL_FILE_RECORD_KEEP_TIME should be longer than the interval between successive resynchronizations.

If the SQL statement ALTER DATABASE OPEN RESETLOGS is executed from within RMAN a new incarnation record is automatically inserted into the recovery catalog & an implicit RESET DATABASE command is also issued.

List & Report are very useful commands to query the RMAN repository & obtain the necessary information about our backup and recovery operations.

Chapter 8 Objectives

- Duplication Framework
- Duplication Process
- Incremental Standby Refresh

Chapter 8
Duplication

Duplication is the process of creating a full or partial replica of the target (primary) database. By cloning the primary we can also create standby databases.

While duplicating RMAN connects to both the target database and an 'auxiliary' instance. A connection to the recovery catalog is also made if employed.

At the minimum one auxiliary channel needs to be allocated on the auxiliary instance. This channel is used for restoring the relevant backups of the primary database, creating the duplicate database and finally performing the recovery.

The DBA has to ensure disk & tape backups are made available for duplication on the same server or a different server depending on the location of the clone database.

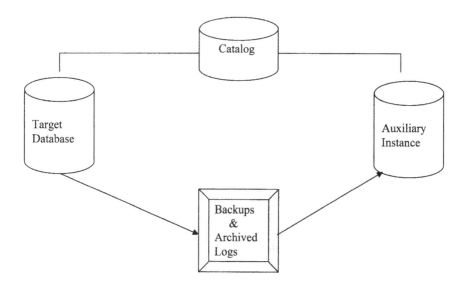

Figure 8-1 Cloning with RMAN

8.1 Modus Operandi

RMAN simplifies the entire process of cloning by intelligently automating the following tasks:

- Creating the control files for the duplicate database

- Restoring the target database datafiles to the duplicate database

- Performing incomplete recovery by using all the available incremental backups and archived redo logs.

- Opening the duplicate database with the RESETLOGS option(online redo logs are created at this time)

- Generating a unique DBID for the duplicate database (as a result this can be registered in the same recovery catalog along with the target database!)

Note: When duplicating for standby the dbid is retained as of the primary.

Can we exclude some portions of the source? If only a subset of database data is desired the DBA can exclude primary database tablespaces from the duplicate database using the SKIP TABLESPACE clause.

Note: Obviously SYSTEM/Sysaux/Undo and default permanent tablespaces can NOT be excluded.

For duplication RMAN utilizes the most current backups of the primary database. Also duplicate database recovery is done until the last available archived log with the most recent SCN is applied.

Recovery can also be controlled with the 'SET UNTIL' clause. You can direct RMAN to recover the duplicate database to a past point in time. The caveat is only the current incarnation of the primary database can be used in this situation.

8.2 Semantics

Let us look at the actual command now.

```
RMAN> run
{ allocate auxiliary channel aux1 device type disk;
  allocate auxiliary channel aux2 device type disk;
  set until time "to_date('2006-07-13:08:10:00', 'YYYY-MM-DD:HH24:MI:SS')";
```

duplicate target database to < 'dbname' >
skip tablespace tbsp1, tbsp2; }

For standby cloning use the FOR STANDBY clause as under:

RMAN> run
{ allocate auxiliary channel aux1 device type disk;
  allocate auxiliary channel aux2 device type disk;
  set until time "to_date('2006-07-13:08:10:00', 'YYYY-MM-DD:HH24:MI:SS')";
  duplicate target database for standby; }

The DBA can also configure channels for restoring backups & archived logs from tape. Below we are using Tivoli Storage Manager/TDP media manager.

RMAN> configure auxiliary channel 1 device type 'sbt_tape' parms
      'ENV=(TDPO_OPTFILE=/usr/tivoli/tsm/client/oracle/bin64/tdpo.opt)';
      configure auxiliary channel 2 device type 'sbt_tape' parms
      'ENV=(TDPO_OPTFILE=/usr/tivoli/tsm/client/oracle/bin64/tdpo.opt)';

Tip: More the channels the merrier (or faster) duplication becomes!

The online redo logs of the duplicate database are named depending upon the clause/option specified while duplicating. Listed below is the order of precedence:

1 LOGFILE clause of DUPLICATE command
2 LOG_FILE_NAME_CONVERT initialization parameter
3 DB_CREATE_ONLINE_DEST_n or DB_CREATE_FILE_DEST or
  DB_RECOVERY_FILE_DEST

Note: If no clause is used then the names are retained as they are meaning the online redo log filenames match one-for-one with those of the target database.

RMAN> duplicate target database to < 'dbname' >
      logfile group 1 ('/u01/app/oracle/oralogs/RMANELSE/redo01a.log',
            '/u02/app/oracle/oralogs/RMANELSE/redo01b.log',
            '/u03/app/oracle/oralogs/RMANELSE/redo01c.log') size 10M reuse,
            group 2 ('/u01/app/oracle/oralogs/RMANELSE/redo02a.log',
            '/u02/app/oracle/oralogs/RMANELSE/redo02b.log',
            '/u03/app/oracle/oralogs/RMANELSE/redo02c.log') size 10M reuse;

> The datafile names of the duplicated database the names are transformed in accordance with the command executed. Again we have the order of precedence as under:
>
> 1 SET NEWNAME FOR DATAFILE in a RUN block that includes both the SET NEWNAME commands and the DUPLICATE command
> 2 CONFIGURE AUXNAME
> 3 DB_FILE_NAME_CONVERT with the DUPLICATE command
> 4 DB_CREATE_FILE_DEST initialization parameter

```
RMAN> duplicate target database to < 'dbname' >
    db_file_name_convert = ('+MY_DG1', '+MY_DG2');
```

Note: You can set multiple conversion pairs in DB_FILE_NAME_CONVERT and LOG_FILE_NAME_CONVERT.

We can also use CONFIGURE AUXNAME to name the datafiles.

```
RMAN> configure auxname for datafile 1
    to '/u01/app/oracle/oradata/RMANELSE/system_01.dbf';
    ...
    ...
duplicate target database to < 'dbname' >;
```

After the duplication is complete remember to clear the configured auxiliary names for the datafiles in the duplicated database to prevent accidental overwrite.

```
RMAN> configure auxname for datafile 1 clear;
```

When duplicating a target database on a remote host maintaining the same directory structure include the NOFILENAMECHECK clause on the DUPLICATE command.

```
RMAN> run
{ allocate auxiliary channel aux1 device type disk;
  allocate auxiliary channel aux2 device type disk;
  duplicate target database to < 'dbname' >
  nofilenamecheck; }
```

8.3 Workshop—Duplicate a Database

We will now go about cloning a database by stepping through the process below. In the following example RACDB is the source database & the duplicate database is called RMANELSE. You will learn to clone a cluster database into a single instance. Archived logs from both the nodes of the source RAC database will be used by RMAN in this process.

Step 1 Create the password file for the duplicate database. From the OS prompt issue this.

$ orapwd file = orapwRMANELSE password = r24rman

This file holding the sys(dba) password should be created in $ORACLE_HOME/dbs. Your startup parameter file also should have remote_login_passwordfile set to 'exclusive'.

Step 2 Establish Oracle Net connectivity

RMAN should be able to connect to all of them: target(primary), duplicate(clone) & recovery catalog instances.

Step 3 Create a client-side initialization parameter file (pfile) for the auxiliary instance.

You can copy pfile of the source database and modify the necessary parameters. The following are worthy of note.
#cluster_database=true
db_name='RMANELSE'
(Also comment out any reference to the second undo tablespace.)

Step 4 Create the server parameter file (spfile) from the client-side file.
$ export ORACLE_SID=RMANELSE

SQL> CREATE SPFILE FROM PFILE;

Note: For both pfile & spfile our location would be $ORACLE_HOME/dbs.

Step 5 Start the auxiliary instance

SQL> STARTUP NOMOUNT;

The target (primary) database should be either mounted or open.

Step 6 Start RMAN and connect to the target, catalog & auxiliary instances.

RMAN> connect target sys/ora2go@racdb;

connected to target database: RACDB (DBID=559768190)

RMAN> connect catalog rman/rwoman@rman4all;

RMAN> connect auxiliary/

connected to auxiliary database: RMANELSE (not mounted)

Step 7 After allocating auxiliary channels clone the target database excluding a few tablespaces. For the auxiliary instance db_create_file_dest initialization parameter is set to the ASM disk group '+MY_DG1'. Archived logs from both the instances of the source RAC database are used.

```
RMAN> run
2> { allocate auxiliary channel aux1 device type disk;
3>   allocate auxiliary channel aux2 device type disk;
4>   duplicate target database to rmanelse
5>   skip tablespace flow_1, soe; }
```

allocated channel: aux1
channel aux1: sid=44 devtype=DISK

allocated channel: aux2
channel aux2: sid=43 devtype=DISK

Starting Duplicate Db at 24-JUN-06
Datafile 7 skipped by request
Datafile 8 skipped by request

contents of Memory Script:
{
    set until scn 3684644;

```
set newname for clone datafile 1 to new;
set newname for clone datafile 2 to new;
set newname for clone datafile 3 to new;
set newname for clone datafile 4 to new;
set newname for clone datafile 5 to new;
set newname for clone datafile 6 to new;
restore
check readonly
clone database
skip tablespace SOE,
FLOW_1;
}
executing Memory Script

executing command: SET until clause

executing command: SET NEWNAME
executing command: SET NEWNAME
executing command: SET NEWNAME
executing command: SET NEWNAME
executing command: SET NEWNAME
executing command: SET NEWNAME

Starting restore at 24-JUN-06

channel aux1: starting datafile backupset restore
channel aux1: specifying datafile(s) to restore from backup set
restoring datafile 00001 to +MY_DG1
restoring datafile 00002 to +MY_DG1
restoring datafile 00003 to +MY_DG1
restoring datafile 00004 to +MY_DG1
restoring datafile 00005 to +MY_DG1
restoring datafile 00006 to +MY_DG1
channel aux1: reading from backup piece +MY_DG1/racdb/backupset/2006_
06_24/nnndf0_tag20060624t155641_0.302.593971001
channel aux1: restored backup piece 1
piece handle=+MY_DG1/racdb/backupset/2006_06_24/nnndf0_tag200606
24t155641_0.302.593971001 tag=TAG20060624T155641
channel aux1: restore complete, elapsed time: 00:02:56
Finished restore at 24-JUN-06
```

sql statement: CREATE CONTROLFILE REUSE SET DATABASE "RMANELSE" RESETLOGS ARCHIVELOG
  MAXLOGFILES   192
  MAXLOGMEMBERS   3
  MAXDATAFILES   1024
  MAXINSTANCES   32
  MAXLOGHISTORY   292
 LOGFILE
  GROUP 1 SIZE 50 M,
  GROUP 2 SIZE 50 M,
  GROUP 3 SIZE 50 M
 DATAFILE
  '+MY_DG1/rmanelse/datafile/system.304.593971515'
 CHARACTER SET AL32UTF8

contents of Memory Script:
{
  switch clone datafile all;
}
executing Memory Script

datafile 2 switched to datafile copy
input datafile copy recid=1 stamp=593971690 filename=+MY_DG1/rmanelse/datafile/undotbs1.286.593971515
datafile 3 switched to datafile copy
input datafile copy recid=2 stamp=593971690 filename=+MY_DG1/rmanelse/datafile/sysaux.281.593971515
datafile 4 switched to datafile copy
input datafile copy recid=3 stamp=593971690 filename=+MY_DG1/rmanelse/datafile/users.283.593971515
datafile 5 switched to datafile copy
input datafile copy recid=4 stamp=593971690 filename=+MY_DG1/rmanelse/datafile/example.282.593971515
datafile 6 switched to datafile copy
input datafile copy recid=5 stamp=593971690 filename=+MY_DG1/rmanelse/datafile/undotbs2.287.593971517

contents of Memory Script:
{
  set until scn 3684644;

```
  recover
  clone database
  delete archivelog
  ;
}
executing Memory Script

executing command: SET until clause
Starting recover at 24-JUN-06
datafile 7 not processed because file is offline
datafile 8 not processed because file is offline

starting media recovery

channel aux1: starting archive log restore to default destination
channel aux1: restoring archive log
archive log thread=1 sequence=84
channel aux1: restoring archive log
archive log thread=2 sequence=50
channel aux1: reading from backup piece +MY_DG1/racdb/backupset/2006_
06_24/annnf0_tag20060624t155929_0.285.593971173
channel aux1: restored backup piece 1
piece handle=+MY_DG1/racdb/backupset/2006_06_24/annnf0_tag20060624t
155929_0.285.593971173 tag=TAG20060624T155929
channel aux1: restore complete, elapsed time: 00:00:01
archive log filename=/u01/app/oracle/product/10.2.0/db_1/dbs/arch1_84_
562151429.dbf thread=1 sequence=84
archive log filename=/u01/app/oracle/product/10.2.0/db_1/dbs/arch2_50_
562151429.dbf thread=2 sequence=50
channel clone_default: deleting archive log(s)
archive log filename=/u01/app/oracle/product/10.2.0/db_1/dbs/arch1_84_
562151429.dbf recid=1 stamp=593971692
channel clone_default: deleting archive log(s)
archive log filename=/u01/app/oracle/product/10.2.0/db_1/dbs/arch2_50_
562151429.dbf recid=2 stamp=593971692
media recovery complete, elapsed time: 00:00:01
Finished recover at 24-JUN-06

contents of Memory Script:
{
```

```
    shutdown clone;
    startup clone nomount;
}
executing Memory Script
```

database dismounted
Oracle instance shut down

connected to auxiliary database (not started)
Oracle instance started

Total System Global Area   100663296 bytes
Fixed Size   1217932 bytes
Variable Size   58722932 bytes
Database Buffers   37748736 bytes
Redo Buffers   2973696 bytes
sql statement: CREATE CONTROLFILE REUSE SET DATABASE
"RMANELSE" RESETLOGS ARCHIVELOG
  MAXLOGFILES   192
  MAXLOGMEMBERS   3
  MAXDATAFILES   1024
  MAXINSTANCES   32
  MAXLOGHISTORY   292
 LOGFILE
  GROUP 1 SIZE 50 M,
  GROUP 2 SIZE 50 M,
  GROUP 3 SIZE 50 M
 DATAFILE
 '+MY_DG1/rmanelse/datafile/system.304.593971515'
 CHARACTER SET AL32UTF8

contents of Memory Script:
{
    set newname for clone tempfile 1 to new;
    switch clone tempfile all;
    catalog clone datafilecopy "+MY_DG1/rmanelse/datafile/undotbs1.286.593971515";
    catalog clone datafilecopy "+MY_DG1/rmanelse/datafile/sysaux.281.593971515";
    catalog clone datafilecopy "+MY_DG1/rmanelse/datafile/users.283.593971515";
    catalog clone datafilecopy "+MY_DG1/rmanelse/datafile/example.282.593971515";
    catalog clone datafilecopy "+MY_DG1/rmanelse/datafile/undotbs2.287.593971517";
```
```

```
   switch clone datafile all;
}
```
executing Memory Script

executing command: SET NEWNAME

renamed temporary file 1 to +MY_DG1 in control file

cataloged datafile copy
datafile copy filename=+MY_DG1/rmanelse/datafile/undotbs1.286.593971515
recid=1 stamp=593971714
cataloged datafile copy
datafile copy filename=+MY_DG1/rmanelse/datafile/sysaux.281.593971515
recid=2 stamp=593971714
cataloged datafile copy
datafile copy filename=+MY_DG1/rmanelse/datafile/users.283.593971515
recid=3 stamp=593971714
cataloged datafile copy
datafile copy filename=+MY_DG1/rmanelse/datafile/example.282.593971515
recid=4 stamp=593971715
cataloged datafile copy
datafile copy filename=+MY_DG1/rmanelse/datafile/undotbs2.287.593971517
recid=5 stamp=593971715

datafile 2 switched to datafile copy
input datafile copy recid=1 stamp=593971714 filename=+MY_DG1/rmanelse/
datafile/undotbs1.286.593971515
datafile 3 switched to datafile copy
input datafile copy recid=2 stamp=593971714 filename=+MY_DG1/rmanelse/
datafile/sysaux.281.593971515
datafile 4 switched to datafile copy
input datafile copy recid=3 stamp=593971714 filename=+MY_DG1/rmanelse/
datafile/users.283.593971515
datafile 5 switched to datafile copy
input datafile copy recid=4 stamp=593971715 filename=+MY_DG1/rmanelse/
datafile/example.282.593971515
datafile 6 switched to datafile copy
input datafile copy recid=5 stamp=593971715 filename=+MY_DG1/rmanelse/
datafile/undotbs2.287.593971517

contents of Memory Script:
{
   Alter clone database open resetlogs;
}
executing Memory Script

database opened

contents of Memory Script:
{
# drop offline and skipped tablespaces
sql clone "drop tablespace SOE including contents cascade constraints";
drop offline and skipped tablespaces
sql clone "drop tablespace FLOW_1 including contents cascade constraints";
}
executing Memory Script

sql statement: drop tablespace SOE including contents cascade constraints

sql statement: drop tablespace FLOW_1 including contents cascade constraints
Finished Duplicate Db at 24-JUN-06

Step 8 Disable the second thread.

SQL> ALTER DATABASE DISABLE INSTANCE 'UNNAMED_
INSTANCE_2';

Step 9 Drop the log groups belonging to that thread.

SQL> ALTER DATABASE DROP LOGFILE GROUP n;

Step 10 Finally drop the second undo tablespace.

SQL> DROP TABLESPACE UNDOTBS2 INCLUDING CONTENTS;

EUREKA! THE REPLICA DATABASE HAS NOW INCARNATED!!

8.4 Incremental Backups for Standby Refresh

The DBA can apply incremental backups of the target database to the standby database.

This synchronization of the standby with its primary database is facilitated by RMAN through the creation of an incremental backup taken at the primary. This backup contains all the changed database blocks since the standby was created or last refreshed. We can then apply this incremental backup to the standby database to effect the resynchronization.

The incremental backup is created at the primary database as noted below.

```
RMAN> backup incremental from scn < scn > database format
      '/orabkup/incr_sby_%U';
```

You can take advantage of this new capability to toggle the physical standby database between managed recovery & reporting modes. Use the Flashback Database to undo any changes after the standby database has been used for reporting and/or testing. An incremental backup can be then used to resynchronize the standby with the primary. At this stage the physical standby database can again be placed in managed recovery mode.

RMAN includes all the database blocks changed at SCNs greater than or equal to the SCN specified in the incremental backup.

Caution: This incremental backup is NOT usable for primary database recovery.

The DBA can follow the procedure defined here for standby refresh:

- Create the incremental backup at the primary

- Make the incremental backup available at the standby

- Catalog the incremental backup at the standby

    RMAN> catalog start with '/orabkup/';
    (/orabkup is the folder with the incremental backups in this example)
- Apply the incremental backup to the standby
    (The standby database should now be in mounted state.)

RMAN> recover database noredo;

Now managed recovery can be restarted at the standby. Redo logs needed at the standby with changes after the incremental are also automatically applied.

Chapter 8 Recapitulation

Duplication is the process of creating a full or partial replica of the target (primary) database. By cloning the primary we can also create standby databases.

At the minimum one auxiliary channel needs to be allocated on the auxiliary instance. This channel is used for restoring the relevant backups of the primary database, creating the duplicate database and finally performing the recovery.

If only a subset of database data is desired the DBA can exclude primary database tablespaces from the duplicate database using the SKIP TABLESPACE clause.

Recovery can also be controlled with the 'SET UNTIL' clause. You can direct RMAN to recover the duplicate database to a past point in time.

The datafile names of the duplicated database the names are transformed in accordance with the command executed. We have the order of precedence as under:

1 SET NEWNAME FOR DATAFILE in a RUN block that includes both the SET NEWNAME commands and the DUPLICATE command
2 CONFIGURE AUXNAME
3 DB_FILE_NAME_CONVERT with the DUPLICATE command
4 DB_CREATE_FILE_DEST initialization parameter

After the duplication is complete remember to clear the configured auxiliary names for the datafiles in the duplicated database to prevent accidental overwrite.

When duplicating a target database on a remote host maintaining the same directory structure include the NOFILENAMECHECK clause on the DUPLICATE command.

The synchronization of the standby with its primary database is facilitated by RMAN through the creation of an incremental backup taken at the primary. This backup contains all the changed database blocks since the standby was created or last refreshed. We can then apply this incremental backup to the standby database to effect the resynchronization.

Chapter 9 Objectives

- TSPITR Explained
- Data Dependencies
- Process Demonstrated
- Troubleshooting
- Image Copies

Chapter 9
TSPITR with RMAN

Tablespace Point-In-Time Recovery more often known as TSPITR is a challenging recovery task which could get involved and complicated.

RMAN automates tablespace point-in-time recovery & makes it easier on the DBA. Without RMAN this certainly is a labor intensive effort.

You can recover one or more tablespaces in the target database to an earlier time compared to the rest of the database in an efficient manner.

This is the diagrammatic depiction of this process.

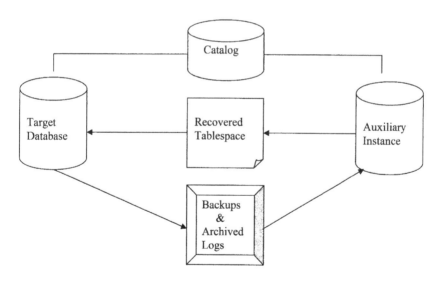

Figure 9-1 TSPITR with RMAN

Let us understand the conceptual framework here.

Using backup sets & archived redo logs of the target database the tablespace is reconstructed by RMAN to the desired date. The actual recovery however is performed in the auxiliary instance. Datafiles of the tablespace being recovered form the recovery set. The auxiliary set is made up of a backup of the SYSTEM tablespace & undo tablespaces of the target database. At the end of successful TSPITR the recovered tablespace is made part of the target database.

Note: A temporary tablespace may also be involved.

The auxiliary instance is like any other regular database. We may also designate an auxiliary destination which is a transient holding area on the disk. After the completion of TSPITR this area can be cleaned out.

9.1 Modus Operandi

RMAN performs several functions during this process. The salient ones are listed below.

- Creates the auxiliary instance
- Target database tablespaces (for recovery) are taken offline
- Restores a backup control file from an earlier time than the target time to the auxiliary instance
- The relevant datafiles are restored to the auxiliary instance
- Recovers the restored datafiles to the indicated time in the auxiliary instance
- The auxiliary database is opened with the RESETLOGS option
- Exports the dictionary metadata of objects from the recovered tablespaces
- The auxiliary instance is shutdown
- Updates the target database control files to point to the recovered datafiles
- The dictionary metadata of objects from the recovered tablespaces is imported from the auxiliary instance into the target database
- Removes all the auxiliary files

The DBA can specify the auxiliary destination & configure channels for the target database.

After successful completion of TSPITR the DBA should back up the recovered tablespaces before bringing them online.

9.2 Why TSPITR?

The DBA can undo the effect of an erroneous TRUNCATE TABLE statement or restore the pre image data after an incorrect batch job (subject to the fact this affects only some tablespaces & not the entire database).

Note: You will NOT be able to recover dropped tablespaces using this methodology.

Can we perform TSPITR on any tablespace? Well, as always some exclusions apply☺.

> The following tablespaces listed are not eligible for TSPITR:
>
> Tablespaces with external tables, nested tables or tables of VARRAY columns
> Tablespaces containing materialized views or materialized view logs
> Tablespaces housing SYS objects or undo segments
> Tablespaces not holding all the partitions of partitioned tables

The DBA should be aware of another limitation of TSPITR which is better explained with an example.

Suppose we performed TSPITR & brought the recovered tablespace(s) online at 12 noon today. Then the backups of the recovered tablespaces created before 12 noon today are rendered unusable for target database recovery with the current control file if recovery is needed later to any point in time earlier than or equal to 12 noon today. In such a scenario the DBA can only perform point-in-time recovery of the entire target database after restoring a backup control file.

Please be aware it is of paramount importance you choose the right target time for TSPITR. You may want to use the different Flashback features to analyze the data at various points in time to zero in on the correct TSPITR target time.

Note: If a recovery catalog is not employed you will NOT be able to perform multiple TSPITR operations to different target times.

9.3 Identifying Data Dependencies

Before RMAN can start TSPITR the DBA needs to resolve all the outgoing foreign key constraint relationships for objects in the tablespaces to be recovered. Instead of including the external tablespaces also in the recovery set or severing the relationships we can just disable the relationship only for the duration of TSPITR.

Tip: Remember to recreate the severed or re-enable the disabled relationships after completing TSPITR.

You can query the TS_PITR_CHECK view to identify the relationships between objects that go beyond the recovery set tablespaces. Only when no rows are returned for the external tablespaces we are ready to begin TSPITR.

SQL> desc ts_pitr_check

Name	Null?	Type
OBJ1_OWNER		VARCHAR2(30)
OBJ1_NAME		VARCHAR2(30)
OBJ1_SUBNAME		VARCHAR2(30)
OBJ1_TYPE		VARCHAR2(16)
TS1_NAME		VARCHAR2(30)
OBJ2_NAME		VARCHAR2(30)
OBJ2_SUBNAME		VARCHAR2(30)
OBJ2_TYPE		VARCHAR2(15)
OBJ2_OWNER		VARCHAR2(30)
TS2_NAME		VARCHAR2(30)
CONSTRAINT_NAME		VARCHAR2(30)
REASON		VARCHAR2(81)

Tip: You may want to format the columns for this query.

In this query we check 2 tablespaces called tbsp1 and tbsp2.

```
SQL> SELECT * FROM TS_PITR_CHECK WHERE
2> (TS1_NAME IN ('tbsp1', 'tbsp2')
3>  AND TS2_NAME NOT IN ('tbsp1', 'tbsp2'))
4> OR
```

5> (TS1_NAME NOT IN ('tbsp1', 'tbsp2')
6> AND TS2_NAME IN ('tbsp1', 'tbsp2'));

Below are a few reasons for TSPITR ineligibility:

- Tables and associated indexes not fully contained in the recovery set

- Queue tables not allowed in the recovery set

- Master tables used for replication not allowed in the recovery set

Let me suggest some remedial measures for the DBA to remove hurdles concerning tablespaces not qualifying for TSPITR. Look at these examples.

SQL> DROP TABLE OE.ACTION_TABLE CASCADE CONSTRAINTS;

ORA-22914: DROP of nested tables not supported

SQL> SELECT PARENT_TABLE_NAME FROM USER_NESTED_TABLES WHERE TABLE_NAME = 'ACTION_TABLE';

PARENT_TABLE_NAME

PURCHASEORDER

SQL> DROP TABLE PURCHASEORDER CASCADE CONSTRAINTS;

Table dropped.

SQL> DROP TABLE WB_RT_SERVICE_QUEUE_TAB;

ORA-24005: must use DBMS_AQADM.DROP_QUEUE_TABLE to drop queue tables

SQL>   EXEC   DBMS_AQADM.DROP_QUEUE_TABLE('WB_RT_ SERVICE_QUEUE_TAB');
BEGIN   DBMS_AQADM.DROP_QUEUE_TABLE('WB_RT_SERVICE_ QUEUE_TAB'); END;

ORA-24012: cannot drop QUEUE_TABLE, some queues in OWB_OWNER.WB_RT_SERVICE_QUEUE_TAB have not been dropped

ORA-06512: at "SYS.DBMS_AQADM", line 197

SQL> EXEC DBMS_AQADM.DROP_QUEUE_TABLE('WB_RT_SERVICE_
QUEUE_TAB',
true, true);

PL/SQL procedure successfully completed.

Caution: After TSPITR objects created after the target time in the recovered tablespaces are NOT retained. However such objects can be preserved by exporting them before TSPITR and importing them afterwards.

The TS_PITR_OBJECTS_TO_BE_DROPPED view comes in handy for identifying such objects.

SQL> SELECT OWNER, NAME, TABLESPACE_NAME,
2> TO_CHAR(CREATION_TIME, 'YYYY-MM-DD:HH24:MI:SS')
3> FROM TS_PITR_OBJECTS_TO_BE_DROPPED
4> WHERE TABLESPACE_NAME = 'AUXDATA'
5> AND CREATION_TIME > TO_DATE('2006-07-13:08:10:00',
6> 'YYYY-MM-DD:HH24:MI:SS')
7> ORDER BY TABLESPACE_NAME, CREATION_TIME;

9.4 Workshop—Perform TSPITR with RMAN

Let us illustrate the TSPITR process using auxdata tablespace in the target database.

SQL> CREATE TABLE WAREHOUSES_TSPITR(WAREHOUSE_ID NUMBER(2), WAREHOUSE_NAME VARCHAR2(15)) TABLESPACE AUXDATA;

Table created.

We populate this table now & check the contents.

SQL> SELECT * FROM WAREHOUSES_TSPITR;

```
WAREHOUSE_ID WAREHOUSE_NAME
------------          ----------
    1                Bangalore
    2                New Jersey
    3                Detroit
    4                Lexington
    5                Atlanta
    6                Raleigh
    7                Dallas
    8                Denver
    9                Aspen
   10                Allentown
```

10 rows selected.

```
SQL> set time on
08:10:07 SQL> TRUNCATE TABLE WAREHOUSES_TSPITR;
```

Table truncated.

Oops! How do we get the table data back now? The mantra to come to our rescue is TSPITR.

We ensure the query against both TS_PITR_CHECK & TS_PITR_OBJECTS_TO_BE_DROPPED return no rows.

```
SQL> SELECT * FROM TS_PITR_CHECK WHERE
2> (TS1_NAME IN ('AUXDATA')
3>  AND TS2_NAME NOT IN ('AUXDATA'))
4> OR
5> (TS1_NAME NOT IN ('AUXDATA')
6>  AND TS2_NAME IN ('AUXDATA'));
```

Now we are ready to start the TSPITR engine!

```
$ export ORACLE_SID=RMANELSE
```

Step 1: Start RMAN and connect to both the target & catalog databases.

Caution: Ensure you do NOT use 'connect auxiliary ...' here. By not using that clause you force RMAN to create an auxiliary instance automatically.

```
$ rman
RMAN> connect target;

connected to target database: RMANELSE (DBID=1826602558)

RMAN> connect catalog rman/rwoman@rman4all;

connected to recovery catalog database
```

Step 2: Decrypt the encrypted backup by supplying the password.

```
RMAN> set decryption identified by 'rman2secure';
executing command: SET decryption
```

Step 3: Recover the tablespace where the table resides. Always use the to_date function mask to override any default NLS_DATE_FORMAT setting. If you recall the table was truncated just after 8.10 am.

```
RMAN> recover tablespace auxdata until time "to_date('2006-07-13:08:10:00',
'YYYY-MM-DD:HH24:MI:SS')"
auxiliary destination '/u01/app/oracle/admin/RMANELSE/aux_dest';

Starting recover at 13-JUL-06
allocated channel: ORA_DISK_1
channel ORA_DISK_1: sid=25 devtype=DISK

Creating automatic instance, with SID='pjEj'

initialization parameters used for automatic instance:
db_name=RMANELSE
compatible=10.2.0.1.0
db_block_size=8192
db_files=200
db_unique_name=tspitr_RMANELSE_pjEj
large_pool_size=1M
shared_pool_size=110M
#No auxiliary parameter file used
```

db_create_file_dest=/u01/app/oracle/admin/RMANELSE/aux_dest
control_files=/u01/app/oracle/admin/RMANELSE/aux_dest/cntrl_tspitr_RMA
NELSE_pjEj.f

starting up automatic instance RMANELSE

Oracle instance started

Total System Global Area   201326592 bytes

Fixed Size   1218508 bytes
Variable Size   146802740 bytes
Database Buffers   50331648 bytes
Redo Buffers   2973696 bytes
Automatic instance created

contents of Memory Script:
{
# set the until clause
set until time "to_date('2006-07-13:08:10:00', 'YYYY-MM-DD:HH24:MI:SS')";
restore the controlfile
restore clone controlfile;
mount the controlfile
sql clone 'alter database mount clone database';
archive current online log for tspitr to a resent until time
sql 'alter system archive log current';
avoid unnecessary autobackups for structural changes during TSPITR
sql 'begin dbms_backup_restore.AutoBackupFlag(FALSE); end;';
resync catalog after controlfile restore
resync catalog;
}
executing Memory Script

executing command: SET until clause

Starting restore at 13-JUL-06
allocated channel: ORA_AUX_DISK_1
channel ORA_AUX_DISK_1: sid=34 devtype=DISK

channel ORA_AUX_DISK_1: starting datafile backupset restore

channel ORA_AUX_DISK_1: restoring control file
channel ORA_AUX_DISK_1: reading from backup piece +MY_DG1/rmanelse/
autobackup/2006_07_12/s_595634175.261.595634179
channel ORA_AUX_DISK_1: restored backup piece 1
piece   handle=+MY_DG1/rmanelse/autobackup/2006_07_12/s_595634175
.261.595634179 tag=TAG20060712T215615
channel ORA_AUX_DISK_1: restore complete, elapsed time: 00:00:08
output   filename=/u01/app/oracle/admin/RMANELSE/aux_dest/cntrl_tspitr_
RMANELSE_pjEj.f
Finished restore at 13-JUL-06

sql statement: alter database mount clone database
sql statement: alter system archive log current
sql statement: begin dbms_backup_restore.AutoBackupFlag(FALSE); end;

starting full resync of recovery catalog
full resync complete
released channel: ORA_DISK_1
released channel: ORA_AUX_DISK_1

contents of Memory Script:
{
# generated tablespace point-in-time recovery script
# set the until clause
set until time "to_date('2006-07-13:08:10:00', 'YYYY-MM-DD:HH24:MI:SS')";
plsql <<<— tspitr_2
declare
  sqlstatement   varchar2(512);
  offline_not_needed exception;
  pragma exception_init(offline_not_needed, -01539);
begin
  sqlstatement:= 'alter tablespace' || 'AUXDATA' || 'offline for recover';
  krmicd.writeMsg(6162, sqlstatement);
  krmicd.execSql(sqlstatement);
exception
  when offline_not_needed then
    null;
end; >>>;
set an omf destination filename for restore
set newname for clone datafile 1 to new;

```
# set an omf destination filename for restore
set newname for clone datafile 2 to new;
# set an omf destination tempfile
set newname for clone tempfile 1 to new;
# set a destination filename for restore
set newname for datafile 6 to
 "+MY_DG1/rmanelse/datafile/auxdata.276.595634175";
# rename all tempfiles
switch clone tempfile all;
# restore the tablespaces in the recovery set plus the auxiliary tablespaces
restore clone datafile 1, 2, 6;
switch clone datafile all;
#online the datafiles restored or flipped
sql clone "alter database datafile 1 online";
#online the datafiles restored or flipped
sql clone "alter database datafile 2 online";
#online the datafiles restored or flipped
sql clone "alter database datafile 6 online";
# make the controlfile point at the restored datafiles, then recover them
recover clone database tablespace "AUXDATA", "SYSTEM", "UNDOTBS1"
delete archivelog;
alter clone database open resetlogs;
# PLUG HERE the creation of a temporary tablespace if export fails due to lack
# of temporary space.
# For example in Unix these two lines would do that:
#sql clone "create tablespace aux_tspitr_tmp
#       datafile "/tmp/aux_tspitr_tmp.dbf" size 500K";
}
executing Memory Script

executing command: SET until clause

sql statement: alter tablespace AUXDATA offline for recover

executing command: SET NEWNAME
executing command: SET NEWNAME
executing command: SET NEWNAME
executing command: SET NEWNAME
```

renamed temporary file 1 to/u01/app/oracle/admin/RMANELSE/aux_dest/
TSPITR_RMANELSE_PJEJ/datafile/o1_mf_temp_%u_.tmp in control file

Starting restore at 13-JUL-06
allocated channel: ORA_AUX_DISK_1
channel ORA_AUX_DISK_1: sid=36 devtype=DISK

creating datafile fno=6 name=+MY_DG1/rmanelse/datafile/auxdata.276
.595634175
channel ORA_AUX_DISK_1: starting datafile backupset restore
channel ORA_AUX_DISK_1: specifying datafile(s) to restore from backup set
restoring datafile 00001 to/u01/app/oracle/admin/RMANELSE/aux_dest/
TSPITR_RMANELSE_PJEJ/datafile/o1_mf_system_%u_.dbf
restoring datafile 00002 to/u01/app/oracle/admin/RMANELSE/aux_dest/
TSPITR_RMANELSE_PJEJ/datafile/o1_mf_undotbs1_%u_.dbf
channel ORA_AUX_DISK_1: reading from backup piece +MY_DG1/rmanelse/
backupset/2006_06_30/nnndn0_tag20060630t111950_0.292.594472791
channel ORA_AUX_DISK_1: restored backup piece 1
piece handle=+MY_DG1/rmanelse/backupset/2006_06_30/nnndn0_tag2006
0630t111950_0.292.594472791 tag=TAG20060630T111950
channel ORA_AUX_DISK_1: restore complete, elapsed time: 00:02:06
Finished restore at 13-JUL-06

datafile 1 switched to datafile copy
input datafile copy recid=16 stamp=595671526 filename=/u01/app/oracle/admin/
RMANELSE/aux_dest/TSPITR_RMANELSE_PJEJ/datafile/o1_mf_system_
2cdgf94c_.dbf
datafile 2 switched to datafile copy
input datafile copy recid=17 stamp=595671526 filename=/u01/app/oracle/admin/
RMANELSE/aux_dest/TSPITR_RMANELSE_PJEJ/datafile/o1_mf_undotbs1_
2cdgf97o_.dbf

sql statement: alter database datafile 1 online
sql statement: alter database datafile 2 online
sql statement: alter database datafile 6 online
Starting recover at 13-JUL-06
using channel ORA_AUX_DISK_1

starting media recovery

archive log thread 1 sequence 1 is already on disk as file/u01/app/oracle/admin/
RMANELSE/arch/1_1_593971715.dbf

archive log thread 1 sequence 2 is already on disk as file/u01/app/oracle/admin/
RMANELSE/arch/1_2_593971715.dbf

archive log thread 2 sequence 3 is already on disk as file/u01/app/oracle/admin/
RMANELSE/arch/2_3_593971715.dbf

archive log thread 2 sequence 4 is already on disk as file/u01/app/oracle/admin/
RMANELSE/arch/2_4_593971715.dbf

media recovery complete, elapsed time: 00:01:08
Finished recover at 13-JUL-06

database opened

contents of Memory Script:
{
# export the tablespaces in the recovery set
host 'exp userid =\"/@\(DESCRIPTION=\(ADDRESS=\(PROTOCOL=beq\)\
(PROGRAM=/u01/app/oracle/product/10.2.0/db_1/bin/oracle\)\(ARGV0=
oraclepjEj\)\)\(ARGS=^'\(DESCRIPTION=\(LOCAL=YES\)\(ADDRESS=\
(PROTOCOL=beq\)\)\)^'\)\)\(ENVS=^'ORACLE_SID=pjEj^'\)\)\(CONNECT_
DATA=\(SID=pjEj\)\)\) as sysdba\" point_in_time_recover=y tablespaces=
AUXDATA file=
tspitr_a.dmp';
shutdown clone before import
shutdown clone immediate
import the tablespaces in the recovery set
host 'imp userid =\"/@ as sysdba\" point_in_time_recover=y file=
tspitr_a.dmp';
online/offline the tablespace imported
sql "alter tablespace AUXDATA online";
sql "alter tablespace AUXDATA offline";
enable autobackups in case user does open resetlogs from RMAN after TSPITR
sql 'begin dbms_backup_restore.AutoBackupFlag(TRUE); end;';
resync catalog after tspitr finished
resync catalog;
}
executing Memory Script

host command complete
database closed
database dismounted
Oracle instance shut down

host command complete

sql statement: alter tablespace AUXDATA online
sql statement: alter tablespace AUXDATA offline
sql statement: begin dbms_backup_restore.AutoBackupFlag(TRUE); end;

starting full resync of recovery catalog
full resync complete

Removing automatic instance
Automatic instance removed
auxiliary instance file/u01/app/oracle/admin/RMANELSE/aux_dest/cntrl_tspitr_RMANELSE_pjEj.f deleted
auxiliary instance file/u01/app/oracle/admin/RMANELSE/aux_dest/TSPITR_RMANELSE_PJEJ/datafile/o1_mf_system_2cdgf94c_.dbf deleted
auxiliary instance file/u01/app/oracle/admin/RMANELSE/aux_dest/TSPITR_RMANELSE_PJEJ/datafile/o1_mf_undotbs1_2cdgf97o_.dbf deleted
auxiliary instance file/u01/app/oracle/admin/RMANELSE/aux_dest/TSPITR_RMANELSE_PJEJ/datafile/o1_mf_temp_2cdgn30m_.tmp deleted
auxiliary instance file/u01/app/oracle/admin/RMANELSE/aux_dest/TSPITR_RMANELSE_PJEJ/onlinelog/o1_mf_1_2cdgmjg5_.log deleted
auxiliary instance file/u01/app/oracle/admin/RMANELSE/aux_dest/TSPITR_RMANELSE_PJEJ/onlinelog/o1_mf_2_2cdgml8x_.log deleted
auxiliary instance file/u01/app/oracle/admin/RMANELSE/aux_dest/TSPITR_RMANELSE_PJEJ/onlinelog/o1_mf_3_2cdgmn7l_.log deleted
Finished recover at 13-JUL-06

Export: Release 10.2.0.1.0—Production on Thu Jul 13 08:20:31 2006

Copyright (c) 1982, 2005, Oracle. All rights reserved.

Connected to: Oracle Database 10g Enterprise Edition Release 10.2.0.1.0—Production
With the Partitioning, Real Application Clusters, Oracle Label Security, OLAP and Data Mining Scoring Engine options

Export done in US7ASCII character set and AL16UTF16 NCHAR character set
server uses AL32UTF8 character set (possible charset conversion)
Note: table data (rows) will not be exported

About to export Tablespace Point-in-time Recovery objects …
For tablespace AUXDATA …
. exporting cluster definitions
. exporting table definitions
. exporting table   WAREHOUSES_TSPITR
. exporting referential integrity constraints
. exporting triggers
. end point-in-time recovery
Export terminated successfully without warnings.

Import: Release 10.2.0.1.0—Production on Thu Jul 13 08:20:53 2006

Copyright (c) 1982, 2005, Oracle. All rights reserved.

Connected to: Oracle Database 10g Enterprise Edition Release 10.2.0.1.0—
Production
With the Partitioning, Real Application Clusters, Oracle Label Security, OLAP
and Data Mining Scoring Engine options

Export file created by EXPORT:V10.02.01 via conventional path
About to import Tablespace Point-in-time Recovery objects …
import done in US7ASCII character set and AL16UTF16 NCHAR character set
import server uses AL32UTF8 character set (possible charset conversion)
. importing SYS's objects into SYS
. importing OE's objects into OE
. importing table   "WAREHOUSES_TSPITR"
. importing SYS's objects into SYS
Import terminated successfully without warnings.

Did we get our table data back now? Not yet!

SQL> SELECT * FROM WAREHOUSES_TSPITR;

ORA-00376: file 6 cannot be read at this time
ORA-01110: data file 6: '+MY_DG1/rmanelse/datafile/auxdata.276.595634175'

We determine its status by querying v$datafile. Since it is marked offline we will bring it online.

Step 5: Bring the tablespace online.

SQL> ALTER TABLESPACE AUXDATA ONLINE;

Tablespace altered.

SQL> SELECT * FROM WAREHOUSES_TSPITR;

WAREHOUSE_ID WAREHOUSE_NAME
------------   ----------
1	Bangalore
2	New Jersey
3	Detroit
4	Lexington
5	Atlanta
6	Raleigh
7	Dallas
8	Denver
9	Aspen
10	Allentown

10 rows selected.

VOILA! Mission Accomplished—Our TSPITR is Successful!!

What do we find in the target database alert log?

```
============================================================
Thu Jul 13 08:13:05 2006
Shutting down archive processes
Thu Jul 13 08:13:10 2006
ARCH shutting down
ARC2: Archival stopped
Thu Jul 13 08:16:04 2006
An auxiliary instance is being automatically created to perform TSPITR
The ORACLE_SID of the auxiliary instance is: pjEj
If for any reason this instance is not removed automatically
```

Do the following for Windows platform
 - Connect to target instance used for TSPITR
 SQL> execute dbms_backup_restore.manageAuxInstance('pjEj',1)
Do the following for non-Windows platform
 - Set your ORACLE_SID to: pjEj
 - sqlplus '/as sysdba'
 SQL> shutdown abort
Thu Jul 13 08:16:23 2006
Thread 1 advanced to log sequence 10
 Current log# 1 seq# 10 mem# 0:
+MY_DG1/rmanelse/onlinelog/group_1.277.593971731
Thu Jul 13 08:16:37 2006
alter tablespace AUXDATA offline for recover
Thu Jul 13 08:16:37 2006
Completed: alter tablespace AUXDATA offline for recover
Thu Jul 13 08:20:56 2006
Memory Notification: Library Cache Object loaded into SGA
Heap size 4631K exceeds notification threshold (2048K)
KGL object name:SELECT count(*) FROM straddling_rs_objects,sys.obj$
o1,sys.obj$ o2 WHERE ((ts1 IN (9) AND ts2 NOT IN (9)) OR (ts2 IN (9)
AND ts1 NOT IN (9))) AND o1.obj#=object1 AND o2.obj#=object2 AND
bitand(o1.flags, 128)=0 AND (o2.flags IS NULL OR bitand(o2.flags, 128)=0)
Thu Jul 13 08:21:48 2006
alter tablespace AUXDATA online
Thu Jul 13 08:21:51 2006
Completed: alter tablespace AUXDATA online
Thu Jul 13 08:21:52 2006
alter tablespace AUXDATA offline
Completed: alter tablespace AUXDATA offline
Auxiliary instance with ORACLE_SID: pjEj has been shutdown
Thu Jul 13 08:46:08 2006
alter tablespace auxdata online
Thu Jul 13 08:46:09 2006
Starting control autobackup
Control autobackup written to DISK device
     handle '+MY_DG1/rmanelse/autobackup/2006_07_13/s_595673169.290
.595673173'
Completed: alter tablespace auxdata online
===

9.5 Troubleshooting

If TSPITR fails due to insufficient sort area during export we will need to edit the recover.bsq file located in $ORACLE_HOME/rdbms/admin.

```
# PLUG HERE the creation of a temporary tablespace if export fails due to lack
# of temporary space.
# For example in Unix these two lines would do that:
# sql clone "create tablespace aux_tspitr_tmp
#           datafile "/tmp/aux_tspitr_tmp.dbf" size 500K";
```

Uncomment the last two lines and modify the statement. Repeat TSPITR with larger tablespace until the export succeeds.

During TSPITR if RMAN is not able to identify the undo tablespaces (if they differ at the target time of recovery & the present time) you must specify the undo tablespace clause in the recover statement. Here undotbs2 is the undo tablespace in the database at the recovery time.

```
RMAN> recover tablespace auxdata until time "to_date('2006-07-13:08:10:00',
'YYYY-MM-DD:HH24:MI:SS')"
auxiliary destination '/u01/app/oracle/admin/RMANELSE/aux_dest'
undo tablespace 'undotbs2';
```

9.6 Using Image Copies

TSPITR can be made faster by using RMAN image copies of datafiles on disk compared to restoring from tape backupsets. The DBA can use the CONFIGURE AUXNAME command for both the recovery set & auxiliary set datafile image copies. Also for auxiliary set datafile copies you can use the SET NEWNAME command.

If the relevant datafile copy is available RMAN uncatalogs the image copy from the target instance repository and then catalogs it into the auxiliary instance.

```
RMAN> configure auxname for datafile 1 to '/aux_dest/system_1.dbf';
      ...
RMAN> recover tablespace auxdata1, auxdata2;
```

If TSPITR is anticipated on a regular basis (God forbid!) the DBA can establish a process as under:

- Configure the AUXNAME for the both the recovery set & auxiliary set datafiles.

- Do BACKUP AS COPY DATAFILE n FORMAT auxname regularly to maintain the updated image copy. A faster method would be to use an incrementally updated backup strategy to keep the copies up to date.

- Specify a target time for TSPITR since the last update of the image copies.

The caveat is it may be impossible to predict the full set of tablespaces needed for TSPITR.

If the image copy (with a SCN before target time) exists for an auxiliary set datafile in the location indicated by SET NEWNAME it will be used for TSPITR. If no such copy exists RMAN will restore a copy from the backup.

The same rule is applicable to the situation when CONFIGURE AUXNAME for an auxiliary set datafile is used.

Note: The currently configured auxnames can be displayed using the SHOW AUXNAME command.

Chapter 9 Recapitulation

By employing RMAN for TSPITR you can recover one or more tablespaces in the target database to an earlier time compared to the rest of the database in an efficient manner.

Using backup sets & archived redo logs of the target database the tablespace is reconstructed by RMAN to the desired date. The actual recovery however is performed in the auxiliary instance. Datafiles of the tablespace being recovered form the recovery set. The auxiliary set is made up of a backup of the SYSTEM tablespace & undo tablespaces of the target database.

After successful completion of TSPITR the DBA should back up the recovered tablespaces before bringing them online.

The DBA can undo the effect of an erroneous TRUNCATE TABLE statement or restore the pre image data after an incorrect batch job (subject to the fact this affects only some tablespaces & not the entire database).

The following tablespaces listed are not eligible for TSPITR:
Tablespaces with external tables, nested tables or tables of VARRAY columns
Tablespaces containing materialized views or materialized view logs
Tablespaces housing SYS objects or undo segments
Tablespaces not holding all the partitions of partitioned tables

Please be aware it is of paramount importance you choose the right target time for TSPITR. You may want to use the different Flashback features to analyze the data at various points in time to zero in on the correct TSPITR target time.

If a recovery catalog is not employed you will NOT be able to perform multiple TSPITR operations to different target times.

You can query the TS_PITR_CHECK view to identify the relationships between objects that go beyond the recovery set tablespaces. Only when no rows are returned for the external tablespaces we are ready to begin TSPITR.

After TSPITR objects created after the target time in the recovered tablespaces are NOT retained. However such objects can be preserved by exporting them before TSPITR and importing them afterwards.

If TSPITR fails due to insufficient sort area during export we will need to edit the recover.bsq file located in $ORACLE_HOME/rdbms/admin.

TSPITR can be made faster by using RMAN image copies of datafiles on disk compared to restoring from tape backupsets.

Chapter 10 Objectives

- RMAN for Tablespace Transport
- Understanding Transportable Tablespaces
- RMAN Transport Process

Chapter 10
Transportable Tablespaces from RMAN Backups

The DBA may be aware transportable tablespaces can make data refresh extremely fast and are very ideally suited for moving large chunks of data. The author has performed these refreshes achieving huge time savings. But like many good things in life this comes at a price: The production database will not be fully available to the users as all transportable tablespaces are not updatable during the process. This was the case until Oracle version 10.2.

Now RMAN comes to our rescue yet another time! By creating transportable tablespace sets from RMAN backups the DBA can keep the production database fully available as live tablespaces are NOT placed in read-only mode.

RMAN also facilitates transporting tablespaces as of a target point in time. This is very useful for time based reporting.

The DBA will need the archived redo logs and backups of the source database.

RMAN creates the auxiliary instance on the same server as the source database. This is the transient holding area to perform the restore and recovery of the tablespaces being transported. On successful completion of tablespace transport this area is cleaned out by RMAN.

RMAN will use a copy of the SYSTEM, Sysaux tablespaces & Undo tablespace(s) from the source database to perform recovery.

RMAN generates the transportable set consisting of the datafiles from the tablespaces being transported and an expdp metadata dump file to be used for importing into the destination database.

10.1 Modus Operandi

RMAN performs several functions during this process. The salient ones are listed below.

- First an auxiliary database instance is created & started in NOMOUNT mode using a RMAN generated initialization parameter file. Then RMAN mounts the auxiliary instance using a restored backup of the source database control file.

- Now the relevant source database (backup) datafiles are restored. Then RMAN updates the auxiliary instance control file to point to the restored datafiles.

- Database point-in-time recovery is done at the auxiliary instance. After the recovery completion the auxiliary database is opened with the RESETLOGS clause.

- The recovered tablespaces (in the auxiliary instance) are placed into read-only mode.

- Transportable tablespace metadata is generated by expdp resulting in a dump file.

- If all of the above tasks are successful RMAN shuts down the auxiliary instance and removes all the transient files.

Note: RMAN also generates the sample impdp script (impscript.sql) to be used for plugging in the transported tablespaces into the target database.

10.2 Exclusions

Do all tablespaces qualify for transport? Not really.

Tablespaces holding these objects are NOT eligible for transport:

Tablespaces with external tables, nested tables or tables of VARRAY columns
Tablespaces containing materialized views or materialized view logs
Tablespaces housing SYS objects or undo segments
Tablespaces not holding all the partitions of partitioned tables

---

10.3 Quick Primer—Transportable Tablespaces

Now we will briefly touch upon the conceptual framework of Transportable Tablespaces.

Firstly we need to check the containment of the transportable set. To determine whether a set of tablespaces is self-contained, you can invoke the TRANSPORT_SET_CHECK procedure in the Oracle supplied package DBMS_TTS. When you invoke the DBMS_TTS package, you specify the list of tablespaces in the transportable set to be checked for self containment. You can optionally specify if constraints must be included. For strict or full containment, you must additionally set the FULL_CHECK parameter to TRUE.

```
PROCEDURE TRANSPORT_SET_CHECK
Argument Name           Type              In/Out Default?
----------------------- ----------------- ------ --------
TS_LIST                 CLOB              IN
INCL_CONSTRAINTS        BOOLEAN           IN     DEFAULT
FULL_CHECK              BOOLEAN           IN     DEFAULT
```

Execution of this procedure populates the TRANSPORT_SET_VIOLATIONS view. You can then query this to determine any violations which must be resolved before transporting the tablespaces of interest.

At the source database execute this procedure as the sys(dba) user.

```
SQL> set serveroutput on
SQL> execute DBMS_TTS.TRANSPORT_SET_CHECK('tbsp1,tbsp2');

SQL>SELECT * FROM TRANSPORT_SET_VIOLATIONS;
```

If a table & its indexes are not contained within the tablespaces targeted for transport that situation would be deemed a violation in this context. To illustrate, let us suppose table t1 of tbsp1 has an index in tbsp3. Since we are not including tbsp3 in our transportable set in the above example this violation will be noted in this view.

When no violations are found the DBA should place all the tablespaces in the transportable set in read-only mode.

SQL> ALTER TABLESPACE TBSP1 READ ONLY;
SQL> ALTER TABLESPACE TBSP2 READ ONLY;

Now export the metadata using expdp utility. Create a parameter file with these entries.

```
$ cat expdp_tbsp.par
transport_tablespaces=(tbsp1,tsbp2)
transport_full_check=y
directory=dpdest
dumpfile=exp_tbsp.dmp
logfile=exp_tbsp.log

$ expdp parfile=expdp_tbsp.par
```

Copy all the datafiles of the transportable set to the destination environment directly or stage them first in a transient location on the source platform itself before onward transmission to the final destination. After the files have been copied you can place the tablespaces in normal read write mode.

SQL> ALTER TABLESPACE TBSP1 READ WRITE;
SQL> ALTER TABLESPACE TBSP2 READ WRITE;

At the destination database we need to drop any pre-existing tablespaces with the same names first.

SQL> DROP TABLESPACE TBSP1 INCLUDING CONTENTS AND DATAFILES CASCADE CONSTRAINTS;
SQL> DROP TABLESPACE TBSP2 INCLUDING CONTENTS AND DATAFILES CASCADE CONSTRAINTS;

Now the DBA can import the transportable set of tablespaces.
Now import the metadata using impdp utility. Create a parameter file with these entries.

```
$ cat impdb_tbsp.par
logfile=impdp_tbsp.log
directory=dpdest
dumpfile=expdp_tbsp.dmp
transport_datafiles=('/oradata/tbsp1/data01.dbf', '/oradata/tbsp2/data01.dbf')
```

$ impdp parfile=impdp_tbsp.par

After importing the transportable set you can place the tablespaces in normal read write mode.

SQL> ALTER TABLESPACE TBSP1 READ WRITE;
SQL> ALTER TABLESPACE TBSP2 READ WRITE;

10.4 Workshop—Generate Transportable Set Using RMAN Backup

Let us now perform schema/data refresh deploying RMAN backups for transportable tablespaces.

$ export ORACLE_SID=RMANELSE

Step 1: Since we will be employing expdp & impdp in this process the DBA needs to create a directory object in the database.

SQL> CREATE OR REPLACE DIRECTORY DPDEST AS '/home/oracle/ram';

Directory created.

Step 2: Start RMAN & connect to both the target & catalog databases.

$ rman
RMAN> connect target;

connected to target database: RMANELSE (DBID=1826602558)

RMAN> connect catalog rman/rwoman@rman4all;

connected to recovery catalog database

Step 3: Decrypt any encrypted backup by supplying the password.

RMAN> set decryption identified by 'rman2secure';

executing command: SET decryption

Step 4: Check & resolve any reported violations.
(Execute DBMS_TTS.TRANSPORT_SET_CHECK and Query
TRANSPORT_SET_VIOLATIONS)

Step 5: Transport the tablespaces AFTER confirming no violations exist.

Always use the to_date function mask to override any default NLS_DATE_ FORMAT setting. The dump file & export log will be placed in the data pump directory while the impdp_tbsp.sql script will be created in the tablespace destination.

RMAN> transport tablespace auxdata
2> tablespace destination '/u01/app/oracle/admin/RMANELSE/tbsp_dest'
3> auxiliary destination '/u01/app/oracle/admin/RMANELSE/aux_dest'
4> until time "to_date('2006-07-13:11:15:00', 'yyyy-mm-dd:hh24:mi:ss')"
5> datapump directory dpdest
6> dump file 'expdp_tbsp.dmp'
7> import script 'impdp_tbsp.sql'
8> export log 'expdp_tbsp.log';

Creating automatic instance, with SID='kpmd'

initialization parameters used for automatic instance:
db_name=RMANELSE
compatible=10.2.0.1.0
db_block_size=8192
db_files=200
db_unique_name=tspitr_RMANELSE_kpmd
large_pool_size=1M
shared_pool_size=110M
#No auxiliary parameter file used
db_create_file_dest=/u01/app/oracle/admin/RMANELSE/aux_dest
control_files=/u01/app/oracle/admin/RMANELSE/aux_dest/cntrl_tspitr_RMA
NELSE_kpmd.f

starting up automatic instance RMANELSE

Oracle instance started

Total System Global Area   201326592 bytes

Fixed Size   1218508 bytes
Variable Size   146802740 bytes
Database Buffers   50331648 bytes
Redo Buffers   2973696 bytes
Automatic instance created

This is the auxiliary instance.

contents of Memory Script:
{
# set the until clause
set until time "to_date('2006-07-13:11:15:00', 'yyyy-mm-dd:hh24:mi:ss')";
restore the controlfile
restore clone controlfile;
mount the controlfile
sql clone 'alter database mount clone database';
archive current online log for tspitr to a resent until time
sql 'alter system archive log current';
avoid unnecessary autobackups for structural changes during TSPITR
sql 'begin dbms_backup_restore.AutoBackupFlag(FALSE); end;';
resync catalog after controlfile restore
resync catalog;
}
executing Memory Script

executing command: SET until clause

Starting restore at 13-JUL-06
allocated channel: ORA_AUX_DISK_1
channel ORA_AUX_DISK_1: sid=34 devtype=DISK

channel ORA_AUX_DISK_1: starting datafile backupset restore
channel ORA_AUX_DISK_1: restoring control file
channel ORA_AUX_DISK_1: reading from backup piece +MY_DG1/rmanelse/
autobackup/2006_07_13/s_595678065.297.595678069
channel ORA_AUX_DISK_1: restored backup piece 1
piece handle=+MY_DG1/rmanelse/autobackup/2006_07_13/s_595678065
.297.595678069 tag=TAG20060713T100745
channel ORA_AUX_DISK_1: restore complete, elapsed time: 00:00:07

output filename=/u01/app/oracle/admin/RMANELSE/aux_dest/cntrl_tspitr_
RMANELSE_kpmd.f
Finished restore at 13-JUL-06

sql statement: alter database mount clone database
sql statement: alter system archive log current
sql statement: begin dbms_backup_restore.AutoBackupFlag(FALSE); end;

starting full resync of recovery catalog
full resync complete
released channel: ORA_AUX_DISK_1

contents of Memory Script:
{
# generated tablespace point-in-time recovery script
# set the until clause
set until time "to_date('2006-07-13:11:15:00', 'yyyy-mm-dd:hh24:mi:ss')";
set an omf destination filename for restore
set newname for clone datafile 1 to new;
set an omf destination filename for restore
set newname for clone datafile 2 to new;
set an omf destination filename for restore
set newname for clone datafile 3 to new;
set an omf destination tempfile
set newname for clone tempfile 1 to new;
set a destination filename for restore
set newname for datafile 6 to
  "/u01/app/oracle/admin/RMANELSE/tbsp_dest/auxdata.276.595634175";
rename all tempfiles
switch clone tempfile all;
restore the tablespaces in the recovery set plus the auxiliary tablespaces
restore clone datafile 1, 2, 3, 6;
switch clone datafile all;
#online the datafiles restored or flipped
sql clone "alter database datafile 1 online";
#online the datafiles restored or flipped
sql clone "alter database datafile 2 online";
#online the datafiles restored or flipped
sql clone "alter database datafile 3 online";
#online the datafiles restored or flipped

```
sql clone "alter database datafile 6 online";
# make the controlfile point at the restored datafiles, then recover them
recover clone database tablespace "AUXDATA", "SYSTEM", "UNDOTBS1",
"SYSAUX" delete archivelog;
alter clone database open resetlogs;
# PLUG HERE the creation of a temporary tablespace if export fails due to lack
# of temporary space.
# For example in Unix these two lines would do that:
#sql clone "create tablespace aux_tspitr_tmp
#          datafile "/tmp/aux_tspitr_tmp.dbf" size 500K";
}
executing Memory Script

executing command: SET until clause

executing command: SET NEWNAME
executing command: SET NEWNAME
executing command: SET NEWNAME
executing command: SET NEWNAME
executing command: SET NEWNAME


renamed temporary file 1 to/u01/app/oracle/admin/RMANELSE/aux_dest/
TSPITR_RMANELSE_KPMD/datafile/o1_mf_temp_%u_.tmp in control file

Starting restore at 13-JUL-06
allocated channel: ORA_AUX_DISK_1
channel ORA_AUX_DISK_1: sid=36 devtype=DISK

channel ORA_AUX_DISK_1: starting datafile backupset restore
channel ORA_AUX_DISK_1: specifying datafile(s) to restore from backup set
restoring datafile 00001 to/u01/app/oracle/admin/RMANELSE/aux_dest/
TSPITR_RMANELSE_KPMD/datafile/o1_mf_system_%u_.dbf
restoring datafile 00002 to/u01/app/oracle/admin/RMANELSE/aux_dest/
TSPITR_RMANELSE_KPMD/datafile/o1_mf_undotbs1_%u_.dbf
restoring datafile 00003 to/u01/app/oracle/admin/RMANELSE/aux_dest/
TSPITR_RMANELSE_KPMD/datafile/o1_mf_sysaux_%u_.dbf
channel ORA_AUX_DISK_1: reading from backup piece +MY_DG1/rmanelse/
backupset/2006_06_30/nnndn0_tag20060630t111950_0.292.594472791
channel ORA_AUX_DISK_1: restored backup piece 1
```

piece handle=+MY_DG1/rmanelse/backupset/2006_06_30/nnndn0_tag2006 0630t111950_0.292.594472791 tag=TAG20060630T111950
channel ORA_AUX_DISK_1: restore complete, elapsed time: 00:02:15
channel ORA_AUX_DISK_1: starting datafile backupset restore
channel ORA_AUX_DISK_1: specifying datafile(s) to restore from backup set
restoring datafile 00006 to/u01/app/oracle/admin/RMANELSE/tbsp_dest/ auxdata.276.595634175
channel ORA_AUX_DISK_1: reading from backup piece +MY_DG1/rmanelse/ backupset/2006_07_13/nnndf0_tag20060713t101513_0.296.595678515
channel ORA_AUX_DISK_1: restored backup piece 1
piece handle=+MY_DG1/rmanelse/backupset/2006_07_13/nnndf0_tag2006 0713t101513_0.296.595678515 tag=TAG20060713T101513
channel ORA_AUX_DISK_1: restore complete, elapsed time: 00:00:01
Finished restore at 13-JUL-06

datafile 1 switched to datafile copy
input datafile copy recid=18 stamp=595687445 filename=/u01/app/oracle/admin/ RMANELSE/aux_dest/TSPITR_RMANELSE_KPMD/datafile/o1_mf_system_ 2cdxyjk9_.dbf
datafile 2 switched to datafile copy
input datafile copy recid=19 stamp=595687446 filename=/u01/app/oracle/admin/ RMANELSE/aux_dest/TSPITR_RMANELSE_KPMD/datafile/o1_mf_undotbs 1_2cdxyjoj_.dbf
datafile 3 switched to datafile copy
input datafile copy recid=20 stamp=595687446 filename=/u01/app/oracle/admin/ RMANELSE/aux_dest/TSPITR_RMANELSE_KPMD/datafile/o1_mf_sysaux_2 cdxyjlj_.dbf
datafile 6 switched to datafile copy
input datafile copy recid=21 stamp=595687446 filename=/u01/app/oracle/admin/ RMANELSE/tbsp_dest/auxdata.276.595634175

sql statement: alter database datafile 1 online
sql statement: alter database datafile 2 online
sql statement: alter database datafile 3 online
sql statement: alter database datafile 6 online

Starting recover at 13-JUL-06
using channel ORA_AUX_DISK_1

starting media recovery

archive log thread 1 sequence 1 is already on disk as file/u01/app/oracle/admin/
RMANELSE/arch/1_1_593971715.dbf
archive log thread 1 sequence 2 is already on disk as file/u01/app/oracle/admin/
RMANELSE/arch/1_2_594484678.dbf
archive log thread 2 sequence 3 is already on disk as file/u01/app/oracle/admin/
RMANELSE/arch/2_3_593971715.dbf
archive log thread 2 sequence 4 is already on disk as file/u01/app/oracle/admin/
RMANELSE/arch/2_4_594484678.dbf

media recovery complete, elapsed time: 00:02:01
Finished recover at 13-JUL-06

database opened

contents of Memory Script:
{
#mark read only the tablespace that will be exported
sql clone "alter tablespace AUXDATA read only";
export the tablespaces in the recovery set
host 'expdp userid=\"/@\(DESCRIPTION=\(ADDRESS=\(PROTOCOL=
beq\)\(PROGRAM=/u01/app/oracle/product/10.2.0/db_1/bin/oracle\)\(ARGV
0=oraclekpmd\)\(ARGS=^'\(DESCRIPTION=\(LOCAL=YES\)\(ADDRESS=\
(PROTOCOL=beq\)\)\)^'\)\)\(ENVS=^'ORACLE_SID=kpmd^'\)\)\(CONNECT_
DATA=\(SID=kpmd\)\)\) as sysdba\" transport_tablespaces=
AUXDATA dumpfile=
expdp_tbsp.dmp directory=
dpdest logfile=
expdp_tbsp.log';
}
executing Memory Script

sql statement: alter tablespace AUXDATA read only

host command complete
/*
   The following command may be used to import the tablespaces.
   Substitute values for <logon> and <directory>.
   impdp <logon> directory=<directory> dumpfile= 'expdp_tbsp.dmp'
transport_datafiles=/u01/app/oracle/admin/RMANELSE/tbsp_dest/auxdata.27
6.595634175

```
*/
------------------------------------------------------------
-- Start of sample PL/SQL script for importing the tablespaces
------------------------------------------------------------
-- creating directory objects
CREATE DIRECTORY STREAMS$DIROBJ$1 AS '/u01/app/oracle/admin/
RMANELSE/tbsp_dest/';
/* PL/SQL Script to import the exported tablespaces */
DECLARE
  -- the datafiles
  tbs_files    dbms_streams_tablespace_adm.file_set;
  cvt_files    dbms_streams_tablespace_adm.file_set;
  -- the dumpfile to import
  dump_file    dbms_streams_tablespace_adm.file;
  dp_job_name  VARCHAR2(30) := NULL;
  -- names of tablespaces that were imported
  ts_names     dbms_streams_tablespace_adm.tablespace_set;
BEGIN
  -- dump file name and location
  dump_file.file_name := 'expdp_tbsp.dmp';
  dump_file.directory_object := 'dpdest';
  -- forming list of datafiles for import
  tbs_files( 1).file_name := 'auxdata.276.595634175';
  tbs_files( 1).directory_object := 'STREAMS$DIROBJ$1';
  -- import tablespaces
  dbms_streams_tablespace_adm.attach_tablespaces(
    datapump_job_name    => dp_job_name,
    dump_file            => dump_file,
    tablespace_files     => tbs_files,
    converted_files      => cvt_files,
    tablespace_names     => ts_names);
  -- output names of imported tablespaces
  IF ts_names IS NOT NULL AND ts_names.first IS NOT NULL THEN
    FOR i IN ts_names.first .. ts_names.last LOOP
      dbms_output.put_line('imported tablespace'|| ts_names(i));
    END LOOP;
  END IF;
END;
/
-- dropping directory objects
```

DROP DIRECTORY STREAMS$DIROBJ$1;
```
----------------------------------------------------------
```
-- End of sample PL/SQL script
```
----------------------------------------------------------
```

Removing automatic instance
shutting down automatic instance
Oracle instance shut down
Automatic instance removed
auxiliary instance file/u01/app/oracle/admin/RMANELSE/aux_dest/cntrl_tspitr_RMANELSE_kpmd.f deleted
auxiliary instance file/u01/app/oracle/admin/RMANELSE/aux_dest/TSPITR_RMANELSE_KPMD/datafile/o1_mf_system_2cdxyjk9_.dbf deleted
auxiliary instance file/u01/app/oracle/admin/RMANELSE/aux_dest/TSPITR_RMANELSE_KPMD/datafile/o1_mf_undotbs1_2cdxyjoj_.dbf deleted
auxiliary instance file/u01/app/oracle/admin/RMANELSE/aux_dest/TSPITR_RMANELSE_KPMD/datafile/o1_mf_sysaux_2cdxyjlj_.dbf deleted
auxiliary instance file/u01/app/oracle/admin/RMANELSE/aux_dest/TSPITR_RMANELSE_KPMD/datafile/o1_mf_temp_2cdy73gh_.tmp deleted
auxiliary instance file/u01/app/oracle/admin/RMANELSE/aux_dest/TSPITR_RMANELSE_KPMD/onlinelog/o1_mf_1_2cdy6klg_.log deleted
auxiliary instance file/u01/app/oracle/admin/RMANELSE/aux_dest/TSPITR_RMANELSE_KPMD/onlinelog/o1_mf_2_2cdy6mbv_.log deleted
auxiliary instance file/u01/app/oracle/admin/RMANELSE/aux_dest/TSPITR_RMANELSE_KPMD/onlinelog/o1_mf_3_2cdy6oht_.log deleted

Export: Release 10.2.0.1.0—Production on Thursday, 13 July, 2006 12:46:44

Copyright (c) 2003, 2005, Oracle. All rights reserved.
Connected to: Oracle Database 10g Enterprise Edition Release 10.2.0.1.0—Production
With the Partitioning, Real Application Clusters, Oracle Label Security, OLAP and Data Mining Scoring Engine options
Starting "SYS"."SYS_EXPORT_TRANSPORTABLE_01": userid="/*******@(DESCRIPTION=(ADDRESS=(PROTOCOL=beq)
(PROGRAM=/u01/app/oracle/product/10.2.0/db_1/bin/oracle)(ARGV0=oraclekpmd)(ARGS=\(DESCRIPTION=\(LOCAL=YES\)\
(ADDRESS=\(PROTOCOL=beq\)\)\))(ENVS=ORACLE_SID=kpmd))(CONNECT_DATA=(SID=kpmd))) AS SYSDBA" transport_tablespaces= AUXDATA dumpfile=expdp_tbsp.dmp directory=dpdest logfile=expdp_tbsp.log

Processing object type TRANSPORTABLE_EXPORT/PLUGTS_BLK
Processing object type TRANSPORTABLE_EXPORT/TABLE
Processing object type TRANSPORTABLE_EXPORT/POST_INSTANCE/ PLUGTS_BLK
Master table "SYS"."SYS_EXPORT_TRANSPORTABLE_01" successfully loaded/unloaded
****
Dump file set for SYS.SYS_EXPORT_TRANSPORTABLE_01 is:
  /home/oracle/ram/expdp_tbsp.dmp
Job "SYS"."SYS_EXPORT_TRANSPORTABLE_01" successfully completed at 12:47:35

We now have generated the transportable tablespace set ready for import into the destination database.

Step 6: Create a parameter file impdp_tbsp.par to work with impdp.

```
$ cat impdp_tbsp.par
logfile=impdp_tbsp.log
directory=dpdest
dumpfile=expdp_tbsp.dmp
transport_datafiles=/u01/app/oracle/admin/RMANELSE/tbsp_dest/auxdata.27
6.595634175
```

Step 7: Import the transported tablespaces.

Set the ORACLE_SID environment variable to point to the destination database. Create the directory object in this database also.
SQL> CREATE OR REPLACE DIRECTORY DPDEST AS '/home/oracle/ram';

Import will fail with ORA-39070/87 if the directory object does not exist in the destination database.

You must create the user (with the necessary privileges) whose objects reside in the transportable tablespace set.

```
$ impdp parfile=impdp_tbsp.par
```

Import: Release 10.2.0.1.0—Production on Wednesday, 19 July, 2006 18:59:54

Copyright (c) 2003, 2005, Oracle. All rights reserved.

Username:/as sysdba

Connected to: Oracle Database 10g Enterprise Edition Release 10.2.0.1.0—Production
With the Partitioning, Real Application Clusters, Oracle Label Security, OLAP and Data Mining Scoring Engine options
Master table "SYS"."SYS_IMPORT_TRANSPORTABLE_01" successfully loaded/unloaded
Starting "SYS"."SYS_IMPORT_TRANSPORTABLE_01":/******** AS SYSDBA parfile=impdp_tbsp.par
Processing object type TRANSPORTABLE_EXPORT/PLUGTS_BLK
Processing object type TRANSPORTABLE_EXPORT/TABLE
Processing object type TRANSPORTABLE_EXPORT/POST_INSTANCE/PLUGTS_BLK
Job "SYS"."SYS_IMPORT_TRANSPORTABLE_01" successfully completed at 19:00:10

How do you verify the tablespace status in the destination database?

SQL> SELECT TABLESPACE_NAME FROM DBA_TABLESPACES WHERE PLUGGED_IN='YES';

TABLESPACE_NAME

AUXDATA

PRESTO! We expediently refreshed the destination database!!

Excerpts from the alert log of destination database:

```
================================================================
Wed Jul 19 18:59:58 2006
The value (30) of MAXTRANS parameter ignored. kupprdp: master process DM00 started with pid=22, OS id=3755
     to execute—SYS.KUPM$MCP.MAIN('SYS_IMPORT_TRANSPORTABLE_01', 'SYS', 'KUPC$C_1_20060719185958', 'KUPC$S_1_20060719185958', 0);
kupprdp: worker process DW01 started with worker id=1, pid=25, OS id=3797
```

to execute—SYS.KUPW$WORKER.MAIN('SYS_IMPORT_TRANSPORTABLE
_01', 'SYS');
Plug in tablespace AUXDATA with datafile
  '/u01/app/oracle/admin/RMANELSE/tbsp_dest/auxdata.276.595634175'
===

Tip: Alter the plugged in tablespace to read write mode now.

10.5 Troubleshooting

You can use an auxiliary instance parameter file to increase the
SHARED_POOL_SIZE value if needed for expdp.

RMAN> run
   { set auxiliary instance parameter file to '/home/oracle/ram/auxinstparams.ora';
   transport tablespace …}

Chapter 10 Recapitulation

By creating transportable tablespace sets from RMAN backups the DBA can keep the production database fully available as live tablespaces are NOT placed in read-only mode.

RMAN also facilitates transporting tablespaces as of a target point in time. This is very useful for time based reporting.

RMAN generates the transportable set consisting of the datafiles from the tablespaces being transported and an expdp metadata dump file to be used for importing into the destination database.

Tablespaces holding these objects are NOT eligible for transport:
Tablespaces with external tables, nested tables or tables of VARRAY columns
Tablespaces containing materialized views or materialized view logs
Tablespaces housing SYS objects or undo segments
Tablespaces not holding all the partitions of partitioned tables

To determine whether a set of tablespaces is self-contained, you can invoke the TRANSPORT_SET_CHECK procedure in the Oracle supplied package DBMS_TTS.

You can use an auxiliary instance parameter file to increase the SHARED_POOL_SIZE value if needed for expdp.

Chapter 11 Objectives

- Tablespace/Datafile Transport
- Database Transport
- Bidirectional ASM Conversion

Chapter 11
Cross Platform Transport

In the last chapter we delved into the realm of transportable tablespaces. Here we will cover the next logical progression of the transportable concept: Migration of data across multiple operating systems.

Can RMAN do this? The answer is in the affirmative. The DBA can transport the entire database or just a few tablespaces across different platforms.

RMAN can convert the database for transport from the source platform to the destination platform. The source and destination platforms must share the same endian format meaning both of them shall be either 'Big' or 'Little'.

However we can transport tablespaces between databases even when the endian formats of the source host & the destination host do not match. RMAN makes this possible by converting datafiles in the transportable tablespace set.

11.1 Tablespace/Datafile Transport

We will now focus on the transport of individual datafiles or tablespaces. The DBA has 2 options:

- use the CONVERT TABLESPACE command on the source server
- use the CONVERT DATAFILE command on the destination server

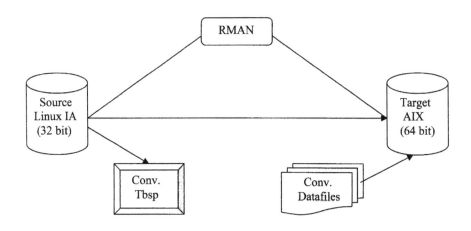

Figure 11-1 Tablespace/Datafile Conversion

RMAN> convert tablespace tbsp_1, tbsp_2
            to platform < 'platform_name' > format < 'format_string' >;

What are the various platform names recognized by RMAN? Let us query the dynamic view V$TRANSPORTABLE_PLATFORM to find out.

SQL> set pagesize 20;
SQL> column platform_id format 99 heading 'ID';
SQL> column platform_name format a40 heading 'PLATFORM';
SQL> column endian_format format a10 heading 'FORMAT';

SQL> SELECT * FROM V$TRANSPORTABLE_PLATFORM ORDER BY 1;

ID	PLATFORM	FORMAT
1	Solaris[tm] OE (32-bit)	Big
2	Solaris[tm] OE (64-bit)	Big
3	HP-UX (64-bit)	Big
4	HP-UX IA (64-bit)	Big
5	HP Tru64 UNIX	Little
6	AIX-Based Systems (64-bit)	Big
7	Microsoft Windows IA (32-bit)	Little
8	Microsoft Windows IA (64-bit)	Little
9	IBM zSeries Based Linux	Big

10 Linux IA (32-bit)	Little
11 Linux IA (64-bit)	Little
12 Windows 64-bit for AMD	Little
13 Linux 64-bit for AMD	Little
15 HP Open VMS	Little
16 Apple Mac OS	Big
17 Solaris Operating System (x86)	Little
18 IBM Power Based Linux	Big

17 rows selected.

Now let us convert the auxdata tablespace on the source.

```
$ export ORACLE_SID=RMANELSE
$ rman

RMAN> connect target;

connected to target database: RMANELSE (DBID=1826602558)

RMAN> sql 'alter tablespace auxdata read only';

sql statement: alter tablespace auxdata read only
starting full resync of recovery catalog
full resync complete
RMAN> convert tablespace auxdata
2> to platform 'AIX-Based Systems (64-bit)'
3> format '/u01/app/oracle/admin/RMANELSE/aux_dest/%U';

Starting backup at 19-JUL-06
using channel ORA_DISK_1
channel ORA_DISK_1: starting datafile conversion
input datafile fno=00006 name=+MY_DG1/rmanelse/datafile/auxdata.276
.596229681
converted  datafile=/u01/app/oracle/admin/RMANELSE/aux_dest/data_D-
RMANELSE_I-1826602558_TS-AUXDATA_FNO-6_0ihojgk5
channel ORA_DISK_1: datafile conversion complete, elapsed time: 00:00:03
Finished backup at 19-JUL-06
```

If the target tablespace(s) for conversion are not placed in read only mode RMAN throws the 6599 error. The converted datafiles of the target tablespaces are NOT considered backups at all as they are not recorded in the repository.

Note: If the flash recovery area is configured RMAN will store the converted datafiles in that location.

Let us see what happens if we attempt to convert datafiles instead on the source which is a Linux server.

RMAN> convert datafile '+MY_DG1/rmanelse/datafile/auxdata.276.596229681'
2> to platform 'AIX-Based Systems (64-bit)'
3> format '/home/oracle/ram/%U';

Starting backup at 19-JUL-06
allocated channel: ORA_DISK_1
channel ORA_DISK_1: sid=41 devtype=DISK
RMAN-00571: ===
RMAN-00569: ====== ERROR MESSAGE STACK FOLLOWS =========
RMAN-00571: ===
RMAN-03002: failure of backup command at 07/19/2006 19:50:42
RMAN-06595: platform name 'AIX-Based Systems (64-bit)' does not match database platform name 'Linux IA (32-bit)'

We conclude we can convert ONLY tablespace(s) on the source platform.

The converse is also true meaning we will not be able to convert tablespaces on the destination platform but ONLY datafiles. This is due to the fact the tablespaces will not be recognized by RMAN before import.

The DBA can direct RMAN to convert datafiles on the destination platform.
RMAN> convert datafile df1, df2
        from platform < 'platform_name' >;

11.2 Database Transport

Now let us look at the big picture. Can RMAN facilitate moving an entire database? The answer is YES.

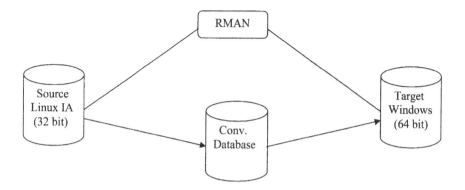

Figure 11-2 Database Conversion

Please be aware the online redo logs and control files of the source database are NOT transported. Also the control files for the newly converted database do not carry over any RMAN repository data from the source database.

Bfiles, Directories and External tables are not transported. But RMAN makes it easier to recreate them on the destination database by listing such objects during conversion.

We will have to use the DBMS_TDB.CHECK_DB function to determine if a database is transportable to the destination platform in its present condition. If this returns true we can then use RMAN to convert the whole database.

The destination platform can be one of the below listed.

SQL> SELECT * FROM V$DB_TRANSPORTABLE_PLATFORM ORDER BY 1;

ID PLATFORM	FORMAT
5 HP Tru64 UNIX	Little
7 Microsoft Windows IA (32-bit)	Little
8 Microsoft Windows IA (64-bit)	Little
10 Linux IA (32-bit)	Little
11 Linux IA (64-bit)	Little
12 Windows 64-bit for AMD	Little
13 Linux 64-bit for AMD	Little

| 15 HP Open VMS | Little |
| 17 Solaris Operating System (x86) | Little |

9 rows selected.

Let us ascertain the readiness of our database for transport. As the sys(dba) user run this piece of code calling the check_db function.

```
SQL> set serveroutput on
SQL> declare
  2 db_conv boolean;
  3 begin
  4 db_conv:=dbms_tdb.check_db('Microsoft Windows IA (32-bit)',0);
  5 end;
  6 /
```

Database is not open in READ-ONLY mode. Open the database in READ-ONLY mode and retry.

PL/SQL procedure successfully completed.

If no messages are output (before 'PL/SQL procedure successfully completed.') then our database is transportable.

What does the DBA do about the non-transportable database objects? Use the check_external function to obtain a report of such objects.

```
SQL> set serveroutput on
SQL> declare
  2 db_conv boolean;
  3 begin
  4 db_conv:=dbms_tdb.check_external;
  5 end;
  6 /
```

The following external tables exist in the database:
SH.SALES_TRANSACTIONS_EXT
The following directories exist in the database:
SYS.DPDEST, SYS.DATA_PUMP_DIR,
SYS.XMLDIR, SYS.MEDIA_DIR, SYS.LOG_FILE_DIR
The following BFILEs exist in the database:

FLOWS_010600.WWV_FLOW_RT_DISTRIBUTIONS$

PL/SQL procedure successfully completed.

Tip: To maximize availability of the production source database you may stage the datafiles in a transient location first before transferring to the destination host.

Once the source database is deemed to be transportable RMAN can take charge to automate and simplify the transport of the entire database by providing these:

- A text initialization parameter file (pfile) for the destination database which can be customized

- A transport script with SQL statements to create the destination database

- A transportable datafiles set (only when opting for conversion on the source host)

- A convert script (only when opting for conversion on the destination host)

11.2.1 Database Conversion (Source)

We will now take up the case of conversion done on the source platform.

RMAN> connect target;

connected to target database: RMANELSE (DBID=1826602558)

RMAN> convert database new database 'RMANYUSE'
2> transport script '/home/oracle/ram/transp_db.sql'
3> to platform 'Microsoft Windows IA (32-bit)'
4> db_file_name_convert ('/u01/app/oracle/admin/RMANELSE/oradata',
5> '/conv_db_stage');

After the conversion you can bounce the source database for opening in normal read write mode. Remember to transfer the converted datafiles to the destination host.

11.2.2 Database Conversion (Destination)

RMAN can also help the DBA to cause minimum impact on the source host by transferring the bulk of conversion to the destination host. Let us explore to see this at work now.

RMAN> connect target;

connected to target database: RMANELSE (DBID=1826602558)

RMAN> convert database on target platform
2> convert script '/home/oracle/ram/conv_file'
3> transport script '/home/oracle/ram/transp_db.sql'
4> new database 'RMANYUSE'
5> format '/u01/app/oracle/admin/RMANELSE/aux_dest/%U';

Starting convert at 20-JUL-06
allocated channel: ORA_DISK_1
channel ORA_DISK_1: sid=40 devtype=DISK

External table SH.SALES_TRANSACTIONS_EXT found in the database

Directory SYS.DPDEST found in the database
Directory SYS.DATA_PUMP_DIR found in the database
Directory SYS.XMLDIR found in the database
Directory SYS.MEDIA_DIR found in the database
Directory SYS.LOG_FILE_DIR found in the database
BFILE FLOWS_010600.WWV_FLOW_RT_DISTRIBUTIONS$ found in the database

User SYS with SYSDBA and SYSOPER privilege found in password file
channel ORA_DISK_1: starting to check datafiles
input datafile fno=00001 name=+MY_DG1/rmanelse/datafile/system.283.594828005
channel ORA_DISK_1: datafile checking complete, elapsed time: 00:00:00
channel ORA_DISK_1: starting to check datafiles
input datafile fno=00003 name=+MY_DG1/rmanelse/datafile/sysaux.286.594828007
channel ORA_DISK_1: datafile checking complete, elapsed time: 00:00:00
channel ORA_DISK_1: starting to check datafiles

input datafile fno=00005 name=+MY_DG1/rmanelse/datafile/example.282.594828007

channel ORA_DISK_1: datafile checking complete, elapsed time: 00:00:00

channel ORA_DISK_1: starting to check datafiles

input datafile fno=00002 name=+MY_DG1/rmanelse/datafile/undotbs1.281.594828007

channel ORA_DISK_1: datafile checking complete, elapsed time: 00:00:00

channel ORA_DISK_1: starting to check datafiles

input datafile fno=00004 name=+MY_DG1/rmanelse/datafile/users.304.594828007

channel ORA_DISK_1: datafile checking complete, elapsed time: 00:00:00

channel ORA_DISK_1: starting to check datafiles

input datafile fno=00006 name=+MY_DG1/rmanelse/datafile/auxdata.276.596229681

channel ORA_DISK_1: datafile checking complete, elapsed time: 00:00:00

Run SQL script/home/oracle/ram/transp_db.sql on the target platform to create database

Edit init.ora file/u01/app/oracle/admin/RMANELSE/aux_dest/init_00hol5ik_1_0.ora. This PFILE will be used to create the database on the target platform

Run RMAN script/home/oracle/ram/conv_file on target platform to convert datafiles

To recompile all PL/SQL modules, run utlirp.sql and utlrp.sql on the target platform

To change the internal database identifier, use DBNEWID Utility

Finished backup at 20-JUL-06

Caution: Please be aware using CONVERT DATABASE ON TARGET PLATFORM does NOT generate converted datafile copies.

The customizable pfile is reproduced here.

```
# Please change the values of the following parameters:
control_files        = "/u01/app/oracle/admin/RMANELSE/aux_dest/cf_D-
RMANYUSE_id-1826602558_00hol5ik"
db_create_file_dest  = "/u01/app/oracle/admin/RMANELSE/aux_dest/+MY
_DG1"
background_dump_dest  = "/u01/app/oracle/admin/RMANELSE/aux_dest/
bdump"
user_dump_dest       = "/u01/app/oracle/admin/RMANELSE/aux_dest/udump"
core_dump_dest       = "/u01/app/oracle/admin/RMANELSE/aux_dest/cdump"
```

```
db_name                 = "RMANYUSE"
# Please review the values of the following parameters:
 __shared_pool_size     = 58720256
 __large_pool_size      = 4194304
 __java_pool_size       = 12582912
 __streams_pool_size    = 0
 __db_cache_size        = 20971520
  log_archive_dest      = "/u01/app/oracle/admin/RMANELSE/arch"
  remote_login_passwordfile= "EXCLUSIVE"
  db_domain             = ""
# The values of the following parameters are from source database:
  processes             = 50
  sga_target            = 100663296
  db_block_size         = 8192
  compatible            = "10.2.0.1.0"
  log_archive_format    = "log%t_%s_%r.arc"
  db_file_multiblock_read_count= 16
  undo_management       = "AUTO"
  job_queue_processes   = 10
  open_cursors          = 100
  pga_aggregate_target  = 11000000
```

The DBA shall transfer the unconverted source datafiles to a staging area at the destination and then execute the convert script.

The convert script generated by RMAN is provided below.

```
RUN {

CONVERT DATAFILE '+MY_DG1/rmanelse/datafile/system.283.594828005'
FROM PLATFORM 'Linux IA (32-bit)'
FORMAT '/u01/app/oracle/admin/RMANELSE/aux_dest/data_
D-RMANELSE_I-
1826602558_TS-SYSTEM_FNO-1_0jhol5ik';

CONVERT DATAFILE '+MY_DG1/rmanelse/datafile/sysaux.286.594828007'
FROM PLATFORM 'Linux IA (32-bit)'
FORMAT '/u01/app/oracle/admin/RMANELSE/aux_dest/data_
D-RMANELSE_I-
1826602558_TS-SYSAUX_FNO-3_0khol5ik';
```

CONVERT DATAFILE '+MY_DG1/rmanelse/datafile/example.282.594828007'
FROM PLATFORM 'Linux IA (32-bit)'
FORMAT '/u01/app/oracle/admin/RMANELSE/aux_dest/data_
D-RMANELSE_I-
1826602558_TS-EXAMPLE_FNO-5_0lhol5ik';

CONVERT DATAFILE '+MY_DG1/rmanelse/datafile/undotbs1.281.594828007'
FROM PLATFORM 'Linux IA (32-bit)'
FORMAT '/u01/app/oracle/admin/RMANELSE/aux_dest/data_
D-RMANELSE_I-
1826602558_TS-UNDOTBS1_FNO-2_0mhol5ik';

CONVERT DATAFILE '+MY_DG1/rmanelse/datafile/users.304.594828007'
FROM PLATFORM 'Linux IA (32-bit)'
FORMAT '/u01/app/oracle/admin/RMANELSE/aux_dest/data_
D-RMANELSE_I-
1826602558_TS-USERS_FNO-4_0nhol5il';

CONVERT DATAFILE '+MY_DG1/rmanelse/datafile/auxdata.276.596229681'
FROM PLATFORM 'Linux IA (32-bit)'
FORMAT '/u01/app/oracle/admin/RMANELSE/aux_dest/data_
D-RMANELSE_I-
1826602558_TS-AUXDATA_FNO-6_0ohol5il';

}

RMAN generates the sql script to create the control file for the destination database as under:

STARTUP NOMOUNT PFILE='/u01/app/oracle/admin/RMANELSE/aux_dest/init_00hol5ik_1_0.ora'
CREATE CONTROLFILE REUSE SET DATABASE "RMANYUSE" RESETLOGS ARCHIVELOG
   MAXLOGFILES 192
   MAXLOGMEMBERS 3
   MAXDATAFILES 1024
   MAXINSTANCES 32
   MAXLOGHISTORY 292
LOGFILE
 GROUP 1 SIZE 50M,

GROUP 2 SIZE 50M,
GROUP 3 SIZE 50M
DATAFILE
  '/u01/app/oracle/admin/RMANELSE/aux_dest/data_D-RMANELSE_I-1826602558_TS-SYSTEM_FNO-1_0jhol5ik',
  '/u01/app/oracle/admin/RMANELSE/aux_dest/data_D-RMANELSE_I-1826602558_TS-UNDOTBS1_FNO-2_0mhol5ik',
  '/u01/app/oracle/admin/RMANELSE/aux_dest/data_D-RMANELSE_I-1826602558_TS-SYSAUX_FNO-3_0khol5ik',
  '/u01/app/oracle/admin/RMANELSE/aux_dest/data_D-RMANELSE_I-1826602558_TS-USERS_FNO-4_0nhol5il',
  '/u01/app/oracle/admin/RMANELSE/aux_dest/data_D-RMANELSE_I-1826602558_TS-EXAMPLE_FNO-5_0lhol5ik'
CHARACTER SET AL32UTF8;

ALTER DATABASE ENABLE BLOCK CHANGE TRACKING
USING FILE '/u01/app/oracle/admin/RMANELSE/blkchgtrk.dbf' REUSE;

-- Initialize the online redo log files.
ALTER DATABASE OPEN RESETLOGS;

-- Files in read-only tablespaces are now named.
ALTER DATABASE RENAME FILE 'MISSING00006'
  TO '/u01/app/oracle/admin/RMANELSE/aux_dest/data_D-RMANELSE_I-1826602558_TS-AUXDATA_FNO-6_0ohol5il';

-- Bring the read-only tablespaces online.
ALTER TABLESPACE "AUXDATA" ONLINE;

ALTER TABLESPACE TEMP ADD TEMPFILE
  SIZE 22020096 AUTOEXTEND ON NEXT 655360 MAXSIZE 32767M;

The DBA can change the internal database identifier (DBID) using the DBNEWID utility.

$ nid target=sys/r24rman as sysdba dbname=RMANYUSE logfile=nid.log

After opening the destination database you may want to recompile all the PL/SQL modules.

SQL> SHUTDOWN IMMEDIATE;

SQL> STARTUP MOUNT;

SQL> ALTER DATABASE OPEN UPGRADE;

SQL> @$ORACLE_HOME/rdbms/admin/utlirp.sql

SQL> SHUTDOWN IMMEDIATE;

SQL> STARTUP

SQL> @$ORACLE_HOME/rdbms/admin/utlrp.sql

To minimize disruption to the production source database we can move the datafiles to an interim location first on the destination host. To illustrate let us suppose we transfer all the source datafiles into/conv_db_stage folder. We want them eventually moved to their final location. To accomplish this modify the convert script as follows:

```
RMAN> convert datafile '/conv_db_stage/auxdata_01.dbf'
    from platform 'Linux IA (32-bit)'
    format '/u01/app/oracle/admin/RMANYUSE/auxdata_01.dbf';
```

11.3 Bidirectional ASM Conversion

RMAN's CONVERT command comes in handy to move datafiles in & out of ASM storage. When no source or destination platform is defined RMAN generates image copies of the individual datafiles in the indicated locations.

Let us convert an ASM datafile to a regular filesystem file.

RMAN> connect target;

connected to target database: RMANELSE (DBID=1826602558)

```
RMAN> convert datafile '+MY_DG1/rmanelse/datafile/auxdata.276.596229681'
2> format '/u01/app/oracle/admin/RMANELSE/aux_dest/%U';
```

Starting backup at 20-JUL-06

allocated channel: ORA_DISK_1
channel ORA_DISK_1: sid=46 devtype=DISK
channel ORA_DISK_1: starting datafile conversion
input filename=+MY_DG1/rmanelse/datafile/auxdata.276.596229681
converted   datafile=/u01/app/oracle/admin/RMANELSE/aux_dest/data_D-
RMANELSE_I-1826602558_TS-AUXDATA_FNO-6_0pholufv
channel ORA_DISK_1: datafile conversion complete, elapsed time: 00:00:04
Finished backup at 20-JUL-06

You can accomplish the conversion in the other direction too.
RMAN> convert datafile '/u01/app/oracle/admin/RMANELSE/oradata/
auxdata_01.dbf', 2> '/u01/app/oracle/admin/RMANELSE/oradata/auxdata_02
.dbf'
3> format '+MY_DG1';

We can also convert tablespaces.

RMAN> convert tablespace auxdata
2> format '/u01/app/oracle/admin/RMANELSE/aux_dest/%U';

Starting backup at 21-JUL-06
allocated channel: ORA_DISK_1
channel ORA_DISK_1: sid=37 devtype=DISK
channel ORA_DISK_1: starting datafile conversion
input datafile fno=00006 name=+MY_DG1/rmanelse/datafile/auxdata.276
.596229681
converted   datafile=/u01/app/oracle/admin/RMANELSE/aux_dest/data_D-
RMANELSE_I-1826602558_TS-AUXDATA_FNO-6_0qhonoqe
channel ORA_DISK_1: datafile conversion complete, elapsed time: 00:00:04
Finished backup at 21-JUL-06

Note: The converted datafiles do NOT belong to the target database.

Chapter 11 Recapitulation

RMAN can convert the database for transport from the source platform to the destination platform. The source and destination platforms must share the same endian format meaning both of them shall be either 'Big' or 'Little'.

However we can transport tablespaces between databases even when the endian formats of the source host & the destination host do not match. RMAN makes this possible by converting datafiles in the transportable tablespace set.

We can query the dynamic view V$TRANSPORTABLE_PLATFORM to list the various platform names recognized by RMAN.

If the target tablespace(s) for conversion are not placed in read only mode RMAN throws the 6599 error.

The converted datafiles of the target tablespaces are NOT considered backups at all as they are not recorded in the repository.

We conclude we can convert ONLY tablespace(s) on the source platform.

The converse is also true meaning we will not be able to convert tablespaces on the destination platform but ONLY datafiles. This is due to the fact the tablespaces will not be recognized by RMAN before import.

Also the control files for the newly converted database do not carry over any RMAN repository data from the source database

Bfiles, Directories and External tables are not transported. But RMAN makes it easier to recreate them on the destination database by listing such objects during conversion.

Once the source database is deemed to be transportable RMAN can automate and simplify the transport of the entire database by providing these:
A text initialization parameter file (pfile) for the destination database which can be customized, a transport script with SQL statements to create the destination database, a transportable datafiles set (only when opting for conversion on the source host) & a convert script (only when opting for conversion on the destination host).

RMAN can also help the DBA to cause minimum impact on the source host by transferring the bulk of conversion to the destination host.

RMAN does NOT generate converted datafile copies while performing CONVERT DATABASE ON TARGET PLATFORM.

RMAN uses the CONVERT command to move datafiles in & out of ASM storage. When no source or destination platform is defined RMAN generates image copies of the individual datafiles in the indicated locations.

The converted datafiles do NOT belong to the target database.

Chapter 12 Objectives

- Non-ASM to ASM Migration
- ASM to non-ASM Migration

Chapter 12
Migration Into & Out of ASM

The DBA knows Automatic Storage Management (ASM) based solution offers an attractive alternative to traditional journal filesystems or raw devices for several database files. As you may be aware we can use ASM for both multi-instance Real Application Cluster (RAC) & non-RAC single instance databases.

In this chapter we will perform migration in both the directions.

i) Non-ASM to ASM
ii) ASM to non-ASM

RMAN is the ONLY tool available to accomplish both the objectives.

Note: Ensure all the tablespaces in the database are in normal read write mode before migration.

12.1 Workshop: Non-ASM to ASM Migration

Employing ASM based storage for our database files is certainly one of the best practices to adopt. Here I detail the process of migrating into ASM based storage.

Step 1: Connect to both the target & catalog databases.

$ export ORACLE_SID=RMANELSE

$ rman

RMAN> connect target;

connected to target database: RMANELSE (DBID=1826602558)

RMAN> connect catalog rman/rwoman@rman4all;

connected to recovery catalog database

Step 2: Perform controlfile autobackup.

RMAN> configure controlfile autobackup on;

old RMAN configuration parameters:
CONFIGURE CONTROLFILE AUTOBACKUP OFF;
new RMAN configuration parameters:
CONFIGURE CONTROLFILE AUTOBACKUP ON;
new RMAN configuration parameters are successfully stored
starting full resync of recovery catalog
full resync complete

RMAN> configure controlfile autobackup format for device type disk to
'/u01/app/oracle/admin/RMANELSE/aux_dest/%F';

new RMAN configuration parameters:
CONFIGURE CONTROLFILE AUTOBACKUP FORMAT FOR DEVICE
TYPE DISK TO '/u01/app/oracle/admin/RMANELSE/aux_dest/%F';
new RMAN configuration parameters are successfully stored
starting full resync of recovery catalog
full resync complete

Step 3: Backup the entire database as image copy into an ASM disk group.

RMAN> backup as copy incremental level 0 database format '+MY_DG1';

Starting backup at 25-JUL-06
allocated channel: ORA_DISK_1
channel ORA_DISK_1: sid=33 devtype=DISK
channel ORA_DISK_1: starting datafile copy
input datafile fno=00001 name=/u01/app/oracle/admin/RMANELSE/aux_dest/
data_D-RMANELSE_I-1826602558_TS-SYSTEM_FNO-1_13hoo4q8
output filename=+MY_DG1/rmanelse/datafile/system.279.596679619 tag=
TAG20060725T002012 recid=33 stamp=596679658
channel ORA_DISK_1: datafile copy complete, elapsed time: 00:00:56
channel ORA_DISK_1: starting datafile copy
input datafile fno=00003 name=/u01/app/oracle/admin/RMANELSE/aux_dest/
data_D-RMANELSE_I-1826602558_TS-SYSAUX_FNO-3_14hoo4rv

output filename=+MY_DG1/rmanelse/datafile/sysaux.289.596679669 tag= TAG20060725T002012 recid=34 stamp=596679700
channel ORA_DISK_1: datafile copy complete, elapsed time: 00:00:35
channel ORA_DISK_1: starting datafile copy
input datafile fno=00005 name=/u01/app/oracle/admin/RMANELSE/aux_dest/ data_D-RMANELSE_I-1826602558_TS-EXAMPLE_FNO-5_15hoo4tn
output filename=+MY_DG1/rmanelse/datafile/example.276.596679707 tag= TAG20060725T002012 recid=35 stamp=596679715
channel ORA_DISK_1: datafile copy complete, elapsed time: 00:00:15
channel ORA_DISK_1: starting datafile copy
input datafile fno=00002 name=/u01/app/oracle/admin/RMANELSE/aux_ dest/data_D-RMANELSE_I-1826602558_TS-UNDOTBS1_FNO- 2_16hoo4ug
output filename=+MY_DG1/rmanelse/datafile/undotbs1.298.596679719 tag= TAG20060725T002012 recid=36 stamp=596679726
channel ORA_DISK_1: datafile copy complete, elapsed time: 00:00:15
channel ORA_DISK_1: starting datafile copy
input datafile fno=00004 name=/u01/app/oracle/admin/RMANELSE/aux_ dest/data_D-RMANELSE_I-1826602558_TS-USERS_FNO-4_17hoo4uv
output filename=+MY_DG1/rmanelse/datafile/users.304.596679735 tag= TAG20060725T002012 recid=37 stamp=596679744
channel ORA_DISK_1: datafile copy complete, elapsed time: 00:00:15
channel ORA_DISK_1: starting datafile copy
input datafile fno=00006 name=/u01/app/oracle/admin/RMANELSE/aux_ dest/data_D-RMANELSE_I-1826602558_TS-AUXDATA_FNO-6_18hoo4ve
output filename=+MY_DG1/rmanelse/datafile/auxdata.281.596679751 tag= TAG20060725T002012 recid=38 stamp=596679751
channel ORA_DISK_1: datafile copy complete, elapsed time: 00:00:01
Finished backup at 25-JUL-06

Starting Control File and SPFILE Autobackup at 25-JUL-06
piece handle=/u01/app/oracle/admin/RMANELSE/aux_dest/c-1826602558- 20060725-00 comment=NONE
Finished Control File and SPFILE Autobackup at 25-JUL-06

Tip: Perform this with multiple channels to speed up the backups.

Step 4: Obtain a consistent backup by archiving the current redo log.

RMAN> sql 'alter system archive log current';

Step 5: Restore the spfile.

RMAN> restore spfile to '+MY_DG1/spfile';

Starting restore at 25-JUL-06
using channel ORA_DISK_1

channel ORA_DISK_1: starting datafile backupset restore
channel ORA_DISK_1: restoring SPFILE
output filename=+MY_DG1
channel ORA_DISK_1: reading from backup piece/u01/app/oracle/admin/
RMANELSE/aux_dest/c-1826602558-20060725-00
channel ORA_DISK_1: restored backup piece 1
piece handle=/u01/app/oracle/admin/RMANELSE/aux_dest/c-1826602558-
20060725-00 tag=TAG20060725T002235
channel ORA_DISK_1: restore complete, elapsed time: 00:00:01
Finished restore at 25-JUL-06

Step 6: Restore the controlfile.

RMAN> restore controlfile to '+MY_DG1';

Starting restore at 25-JUL-06
using channel ORA_DISK_1
channel ORA_DISK_1: starting datafile backupset restore
channel ORA_DISK_1: restoring control file
output filename=+MY_DG1
channel ORA_DISK_1: reading from backup piece/u01/app/oracle/admin/
RMANELSE/aux_dest/c-1826602558-20060725-00
channel ORA_DISK_1: restored backup piece 1
piece handle=/u01/app/oracle/admin/RMANELSE/aux_dest/c-1826602558-
20060725-00 tag=TAG20060725T002235
channel ORA_DISK_1: restore complete, elapsed time: 00:00:04
Finished restore at 25-JUL-06

How do we obtain the actual ASM based controlfile name? You can use the new
ASM command line tool called ASMCMD. Follow this method to find out.

$ .oraenv
ORACLE_SID = [RMANELSE]? +ASM1

```
$ asmcmd
ASMCMD> ls
MY_DG1/
MY_DG2/
ASMCMD> cd my_dg1
ASMCMD> ls
RMANELSE/
ASMCMD> cd rmanelse
ASMCMD> ls
CHANGETRACKING/
CONTROLFILE/
DATAFILE/
ONLINELOG/
TEMPFILE/
ASMCMD> cd controlfile
ASMCMD> ls
Current.282.596682859
```

Step 7: Update the spfile with the new controlfile location.

SQL> ALTER SYSTEM SET CONTROL_FILES = '+MY_DG1/RMANELSE/CONTROLFILE/current.282.596682859' scope = spfile;

Step 8: Configure the flash recovery area (if needed) by defining these 2 parameters

SQL> ALTER SYSTEM SET DB_RECOVERY_FILE_DEST_SIZE = 100G SID = '*';

SQL> ALTER SYSTEM SET DB_RECOVERY_FILE_DEST = '+MY_DG2' SID = '*';

Note: For a RAC database we are setting the parameter values across all the instances/nodes by the denotation: SID = '*'.

Step 9: Shutdown the instance & Mount the database.

We have to bounce the database to use the new CONTROL_FILES location. We then open the controlfile(s) by having the database in mounted state. Now we can update the control file(s) to point to the datafile copies created before.

Step 10: Convert the datafile copies into live database datafiles.

RMAN> switch database to copy;

datafile 1 switched to datafile copy "+MY_DG1/rmanelse/datafile/system
.279.596679619"
datafile 2 switched to datafile copy "+MY_DG1/rmanelse/datafile/undotbs1
.298.596679719"
datafile 3 switched to datafile copy "+MY_DG1/rmanelse/datafile/sysaux.
289.596679669"
datafile 4 switched to datafile copy "+MY_DG1/rmanelse/datafile/users
.304.596679735"
datafile 5 switched to datafile copy "+MY_DG1/rmanelse/datafile/example
.276.596679707"
datafile 6 switched to datafile copy "+MY_DG1/rmanelse/datafile/auxdata
.281.596679751"

Step 11: Perform recovery.

RMAN> recover database;

Starting recover at 25-JUL-06
allocated channel: ORA_DISK_1
channel ORA_DISK_1: sid=40 devtype=DISK

starting media recovery

archive log thread 1 sequence 9 is already on disk as file/u01/app/oracle/admin/
RMANELSE/aux_dest/onredo2_1.log
archive log thread 1 sequence 10 is already on disk as file/u01/app/oracle/admin/
RMANELSE/aux_dest/onredo3_1.log
archive log filename=/u01/app/oracle/admin/RMANELSE/aux_dest/onredo2_
1.log thread=1 sequence=9
archive log filename=/u01/app/oracle/admin/RMANELSE/aux_dest/onredo3_
1.log thread=1 sequence=10
media recovery complete, elapsed time: 00:00:07
Finished recover at 25-JUL-06

Step 12: Update the temporary tablespace location.

RMAN> run
2> { set newname for tempfile 1 to '+MY_DG1';
3> switch tempfile all; }

executing command: SET NEWNAME

renamed temporary file 1 to +MY_DG1 in control file

Note: The new tempfile(s) are created when you open the database.

Step: 13 Disable the flash recovery area on the filesystem. (if configured)

SQL> ALTER DATABASE FLASHBACK OFF;

Step 14: Enable it using ASM based storage. (The DB_RECOVERY_FILE_DEST was defined earlier as the ASM disk group 'MY_DG2'.)

SQL> ALTER DATABASE FLASHBACK ON;

Step 15: Turn off the block change tracking using filesystem based file.

SQL> ALTER DATABASE DISABLE BLOCK CHANGE TRACKING;

Step 16: Turn on the block change tracking using ASM based file.

SQL> ALTER DATABASE ENABLE BLOCK CHANGE TRACKING USING FILE '+MY_DG1';

SQL> SELECT FILENAME FROM V$BLOCK_CHANGE_TRACKING;

FILENAME

+MY_DG1/rmanelse/changetracking/ctf.297.596719319

Now we must open the database with the resetlogs clause. Otherwise you will hit the ORA-01589 error.

Step 17: Open the database initializing the online logs.

RMAN> alter database open resetlogs;

database opened
new incarnation of database registered in recovery catalog
starting full resync of recovery catalog
full resync complete

Step 18: Transfer the online redo logs into ASM based storage.

The last component for migration is the online redo log files. For each thread let us add an ASM based log group & then drop the non-ASM based group. Before we drop any log group we need to query its status to ascertain its eligibility for removal. Only the group marked 'INACTIVE' or 'UNUSED' can be dropped. We will gather the necessary redo log information first.

SQL> SELECT THREAD#, GROUP#, BYTES FROM V$LOG ORDER BY 1;

SQL> SELECT GROUP#, STATUS FROM V$LOG;

```
   GROUP# STATUS
---------- ----------------
        1 CURRENT
        2 INACTIVE
        3 UNUSED
```

SQL> ALTER DATABASE DROP LOGFILE GROUP 2;

Database altered.

SQL> ALTER DATABASE ADD LOGFILE GROUP 2 '+MY_DG1' size 10M;

Database altered.

Tip: Run the command 'alter system switch logfile' to switch out of active log groups preceding their drop.

Repeat the above procedure until all the online logs are moved into ASM diskgroups.

Step 19: Do a sanity check.

Let us do a final reality check of the various database files to confirm their migration into ASM based storage.

SQL> SELECT NAME FROM V$CONTROLFILE;

NAME

+MY_DG1/rmanelse/controlfile/current.282.596682859

SQL> SELECT NAME FROM V$DATAFILE;

NAME

+MY_DG1/rmanelse/datafile/system.279.596679619
+MY_DG1/rmanelse/datafile/undotbs1.298.596679719
+MY_DG1/rmanelse/datafile/sysaux.289.596679669
+MY_DG1/rmanelse/datafile/users.304.596679735
+MY_DG1/rmanelse/datafile/example.276.596679707
+MY_DG1/rmanelse/datafile/auxdata.281.596679751

6 rows selected.

SQL> SELECT MEMBER FROM V$LOGFILE ORDER BY 1;

MEMBER

+MY_DG1/rmanelse/onlinelog/group_1.259.596715151
+MY_DG1/rmanelse/onlinelog/group_2.277.596715079
+MY_DG1/rmanelse/onlinelog/group_3.275.596715797

SQL> SELECT NAME FROM V$TEMPFILE;

NAME

+MY_DG1/rmanelse/tempfile/temp.283.596709727

Step 20: Congratulate yourself—You are awesome!

VOILA!! We now have successfully completed the migration into ASM.

12.2 Workshop: ASM to non-ASM Migration

I wonder why you would have to do this ☹. Anyway let us shift gears to do the migration in the reverse direction.

RMAN> connect target;

connected to target database: RMANELSE (DBID=1826602558)

RMAN> connect catalog rman/rwoman@rman4all;

connected to recovery catalog database

RMAN> backup as copy incremental level 0 database format
2> '/u01/app/oracle/admin/RMANELSE/aux_dest/%U';

Starting backup at 21-JUL-06
using channel ORA_DISK_1
channel ORA_DISK_1: starting datafile copy
input datafile fno=00001 name=+MY_DG1/rmanelse/datafile/system.283
.594828005
output   filename=/u01/app/oracle/admin/RMANELSE/aux_dest/data_D-
RMANELSE_I-1826602558_TS-SYSTEM_FNO-1_13hoo4q8 tag=TAG2006
0721T134856 recid=21 stamp=596382583
channel ORA_DISK_1: datafile copy complete, elapsed time: 00:00:55
channel ORA_DISK_1: starting datafile copy
input datafile fno=00003 name=+MY_DG1/rmanelse/datafile/sysaux.286
.594828007
output   filename=/u01/app/oracle/admin/RMANELSE/aux_dest/data_D-
RMANELSE_I-1826602558_TS-SYSAUX_FNO-3_14hoo4rv tag=TAG2006
0721T134856 recid=22 stamp=596382645
channel ORA_DISK_1: datafile copy complete, elapsed time: 00:00:55
channel ORA_DISK_1: starting datafile copy
input datafile fno=00005 name=+MY_DG1/rmanelse/datafile/example.282
.594828007
output   filename=/u01/app/oracle/admin/RMANELSE/aux_dest/data_D-
RMANELSE_I-1826602558_TS-EXAMPLE_FNO-5_15hoo4tn tag=TAG
20060721T134856 recid=23 stamp=596382662
channel ORA_DISK_1: datafile copy complete, elapsed time: 00:00:25
channel ORA_DISK_1: starting datafile copy

input datafile fno=00002 name=+MY_DG1/rmanelse/datafile/undotbs1.281
.594828007
output filename=/u01/app/oracle/admin/RMANELSE/aux_dest/data_D-
RMANELSE_I-1826602558_TS-UNDOTBS1_FNO-2_16hoo4ug tag=TAG
20060721T134856 recid=24 stamp=596382685
channel ORA_DISK_1: datafile copy complete, elapsed time: 00:00:15
channel ORA_DISK_1: starting datafile copy
input datafile fno=00004 name=+MY_DG1/rmanelse/datafile/users.304
.594828007
output filename=/u01/app/oracle/admin/RMANELSE/aux_dest/data_D-
RMANELSE_I-1826602558_TS-USERS_FNO-4_17hoo4uv tag=TAG2006
0721T134856 recid=25 stamp=596382698
channel ORA_DISK_1: datafile copy complete, elapsed time: 00:00:15
channel ORA_DISK_1: starting datafile copy
input datafile fno=00006 name=+MY_DG1/rmanelse/datafile/auxdata.276
.596229681
output filename=/u01/app/oracle/admin/RMANELSE/aux_dest/data_D-
RMANELSE_I-1826602558_TS-AUXDATA_FNO-6_18hoo4ve tag=TAG
20060721T134856 recid=26 stamp=596382703
channel ORA_DISK_1: datafile copy complete, elapsed time: 00:00:03
Finished backup at 21-JUL-06

RMAN> sql 'alter system archive log current';

Restore the spfile and controlfile.

RMAN> restore spfile to
2> '/u01/app/oracle/product/10.2.0/db_1/dbs/spfileRMANELSE.ora';

Starting restore at 21-JUL-06
allocated channel: ORA_DISK_1
channel ORA_DISK_1: sid=46 devtype=DISK

channel ORA_DISK_1: starting datafile backupset restore
channel ORA_DISK_1: restoring SPFILE
output filename=/u01/app/oracle/product/10.2.0/db_1/dbs/spfileRMANELSE.ora
channel ORA_DISK_1: reading from backup piece/u01/app/oracle/admin/
RMANELSE/aux_dest/c-1826602558-20060721-00
channel ORA_DISK_1: restored backup piece 1

piece handle=/u01/app/oracle/admin/RMANELSE/aux_dest/c-1826602558-20060721-00 tag=TAG20060721T135147
channel ORA_DISK_1: restore complete, elapsed time: 00:00:01
Finished restore at 21-JUL-06

Note: You can also create a text initialization parameter file (pfile) with just one line referencing the server parameter file (spfile). The location defaults to $ORACLE_HOME/dbs unless otherwise indicated.

SPFILE=spfileRMANELSE.ora

SQL> show parameter spfile

/u01/app/oracle/product/10.2.0/db_1/dbs/spfileRMANELSE.ora

SQL> STARTUP NOMOUNT;

SQL> ALTER SYSTEM SET CONTROL_FILES='/home/oracle/ram/rmanelse.ctl' SCOPE = SPFILE SID = '*';

RMAN> restore controlfile to '/home/oracle/ram/rmanelse.ctl';

Starting restore at 21-JUL-06
allocated channel: ORA_DISK_1
channel ORA_DISK_1: sid=44 devtype=DISK

channel ORA_DISK_1: starting datafile backupset restore
channel ORA_DISK_1: restoring control file
output filename=/home/oracle/ram/rmanelse.ctl
channel ORA_DISK_1: reading from backup piece/u01/app/oracle/admin/RMANELSE/aux_dest/c-1826602558-20060721-00
channel ORA_DISK_1: restored backup piece 1
piece handle=/u01/app/oracle/admin/RMANELSE/aux_dest/c-1826602558-20060721-00 tag=TAG20060721T135147
channel ORA_DISK_1: restore complete, elapsed time: 00:00:03
Finished restore at 21-JUL-06
SQL> ALTER SYSTEM SET DB_RECOVERY_FILE_DEST_SIZE = 100G SID = '*';
SQL> ALTER SYSTEM SET DB_RECOVERY_FILE_DEST =/flash_dest SID = '*';

Shutdown & mount the database.

RMAN> switch database to copy;

datafile 1 switched to datafile copy "/u01/app/oracle/admin/RMANELSE/ aux_dest/data_D-RMANELSE_I-1826602558_TS-SYSTEM_FNO- 1_13hoo4q8"
datafile 2 switched to datafile copy "/u01/app/oracle/admin/RMANELSE/ aux_dest/data_D-RMANELSE_I-1826602558_TS-UNDOTBS1_FNO- 2_16hoo4ug"
datafile 3 switched to datafile copy "/u01/app/oracle/admin/RMANELSE/ aux_dest/data_D-RMANELSE_I-1826602558_TS-SYSAUX_FNO- 3_14hoo4rv"
datafile 4 switched to datafile copy "/u01/app/oracle/admin/RMANELSE/ aux_dest/data_D-RMANELSE_I-1826602558_TS-USERS_FNO- 4_17hoo4uv"
datafile 5 switched to datafile copy "/u01/app/oracle/admin/RMANELSE/ aux_dest/data_D-RMANELSE_I-1826602558_TS-EXAMPLE_FNO- 5_15hoo4tn"
datafile 6 switched to datafile copy "/u01/app/oracle/admin/RMANELSE/ aux_dest/data_D-RMANELSE_I-1826602558_TS-AUXDATA_FNO- 6_18hoo4ve"

RMAN> recover database;

Starting recover at 21-JUL-06
allocated channel: ORA_DISK_1
channel ORA_DISK_1: sid=40 devtype=DISK

starting media recovery

archive log thread 1 sequence 20 is already on disk as file +MY_DG1/rmanelse/ onlinelog/group_2.275.593971735
archive log thread 1 sequence 21 is already on disk as file +MY_DG1/rmanelse/ onlinelog/group_3.259.593971739
archive log filename=+MY_DG1/rmanelse/onlinelog/group_2.275.593971735 thread=1 sequence=20
archive log filename=+MY_DG1/rmanelse/onlinelog/group_3.259.593971739 thread=1 sequence=21
media recovery complete, elapsed time: 00:00:04

Finished recover at 21-JUL-06

```
RMAN> run
2> { set newname for tempfile 1 to
3> '/u01/app/oracle/admin/RMANELSE/aux_dest/temp.dbf';
4> switch tempfile all; }
```

The DBA should disable the ASM based flash recovery area. (if configured)

```
SQL> ALTER DATABASE FLASHBACK OFF;
```

Now enable it using the filesystem.

```
SQL> ALTER DATABASE FLASHBACK ON;
```

Do likewise for block change tracking.

```
SQL> ALTER DATABASE DISABLE BLOCK CHANGE TRACKING;
```

```
SQL> ALTER DATABASE ENABLE BLOCK CHANGE TRACKING
USING FILE '/u01/app/oracle/admin/RMANELSE/blkchgtrk.dbf';
```

```
SQL> ALTER DATABASE OPEN RESETLOGS;
```

Database altered.

Lastly we migrate the online redo logs. For each thread let us add a non-ASM based log group & then drop the ASM based group.

```
SQL> SELECT GROUP#, STATUS FROM V$LOG;

  GROUP# STATUS
---------- ----------------
       1 CURRENT
       2 INACTIVE
       3 UNUSED
```

```
SQL> ALTER DATABASE DROP LOGFILE GROUP 2;
```

Database altered.

SQL> ALTER DATABASE ADD LOGFILE GROUP 2
2> ('/u01/app/oracle/admin/RMANELSE/aux_dest/onredo_1.log',
3> '/u01/app/oracle/admin/RMANELSE/aux_dest/onredo_2.log') SIZE 10M;

Database altered.

Repeat the above procedure until all the online logs are moved out of ASM diskgroups.

Now let us confirm the migration for all the database files.

SQL> SELECT NAME FROM V$CONTROLFILE;

/home/oracle/ram/rmanelse.ctl

SQL> SELECT NAME FROM V$DATAFILE;

/u01/app/oracle/admin/RMANELSE/aux_dest/data_D-RMANELSE_I-1826602558_TS-SYSTEM_FNO-1_13hoo4q8

/u01/app/oracle/admin/RMANELSE/aux_dest/data_D-RMANELSE_I-1826602558_TS-UNDOTBS1_FNO-2_16hoo4ug

/u01/app/oracle/admin/RMANELSE/aux_dest/data_D-RMANELSE_I-1826602558_TS-SYSAUX_FNO-3_14hoo4rv

/u01/app/oracle/admin/RMANELSE/aux_dest/data_D-RMANELSE_I-1826602558_TS-USERS_FNO-4_17hoo4uv

/u01/app/oracle/admin/RMANELSE/aux_dest/data_D-RMANELSE_I-1826602558_TS-EXAMPLE_FNO-5_15hoo4tn

/u01/app/oracle/admin/RMANELSE/aux_dest/data_D-RMANELSE_I-1826602558_TS-AUXDATA_FNO-6_18hoo4ve

6 rows selected.

SQL> select group#, member from v$logfile order by 1;

    1
/u01/app/oracle/admin/RMANELSE/aux_dest/onredo1_1.log

    1
/u01/app/oracle/admin/RMANELSE/aux_dest/onredo1_2.log

    2
/u01/app/oracle/admin/RMANELSE/aux_dest/onredo2_2.log

    2
/u01/app/oracle/admin/RMANELSE/aux_dest/onredo2_1.log

    3
/u01/app/oracle/admin/RMANELSE/aux_dest/onredo3_2.log

    3
/u01/app/oracle/admin/RMANELSE/aux_dest/onredo3_1.log

6 rows selected.

SQL> SELECT NAME FROM V$TEMPFILE;

/u01/app/oracle/admin/RMANELSE/aux_dest/temp.dbf

At this juncture our migration out of ASM is complete.

Chapter 12 Recapitulation

RMAN is the ONLY tool available to accomplish the migration into & out of ASM based storage.

Ensure all the tablespaces in the database are in normal read write mode before migration.

Appendix: Recovery Catalog Views

The Recovery Catalog contains 53 views whose structure is presented here.

SQL> desc RC_ARCHIVED_LOG

Name	Null?	Type
DB_KEY	NOT NULL	NUMBER
DBINC_KEY	NOT NULL	NUMBER
DB_NAME	NOT NULL	VARCHAR2(8)
AL_KEY	NOT NULL	NUMBER
RECID	NOT NULL	NUMBER
STAMP	NOT NULL	NUMBER
NAME		VARCHAR2(1024)
THREAD#	NOT NULL	NUMBER
SEQUENCE#	NOT NULL	NUMBER
RESETLOGS_CHANGE#	NOT NULL	NUMBER
RESETLOGS_TIME	NOT NULL	DATE
FIRST_CHANGE#	NOT NULL	NUMBER
FIRST_TIME	NOT NULL	DATE
NEXT_CHANGE#	NOT NULL	NUMBER
NEXT_TIME		DATE
BLOCKS	NOT NULL	NUMBER
BLOCK_SIZE	NOT NULL	NUMBER
COMPLETION_TIME	NOT NULL	DATE
ARCHIVED		VARCHAR2(3)
STATUS	NOT NULL	VARCHAR2(1)
IS_STANDBY		VARCHAR2(3)
DICTIONARY_BEGIN		VARCHAR2(3)
DICTIONARY_END		VARCHAR2(3)
IS_RECOVERY_DEST_FILE	NOT NULL	VARCHAR2(3)
COMPRESSED		VARCHAR2(3)
CREATOR		VARCHAR2(7)

SQL> desc RC_BACKUP_ARCHIVELOG_DETAILS

Name	Null?	Type
BTYPE		CHAR(9)
BTYPE_KEY		NUMBER
SESSION_KEY		NUMBER
SESSION_RECID		NUMBER
SESSION_STAMP		NUMBER
DB_KEY		NUMBER
DB_NAME		VARCHAR2(8)
ID1		NUMBER
ID2		NUMBER
THREAD#		NUMBER
SEQUENCE#		NUMBER
RESETLOGS_CHANGE#		NUMBER
RESETLOGS_TIME		DATE
FIRST_CHANGE#		NUMBER
FIRST_TIME		DATE
NEXT_CHANGE#		NUMBER
NEXT_TIME		DATE
FILESIZE		NUMBER
COMPRESSION_RATIO		NUMBER
FILESIZE_DISPLAY		VARCHAR2(4000)

SQL> desc RC_BACKUP_ARCHIVELOG_SUMMARY

Name	Null?	Type
DB_NAME	NOT NULL	VARCHAR2(8)
DB_KEY		NUMBER
NUM_FILES_BACKED		NUMBER
NUM_DISTINCT_FILES_BACKED		NUMBER
MIN_FIRST_CHANGE#		NUMBER
MAX_NEXT_CHANGE#		NUMBER
MIN_FIRST_TIME		DATE
MAX_NEXT_TIME		DATE
INPUT_BYTES		NUMBER
OUTPUT_BYTES		NUMBER
COMPRESSION_RATIO		NUMBER

INPUT_BYTES_DISPLAY		VARCHAR2(4000)
OUTPUT_BYTES_DISPLAY		VARCHAR2(4000)

SQL> desc RC_BACKUP_CONTROLFILE

Name	Null?	Type
DB_KEY	NOT NULL	NUMBER
DBINC_KEY	NOT NULL	NUMBER
DB_NAME	NOT NULL	VARCHAR2(8)
BCF_KEY	NOT NULL	NUMBER
RECID	NOT NULL	NUMBER
STAMP	NOT NULL	NUMBER
BS_KEY	NOT NULL	NUMBER
SET_STAMP	NOT NULL	NUMBER
SET_COUNT	NOT NULL	NUMBER
RESETLOGS_CHANGE#	NOT NULL	NUMBER
RESETLOGS_TIME	NOT NULL	DATE
CHECKPOINT_CHANGE#	NOT NULL	NUMBER
CHECKPOINT_TIME	NOT NULL	DATE
CREATION_TIME	NOT NULL	DATE
BLOCK_SIZE	NOT NULL	NUMBER
OLDEST_OFFLINE_RANGE	NOT NULL	NUMBER
STATUS		VARCHAR2(1)
BS_RECID		NUMBER
BS_STAMP		NUMBER
BS_LEVEL		NUMBER
COMPLETION_TIME		DATE
CONTROLFILE_TYPE		VARCHAR2(1)
BLOCKS		NUMBER
AUTOBACKUP_DATE		DATE
AUTOBACKUP_SEQUENCE		NUMBER

SQL> desc RC_BACKUP_CONTROLFILE_DETAILS

Name	Null?	Type
BTYPE		CHAR(9)
BTYPE_KEY		NUMBER
SESSION_KEY		NUMBER

SESSION_RECID	NUMBER
SESSION_STAMP	NUMBER
DB_KEY	NUMBER
DB_NAME	VARCHAR2(8)
ID1	NUMBER
ID2	NUMBER
CREATION_TIME	DATE
RESETLOGS_CHANGE#	NUMBER
RESETLOGS_TIME	DATE
CHECKPOINT_CHANGE#	NUMBER
CHECKPOINT_TIME	DATE
FILESIZE	NUMBER
COMPRESSION_RATIO	NUMBER
FILESIZE_DISPLAY	VARCHAR2(4000)

SQL> desc RC_BACKUP_CONTROLFILE_SUMMARY

Name	Null?	Type
DB_NAME	NOT NULL	VARCHAR2(8)
DB_KEY		NUMBER
NUM_FILES_BACKED		NUMBER
NUM_DISTINCT_FILES_BACKED		NUMBER
MIN_CHECKPOINT_CHANGE#		NUMBER
MAX_CHECKPOINT_CHANGE#		NUMBER
MIN_CHECKPOINT_TIME		DATE
MAX_CHECKPOINT_TIME		DATE
INPUT_BYTES		NUMBER
OUTPUT_BYTES		NUMBER
COMPRESSION_RATIO		NUMBER
INPUT_BYTES_DISPLAY		VARCHAR2(4000)
OUTPUT_BYTES_DISPLAY		VARCHAR2(4000)

SQL> desc RC_BACKUP_COPY_DETAILS

Name	Null?	Type
SESSION_KEY		NUMBER
SESSION_RECID		NUMBER
SESSION_STAMP		NUMBER

DB_KEY	NUMBER
DB_NAME	VARCHAR2(8)
RSR_KEY	NUMBER
COPY_KEY	NUMBER
FILE#	NUMBER
NAME	VARCHAR2(1024)
TAG	VARCHAR2(32)
CREATION_CHANGE#	NUMBER
CREATION_TIME	DATE
CHECKPOINT_CHANGE#	NUMBER
CHECKPOINT_TIME	DATE
MARKED_CORRUPT	NUMBER
OUTPUT_BYTES	NUMBER
COMPLETION_TIME	DATE
CONTROLFILE_TYPE	VARCHAR2(1)
KEEP	VARCHAR2(3)
KEEP_UNTIL	DATE
KEEP_OPTIONS	VARCHAR2(10)
IS_RECOVERY_DEST_FILE	VARCHAR2(3)
OUTPUT_BYTES_DISPLAY	VARCHAR2(4000)

SQL> desc RC_BACKUP_COPY_SUMMARY

Name	Null?	Type
DB_NAME	NOT NULL	VARCHAR2(8)
DB_KEY		NUMBER
NUM_COPIES		NUMBER
NUM_DISTINCT_COPIES		NUMBER
MIN_CHECKPOINT_CHANGE#		NUMBER
MAX_CHECKPOINT_CHANGE#		NUMBER
MIN_CHECKPOINT_TIME		DATE
MAX_CHECKPOINT_TIME		DATE
OUTPUT_BYTES		NUMBER
OUTPUT_BYTES_DISPLAY		VARCHAR2(4000)

SQL> desc RC_BACKUP_CORRUPTION

Name	Null?	Type
DB_KEY	NOT NULL	NUMBER
DBINC_KEY	NOT NULL	NUMBER
DB_NAME	NOT NULL	VARCHAR2(8)
RECID	NOT NULL	NUMBER
STAMP	NOT NULL	NUMBER
BS_KEY	NOT NULL	NUMBER
SET_STAMP	NOT NULL	NUMBER
SET_COUNT	NOT NULL	NUMBER
PIECE#	NOT NULL	NUMBER
BDF_KEY	NOT NULL	NUMBER
BDF_RECID	NOT NULL	NUMBER
BDF_STAMP	NOT NULL	NUMBER
FILE#	NOT NULL	NUMBER
CREATION_CHANGE#	NOT NULL	NUMBER
BLOCK#	NOT NULL	NUMBER
BLOCKS	NOT NULL	NUMBER
CORRUPTION_CHANGE#		NUMBER
MARKED_CORRUPT		VARCHAR2(3)
CORRUPTION_TYPE		VARCHAR2(9)

SQL> desc RC_BACKUP_DATAFILE

Name	Null?	Type
DB_KEY	NOT NULL	NUMBER
DBINC_KEY	NOT NULL	NUMBER
DB_NAME	NOT NULL	VARCHAR2(8)
BDF_KEY	NOT NULL	NUMBER
RECID	NOT NULL	NUMBER
STAMP	NOT NULL	NUMBER
BS_KEY	NOT NULL	NUMBER
SET_STAMP	NOT NULL	NUMBER
SET_COUNT	NOT NULL	NUMBER
BS_RECID		NUMBER
BS_STAMP		NUMBER
BACKUP_TYPE		VARCHAR2(1)

INCREMENTAL_LEVEL		NUMBER
COMPLETION_TIME		DATE
FILE#	NOT NULL	NUMBER
CREATION_CHANGE#	NOT NULL	NUMBER
CREATION_TIME		DATE
RESETLOGS_CHANGE#	NOT NULL	NUMBER
RESETLOGS_TIME	NOT NULL	DATE
INCREMENTAL_CHANGE#	NOT NULL	NUMBER
CHECKPOINT_CHANGE#	NOT NULL	NUMBER
CHECKPOINT_TIME	NOT NULL	DATE
ABSOLUTE_FUZZY_CHANGE#		NUMBER
DATAFILE_BLOCKS	NOT NULL	NUMBER
BLOCKS	NOT NULL	NUMBER
BLOCK_SIZE	NOT NULL	NUMBER
STATUS		VARCHAR2(1)
BS_LEVEL		NUMBER
PIECES	NOT NULL	NUMBER
BLOCKS_READ	NOT NULL	NUMBER
MARKED_CORRUPT		NUMBER
USED_CHANGE_TRACKING		VARCHAR2(3)
USED_OPTIMIZATION		VARCHAR2(3)
PCT_NOTREAD		NUMBER

SQL> desc RC_BACKUP_DATAFILE_DETAILS

Name	Null?	Type
BTYPE		CHAR(9)
BTYPE_KEY		NUMBER
SESSION_KEY		NUMBER
SESSION_RECID		NUMBER
SESSION_STAMP		NUMBER
DB_KEY		NUMBER
DB_NAME		VARCHAR2(8)
ID1		NUMBER
ID2		NUMBER
FILE#		NUMBER
CREATION_CHANGE#		NUMBER
CREATION_TIME		DATE
RESETLOGS_CHANGE#		NUMBER

RESETLOGS_TIME	DATE
INCREMENTAL_LEVEL	NUMBER
INCREMENTAL_CHANGE#	NUMBER
CHECKPOINT_CHANGE#	NUMBER
CHECKPOINT_TIME	DATE
MARKED_CORRUPT	NUMBER
FILESIZE	NUMBER
COMPRESSION_RATIO	NUMBER
TS#	NUMBER
TSNAME	VARCHAR2(30)
FILESIZE_DISPLAY	VARCHAR2(4000)

SQL> desc RC_BACKUP_DATAFILE_SUMMARY

Name	Null?	Type
DB_NAME	NOT NULL	VARCHAR2(8)
DB_KEY		NUMBER
NUM_FILES_BACKED		NUMBER
NUM_DISTINCT_FILES_BACKED		NUMBER
NUM_DISTINCT_TS_BACKED		NUMBER
MIN_CHECKPOINT_CHANGE#		NUMBER
MAX_CHECKPOINT_CHANGE#		NUMBER
MIN_CHECKPOINT_TIME		DATE
MAX_CHECKPOINT_TIME		DATE
INPUT_BYTES		NUMBER
OUTPUT_BYTES		NUMBER
COMPRESSION_RATIO		NUMBER
INPUT_BYTES_DISPLAY		VARCHAR2(4000)
OUTPUT_BYTES_DISPLAY		VARCHAR2(4000)

SQL> desc RC_BACKUP_FILES

Name	Null?	Type
PKEY		NUMBER
BACKUP_TYPE		VARCHAR2(32)
FILE_TYPE		VARCHAR2(32)
KEEP		VARCHAR2(3)
KEEP_UNTIL		DATE

KEEP_OPTIONS	VARCHAR2(13)
STATUS	VARCHAR2(16)
FNAME	VARCHAR2(1024)
TAG	VARCHAR2(32)
MEDIA	VARCHAR2(80)
RECID	NUMBER
STAMP	NUMBER
DEVICE_TYPE	VARCHAR2(255)
BLOCK_SIZE	NUMBER
COMPLETION_TIME	DATE
COMPRESSED	VARCHAR2(3)
OBSOLETE	VARCHAR2(3)
BYTES	NUMBER
BS_KEY	NUMBER
BS_COUNT	NUMBER
BS_STAMP	NUMBER
BS_TYPE	VARCHAR2(32)
BS_INCR_TYPE	VARCHAR2(32)
BS_PIECES	NUMBER
BS_COPIES	NUMBER
BS_COMPLETION_TIME	DATE
BS_STATUS	VARCHAR2(16)
BS_BYTES	NUMBER
BS_COMPRESSED	VARCHAR2(3)
BS_TAG	VARCHAR2(1024)
BS_DEVICE_TYPE	VARCHAR2(255)
BP_PIECE#	NUMBER
BP_COPY#	NUMBER
DF_FILE#	NUMBER
DF_TABLESPACE	VARCHAR2(30)
DF_RESETLOGS_CHANGE#	NUMBER
DF_CREATION_CHANGE#	NUMBER
DF_CHECKPOINT_CHANGE#	NUMBER
DF_CKP_MOD_TIME	DATE
RL_THREAD#	NUMBER
RL_SEQUENCE#	NUMBER
RL_RESETLOGS_CHANGE#	NUMBER
RL_FIRST_CHANGE#	NUMBER
RL_FIRST_TIME	DATE

RL_NEXT_CHANGE#   NUMBER
RL_NEXT_TIME   DATE

SQL> desc RC_BACKUP_PIECE

Name	Null?	Type
DB_KEY	NOT NULL	NUMBER
DB_ID	NOT NULL	NUMBER
BP_KEY	NOT NULL	NUMBER
RECID	NOT NULL	NUMBER
STAMP	NOT NULL	NUMBER
BS_KEY	NOT NULL	NUMBER
SET_STAMP	NOT NULL	NUMBER
SET_COUNT	NOT NULL	NUMBER
BACKUP_TYPE		VARCHAR2(1)
INCREMENTAL_LEVEL		NUMBER
PIECE#	NOT NULL	NUMBER
COPY#	NOT NULL	NUMBER
DEVICE_TYPE	NOT NULL	VARCHAR2(255)
HANDLE	NOT NULL	VARCHAR2(1024)
COMMENTS		VARCHAR2(255)
MEDIA		VARCHAR2(80)
MEDIA_POOL		NUMBER
CONCUR		VARCHAR2(3)
TAG		VARCHAR2(32)
START_TIME	NOT NULL	DATE
COMPLETION_TIME	NOT NULL	DATE
ELAPSED_SECONDS		NUMBER
STATUS	NOT NULL	VARCHAR2(1)
BYTES		NUMBER
IS_RECOVERY_DEST_FILE	NOT NULL	VARCHAR2(3)
RSR_KEY		NUMBER
COMPRESSED		VARCHAR2(3)

SQL> desc RC_BACKUP_PIECE_DETAILS

Name	Null?	Type
SESSION_KEY		NUMBER

SESSION_RECID		NUMBER
SESSION_STAMP		NUMBER
DB_NAME		VARCHAR2(8)
DB_KEY	NOT NULL	NUMBER
DB_ID	NOT NULL	NUMBER
BP_KEY		NUMBER
RECID		NUMBER
STAMP		NUMBER
BS_KEY		NUMBER
SET_STAMP		NUMBER
SET_COUNT		NUMBER
BACKUP_TYPE		VARCHAR2(1)
INCREMENTAL_LEVEL		NUMBER
PIECE#		NUMBER
COPY#		NUMBER
DEVICE_TYPE		VARCHAR2(255)
HANDLE		VARCHAR2(1024)
COMMENTS		VARCHAR2(255)
MEDIA		VARCHAR2(80)
MEDIA_POOL		NUMBER
CONCUR		VARCHAR2(3)
TAG		VARCHAR2(32)
START_TIME		DATE
COMPLETION_TIME		DATE
ELAPSED_SECONDS		NUMBER
STATUS		VARCHAR2(1)
BYTES		NUMBER
IS_RECOVERY_DEST_FILE		VARCHAR2(3)
RSR_KEY		NUMBER
COMPRESSED		VARCHAR2(3)
PIECES_PER_SET		NUMBER
SIZE_BYTES_DISPLAY		VARCHAR2(4000)

SQL> desc RC_BACKUP_REDOLOG

Name	Null?	Type
DB_KEY	NOT NULL	NUMBER
DBINC_KEY	NOT NULL	NUMBER
DB_NAME	NOT NULL	VARCHAR2(8)

BRL_KEY	NOT NULL	NUMBER
RECID	NOT NULL	NUMBER
STAMP	NOT NULL	NUMBER
BS_KEY	NOT NULL	NUMBER
SET_STAMP	NOT NULL	NUMBER
SET_COUNT	NOT NULL	NUMBER
BACKUP_TYPE		VARCHAR2(1)
COMPLETION_TIME		DATE
THREAD#	NOT NULL	NUMBER
SEQUENCE#	NOT NULL	NUMBER
RESETLOGS_CHANGE#	NOT NULL	NUMBER
RESETLOGS_TIME	NOT NULL	DATE
FIRST_CHANGE#	NOT NULL	NUMBER
FIRST_TIME	NOT NULL	DATE
NEXT_CHANGE#	NOT NULL	NUMBER
NEXT_TIME	NOT NULL	DATE
BLOCKS	NOT NULL	NUMBER
BLOCK_SIZE	NOT NULL	NUMBER
STATUS		VARCHAR2(1)
BS_RECID		NUMBER
BS_STAMP		NUMBER
PIECES	NOT NULL	NUMBER

SQL> desc RC_BACKUP_SET

Name	Null?	Type
DB_KEY	NOT NULL	NUMBER
DB_ID	NOT NULL	NUMBER
BS_KEY	NOT NULL	NUMBER
RECID		NUMBER
STAMP		NUMBER
SET_STAMP	NOT NULL	NUMBER
SET_COUNT	NOT NULL	NUMBER
BACKUP_TYPE		VARCHAR2(1)
INCREMENTAL_LEVEL		NUMBER
PIECES	NOT NULL	NUMBER
START_TIME		DATE
COMPLETION_TIME		DATE
ELAPSED_SECONDS		NUMBER

STATUS	VARCHAR2(1)
CONTROLFILE_INCLUDED	VARCHAR2(7)
INPUT_FILE_SCAN_ONLY	VARCHAR2(3)
KEEP	VARCHAR2(3)
KEEP_UNTIL	DATE
KEEP_OPTIONS	VARCHAR2(10)

SQL> desc RC_BACKUP_SET_DETAILS

Name	Null?	Type
SESSION_KEY		NUMBER
SESSION_RECID		NUMBER
SESSION_STAMP		NUMBER
DB_KEY		NUMBER
DB_NAME		VARCHAR2(8)
BS_KEY		NUMBER
RECID		NUMBER
STAMP		NUMBER
SET_STAMP		NUMBER
SET_COUNT		NUMBER
BACKUP_TYPE		VARCHAR2(1)
CONTROLFILE_INCLUDED		VARCHAR2(7)
INCREMENTAL_LEVEL		NUMBER
PIECES		NUMBER
START_TIME		DATE
COMPLETION_TIME		DATE
ELAPSED_SECONDS		NUMBER
BLOCK_SIZE		VARCHAR2
KEEP		VARCHAR2(3)
KEEP_UNTIL		DATE
KEEP_OPTIONS		VARCHAR2(10)
DEVICE_TYPE		VARCHAR2(255)
COMPRESSED		VARCHAR2(3)
NUM_COPIES		NUMBER
OUTPUT_BYTES		NUMBER
ORIGINAL_INPUT_BYTES		NUMBER
COMPRESSION_RATIO		NUMBER
STATUS		CHAR(1)
ORIGINAL_INPRATE_BYTES		NUMBER

OUTPUT_RATE_BYTES	NUMBER
ORIGINAL_INPUT_BYTES_DISPLAY	VARCHAR2(4000)
OUTPUT_BYTES_DISPLAY	VARCHAR2(4000)
ORIGINAL_INPRATE_BYTES_DISPLAY	VARCHAR2(4000)
OUTPUT_RATE_BYTES_DISPLAY	VARCHAR2(4000)
TIME_TAKEN_DISPLAY	VARCHAR2(4000)

SQL> desc RC_BACKUP_SET_SUMMARY

Name	Null?	Type
DB_NAME	NOT NULL	VARCHAR2(8)
DB_KEY		NUMBER
NUM_BACKUPSETS		NUMBER
OLDEST_BACKUP_TIME		DATE
NEWEST_BACKUP_TIME		DATE
OUTPUT_BYTES		NUMBER
ORIGINAL_INPUT_BYTES		NUMBER
ORIGINAL_INPRATE_BYTES		NUMBER
OUTPUT_RATE_BYTES		NUMBER
COMPRESSION_RATIO		NUMBER
ORIGINAL_INPUT_BYTES_DISPLAY		VARCHAR2(4000)
OUTPUT_BYTES_DISPLAY		VARCHAR2(4000)
ORIGINAL_INPRATE_BYTES_DISPLAY		VARCHAR2(4000)
OUTPUT_RATE_BYTES_DISPLAY		VARCHAR2(4000)

SQL> desc RC_BACKUP_SPFILE

Name	Null?	Type
DB_KEY	NOT NULL	NUMBER
BSF_KEY	NOT NULL	NUMBER
RECID	NOT NULL	NUMBER
STAMP	NOT NULL	NUMBER
BS_KEY	NOT NULL	NUMBER
SET_STAMP	NOT NULL	NUMBER
SET_COUNT	NOT NULL	NUMBER
MODIFICATION_TIME	NOT NULL	DATE
STATUS		VARCHAR2(1)
BS_RECID		NUMBER

```
BS_STAMP                                    NUMBER
COMPLETION_TIME                             DATE
BYTES                       NOT NULL        NUMBER
```

SQL> desc RC_BACKUP_SPFILE_DETAILS

Name	Null?	Type
SESSION_KEY		NUMBER
SESSION_RECID		NUMBER
SESSION_STAMP		NUMBER
DB_KEY		NUMBER
DB_NAME		VARCHAR2(8)
BS_KEY		NUMBER
SET_STAMP	NOT NULL	NUMBER
SET_COUNT		NUMBER
MODIFICATION_TIME	NOT NULL	DATE
FILESIZE	NOT NULL	NUMBER
FILESIZE_DISPLAY		VARCHAR2(4000)

SQL> desc RC_BACKUP_SPFILE_SUMMARY

Name	Null?	Type
DB_NAME	NOT NULL	VARCHAR2(8)
DB_KEY	NOT NULL	NUMBER
NUM_FILES_BACKED		NUMBER
NUM_DISTINCT_FILES_BACKED		NUMBER
MIN_MODIFICATION_TIME		DATE
MAX_MODIFICATION_TIME		DATE
INPUT_BYTES		NUMBER
INPUT_BYTES_DISPLAY		VARCHAR2(4000)

SQL> desc RC_CHECKPOINT

Name	Null?	Type
DB_KEY	NOT NULL	NUMBER
DBINC_KEY	NOT NULL	NUMBER

DB_NAME	NOT NULL	VARCHAR2(8)
CKP_KEY	NOT NULL	NUMBER
CKP_SCN	NOT NULL	NUMBER
CKP_CF_SEQ	NOT NULL	NUMBER
CKP_TIME		DATE
CKP_TYPE	NOT NULL	VARCHAR2(7)

SQL> desc RC_CONTROLFILE_COPY

Name	Null?	Type
DB_KEY	NOT NULL	NUMBER
DBINC_KEY	NOT NULL	NUMBER
DB_NAME	NOT NULL	VARCHAR2(8)
CCF_KEY	NOT NULL	NUMBER
RECID	NOT NULL	NUMBER
STAMP	NOT NULL	NUMBER
NAME	NOT NULL	VARCHAR2(1024)
TAG		VARCHAR2(32)
RESETLOGS_CHANGE#	NOT NULL	NUMBER
RESETLOGS_TIME	NOT NULL	DATE
CHECKPOINT_CHANGE#	NOT NULL	NUMBER
CHECKPOINT_TIME	NOT NULL	DATE
CREATION_TIME	NOT NULL	DATE
BLOCKS		NUMBER
BLOCK_SIZE	NOT NULL	NUMBER
MIN_OFFR_RECID	NOT NULL	NUMBER
OLDEST_OFFLINE_RANGE	NOT NULL	NUMBER
COMPLETION_TIME	NOT NULL	DATE
STATUS	NOT NULL	VARCHAR2(1)
CONTROLFILE_TYPE		VARCHAR2(1)
KEEP		VARCHAR2(3)
KEEP_UNTIL		DATE
KEEP_OPTIONS		VARCHAR2(10)
IS_RECOVERY_DEST_FILE	NOT NULL	VARCHAR2(3)
RSR_KEY		NUMBER

```
SQL> desc RC_COPY_CORRUPTION
```

Name	Null?	Type
DB_KEY	NOT NULL	NUMBER
DBINC_KEY	NOT NULL	NUMBER
DB_NAME	NOT NULL	VARCHAR2(8)
RECID	NOT NULL	NUMBER
STAMP	NOT NULL	NUMBER
CDF_KEY	NOT NULL	NUMBER
COPY_RECID	NOT NULL	NUMBER
COPY_STAMP	NOT NULL	NUMBER
FILE#	NOT NULL	NUMBER
CREATION_CHANGE#	NOT NULL	NUMBER
BLOCK#	NOT NULL	NUMBER
BLOCKS	NOT NULL	NUMBER
CORRUPTION_CHANGE#		NUMBER
MARKED_CORRUPT		VARCHAR2(3)
CORRUPTION_TYPE		VARCHAR2(9)

```
SQL> desc RC_DATABASE
```

Name	Null?	Type
DB_KEY	NOT NULL	NUMBER
DBINC_KEY		NUMBER
DBID	NOT NULL	NUMBER
NAME	NOT NULL	VARCHAR2(8)
RESETLOGS_CHANGE#	NOT NULL	NUMBER
RESETLOGS_TIME	NOT NULL	DATE

```
SQL> desc RC_DATABASE_BLOCK_CORRUPTION
```

Name	Null?	Type
DB_KEY		NUMBER
DBINC_KEY		NUMBER
FILE#		NUMBER
BLOCK#		NUMBER
BLOCKS		NUMBER

CORRUPTION_CHANGE#	NUMBER
CORRUPTION_TYPE	VARCHAR2(9)

SQL> desc RC_DATABASE_INCARNATION

Name	Null?	Type
DB_KEY		NUMBER
DBID		NUMBER
DBINC_KEY		NUMBER
NAME		VARCHAR2(8)
RESETLOGS_CHANGE#		NUMBER
RESETLOGS_TIME		DATE
CURRENT_INCARNATION		VARCHAR2(3)
PARENT_DBINC_KEY		NUMBER
PRIOR_RESETLOGS_CHANGE#		NUMBER
PRIOR_RESETLOGS_TIME		DATE
STATUS		VARCHAR2(8)

SQL> desc RC_DATAFILE

Name	Null?	Type
DB_KEY	NOT NULL	NUMBER
DBINC_KEY	NOT NULL	NUMBER
DB_NAME	NOT NULL	VARCHAR2(8)
TS#	NOT NULL	NUMBER
TABLESPACE_NAME	NOT NULL	VARCHAR2(30)
FILE#	NOT NULL	NUMBER
CREATION_CHANGE#	NOT NULL	NUMBER
CREATION_TIME		DATE
DROP_CHANGE#		NUMBER
DROP_TIME		DATE
BYTES		NUMBER
BLOCKS		NUMBER
BLOCK_SIZE	NOT NULL	NUMBER
NAME		VARCHAR2(1024)
STOP_CHANGE#		NUMBER
STOP_TIME		DATE
READ_ONLY	NOT NULL	NUMBER

RFILE#		NUMBER
INCLUDED_IN_DATABASE_BACKUP	NOT NULL	VARCHAR2(3)
AUX_NAME		VARCHAR2(1024)
ENCRYPT_IN_BACKUP		VARCHAR2(3)

SQL> desc RC_DATAFILE_COPY

Name	Null?	Type
DB_KEY	NOT NULL	NUMBER
DBINC_KEY	NOT NULL	NUMBER
DB_NAME	NOT NULL	VARCHAR2(8)
CDF_KEY	NOT NULL	NUMBER
RECID	NOT NULL	NUMBER
STAMP	NOT NULL	NUMBER
NAME	NOT NULL	VARCHAR2(1024)
TAG		VARCHAR2(32)
FILE#	NOT NULL	NUMBER
CREATION_CHANGE#	NOT NULL	NUMBER
CREATION_TIME		DATE
RESETLOGS_CHANGE#	NOT NULL	NUMBER
RESETLOGS_TIME	NOT NULL	DATE
INCREMENTAL_LEVEL		NUMBER
CHECKPOINT_CHANGE#	NOT NULL	NUMBER
CHECKPOINT_TIME	NOT NULL	DATE
ABSOLUTE_FUZZY_CHANGE#		NUMBER
RECOVERY_FUZZY_CHANGE#		NUMBER
RECOVERY_FUZZY_TIME		DATE
ONLINE_FUZZY		VARCHAR2(3)
BACKUP_FUZZY		VARCHAR2(3)
BLOCKS	NOT NULL	NUMBER
BLOCK_SIZE	NOT NULL	NUMBER
COMPLETION_TIME	NOT NULL	DATE
STATUS	NOT NULL	VARCHAR2(1)
KEEP		VARCHAR2(3)
KEEP_UNTIL		DATE
KEEP_OPTIONS		VARCHAR2(10)
SCANNED		VARCHAR2(3)
IS_RECOVERY_DEST_FILE	NOT NULL	VARCHAR2(3)
RSR_KEY		NUMBER

MARKED_CORRUPT		NUMBER

SQL> desc RC_LOG_HISTORY

Name	Null?	Type
DB_KEY	NOT NULL	NUMBER
DBINC_KEY	NOT NULL	NUMBER
DB_NAME	NOT NULL	VARCHAR2(8)
RECID	NOT NULL	NUMBER
STAMP	NOT NULL	NUMBER
THREAD#	NOT NULL	NUMBER
SEQUENCE#	NOT NULL	NUMBER
FIRST_CHANGE#	NOT NULL	NUMBER
FIRST_TIME	NOT NULL	DATE
NEXT_CHANGE#	NOT NULL	NUMBER
CLEARED		VARCHAR2(3)

SQL> desc RC_OFFLINE_RANGE

Name	Null?	Type
DB_KEY	NOT NULL	NUMBER
DBINC_KEY	NOT NULL	NUMBER
DB_NAME	NOT NULL	VARCHAR2(8)
RECID		NUMBER
STAMP		NUMBER
FILE#	NOT NULL	NUMBER
CREATION_CHANGE#	NOT NULL	NUMBER
OFFLINE_CHANGE#	NOT NULL	NUMBER
ONLINE_CHANGE#	NOT NULL	NUMBER
ONLINE_TIME	NOT NULL	DATE
CF_CREATE_TIME		DATE

SQL> desc RC_PROXY_ARCHIVEDLOG

Name	Null?	Type
DB_KEY	NOT NULL	NUMBER
DBINC_KEY	NOT NULL	NUMBER

DB_NAME	NOT NULL	VARCHAR2(8)
XAL_KEY	NOT NULL	NUMBER
RECID	NOT NULL	NUMBER
STAMP	NOT NULL	NUMBER
TAG		VARCHAR2(32)
DEVICE_TYPE	NOT NULL	VARCHAR2(255)
HANDLE	NOT NULL	VARCHAR2(1024)
COMMENTS		VARCHAR2(255)
MEDIA		VARCHAR2(80)
MEDIA_POOL		NUMBER
STATUS	NOT NULL	VARCHAR2(1)
THREAD#	NOT NULL	NUMBER
SEQUENCE#	NOT NULL	NUMBER
RESETLOGS_CHANGE#	NOT NULL	NUMBER
RESETLOGS_TIME	NOT NULL	DATE
FIRST_CHANGE#	NOT NULL	NUMBER
FIRST_TIME	NOT NULL	DATE
NEXT_CHANGE#	NOT NULL	NUMBER
NEXT_TIME	NOT NULL	DATE
BLOCKS	NOT NULL	NUMBER
BLOCK_SIZE	NOT NULL	NUMBER
START_TIME	NOT NULL	DATE
COMPLETION_TIME		NOT NULL DATE
ELAPSED_SECONDS		NUMBER
RSR_KEY		NUMBER

SQL> desc RC_PROXY_ARCHIVELOG_DETAILS

Name	Null?	Type
SESSION_KEY		NUMBER
SESSION_RECID		NUMBER
SESSION_STAMP		NUMBER
DB_KEY		NUMBER
DB_NAME		VARCHAR2(8)
COPY_KEY	NOT NULL	NUMBER
THREAD#	NOT NULL	NUMBER
SEQUENCE#	NOT NULL	NUMBER
RESETLOGS_CHANGE#	NOT NULL	NUMBER
RESETLOGS_TIME	NOT NULL	DATE

HANDLE	NOT NULL	VARCHAR2(1024)
MEDIA		VARCHAR2(80)
MEDIA_POOL		NUMBER
TAG		VARCHAR2(32)
FIRST_CHANGE#	NOT NULL	NUMBER
NEXT_CHANGE#	NOT NULL	NUMBER
FIRST_TIME	NOT NULL	DATE
NEXT_TIME	NOT NULL	DATE
OUTPUT_BYTES		NUMBER
COMPLETION_TIME	NOT NULL	DATE
OUTPUT_BYTES_DISPLAY		VARCHAR2(4000)

SQL> desc RC_PROXY_ARCHIVELOG_SUMMARY

Name	Null?	Type
DB_NAME	NOT NULL	VARCHAR2(8)
DB_KEY	NOT NULL	NUMBER
NUM_FILES_BACKED		NUMBER
NUM_DISTINCT_FILES_BACKED		NUMBER
MIN_FIRST_CHANGE#		NUMBER
MAX_NEXT_CHANGE#		NUMBER
MIN_FIRST_TIME		DATE
MAX_NEXT_TIME		DATE
OUTPUT_BYTES		NUMBER
OUTPUT_BYTES_DISPLAY		VARCHAR2(4000)

SQL> desc RC_PROXY_CONTROLFILE

Name	Null?	Type
DB_KEY	NOT NULL	NUMBER
DBINC_KEY	NOT NULL	NUMBER
DB_NAME	NOT NULL	VARCHAR2(8)
XCF_KEY	NOT NULL	NUMBER
RECID	NOT NULL	NUMBER
STAMP	NOT NULL	NUMBER
TAG		VARCHAR2(32)
RESETLOGS_CHANGE#	NOT NULL	NUMBER
RESETLOGS_TIME	NOT NULL	DATE

CHECKPOINT_CHANGE#	NOT NULL	NUMBER
CHECKPOINT_TIME	NOT NULL	DATE
CREATION_TIME	NOT NULL	DATE
BLOCK_SIZE	NOT NULL	NUMBER
BLOCKS		NUMBER
MIN_OFFR_RECID	NOT NULL	NUMBER
OLDEST_OFFLINE_RANGE	NOT NULL	NUMBER
DEVICE_TYPE	NOT NULL	VARCHAR2(255)
HANDLE	NOT NULL	VARCHAR2(1024)
COMMENTS		VARCHAR2(255)
MEDIA		VARCHAR2(80)
MEDIA_POOL		NUMBER
START_TIME	NOT NULL	DATE
COMPLETION_TIME	NOT NULL	DATE
ELAPSED_SECONDS		NUMBER
STATUS	NOT NULL	VARCHAR2(1)
CONTROLFILE_TYPE		VARCHAR2(1)
KEEP		VARCHAR2(3)
KEEP_UNTIL		DATE
KEEP_OPTIONS		VARCHAR2(10)
RSR_KEY		NUMBER

SQL> desc RC_PROXY_COPY_DETAILS

Name	Null?	Type
SESSION_KEY		NUMBER
SESSION_RECID		NUMBER
SESSION_STAMP		NUMBER
DB_KEY		NUMBER
DB_NAME		VARCHAR2(8)
RSR_KEY		NUMBER
COPY_KEY		NUMBER
FILE#		NUMBER
HANDLE		VARCHAR2(1024)
COMMENTS		VARCHAR2(255)
MEDIA		VARCHAR2(80)
MEDIA_POOL		NUMBER
TAG		VARCHAR2(32)
CREATION_CHANGE#		NUMBER

CREATION_TIME	DATE
CHECKPOINT_CHANGE#	NUMBER
CHECKPOINT_TIME	DATE
OUTPUT_BYTES	NUMBER
COMPLETION_TIME	DATE
CONTROLFILE_TYPE	VARCHAR2(1)
KEEP	VARCHAR2(3)
KEEP_UNTIL	DATE
KEEP_OPTIONS	VARCHAR2(10)
OUTPUT_BYTES_DISPLAY	VARCHAR2(4000)

SQL> desc RC_PROXY_COPY_SUMMARY

Name	Null?	Type
DB_NAME	NOT NULL	VARCHAR2(8)
DB_KEY		NUMBER
NUM_COPIES		NUMBER
NUM_DISTINCT_COPIES		NUMBER
MIN_CHECKPOINT_CHANGE#		NUMBER
MAX_CHECKPOINT_CHANGE#		NUMBER
MIN_CHECKPOINT_TIME		DATE
MAX_CHECKPOINT_TIME		DATE
OUTPUT_BYTES		NUMBER
OUTPUT_BYTES_DISPLAY		VARCHAR2(4000)

SQL> desc RC_PROXY_DATAFILE

Name	Null?	Type
DB_KEY	NOT NULL	NUMBER
DBINC_KEY	NOT NULL	NUMBER
DB_NAME	NOT NULL	VARCHAR2(8)
XDF_KEY	NOT NULL	NUMBER
RECID	NOT NULL	NUMBER
STAMP	NOT NULL	NUMBER
TAG		VARCHAR2(32)
FILE#	NOT NULL	NUMBER
CREATION_CHANGE#	NOT NULL	NUMBER
CREATION_TIME		DATE

RESETLOGS_CHANGE#	NOT NULL	NUMBER
RESETLOGS_TIME	NOT NULL	DATE
INCREMENTAL_LEVEL		NUMBER
CHECKPOINT_CHANGE#	NOT NULL	NUMBER
CHECKPOINT_TIME	NOT NULL	DATE
ABSOLUTE_FUZZY_CHANGE#		NUMBER
RECOVERY_FUZZY_CHANGE#		NUMBER
RECOVERY_FUZZY_TIME		DATE
ONLINE_FUZZY		VARCHAR2(3)
BACKUP_FUZZY		VARCHAR2(3)
BLOCKS	NOT NULL	NUMBER
BLOCK_SIZE	NOT NULL	NUMBER
DEVICE_TYPE	NOT NULL	VARCHAR2(255)
HANDLE	NOT NULL	VARCHAR2(1024)
COMMENTS		VARCHAR2(255)
MEDIA		VARCHAR2(80)
MEDIA_POOL		NUMBER
START_TIME	NOT NULL	DATE
COMPLETION_TIME	NOT NULL	DATE
ELAPSED_SECONDS		NUMBER
STATUS	NOT NULL	VARCHAR2(1)
KEEP		VARCHAR2(3)
KEEP_UNTIL		DATE
KEEP_OPTIONS		VARCHAR2(10)
RSR_KEY		NUMBER

SQL> desc RC_REDO_LOG

Name	Null?	Type
DB_KEY	NOT NULL	NUMBER
DBINC_KEY	NOT NULL	NUMBER
DB_NAME	NOT NULL	VARCHAR2(8)
THREAD#	NOT NULL	NUMBER
GROUP#	NOT NULL	NUMBER
NAME	NOT NULL	VARCHAR2(1024)

SQL> desc RC_REDO_THREAD

Name	Null?	Type
DB_KEY	NOT NULL	NUMBER
DBINC_KEY	NOT NULL	NUMBER
DB_NAME	NOT NULL	VARCHAR2(8)
THREAD#	NOT NULL	NUMBER
STATUS	NOT NULL	VARCHAR2(1)
SEQUENCE#	NOT NULL	NUMBER
ENABLE_CHANGE#		NUMBER
ENABLE_TIME		DATE
DISABLE_CHANGE#		NUMBER
DISABLE_TIME		DATE

SQL> desc RC_RESYNC

Name	Null?	Type
DB_KEY	NOT NULL	NUMBER
DBINC_KEY	NOT NULL	NUMBER
DB_NAME	NOT NULL	VARCHAR2(8)
RESYNC_KEY	NOT NULL	NUMBER
CONTROLFILE_CHANGE#	NOT NULL	NUMBER
CONTROLFILE_TIME		DATE
CONTROLFILE_SEQUENCE#	NOT NULL	NUMBER
CONTROLFILE_VERSION	NOT NULL	DATE
RESYNC_TYPE	NOT NULL	VARCHAR2(7)
DB_STATUS		VARCHAR2(7)
RESYNC_TIME	NOT NULL	DATE

SQL> desc RC_RMAN_BACKUP_JOB_DETAILS

Name	Null?	Type
DB_KEY		NUMBER
DB_NAME		VARCHAR2(8)
SESSION_KEY		NUMBER
SESSION_RECID		NUMBER
SESSION_STAMP		NUMBER

COMMAND_ID	VARCHAR2(33)
START_TIME	DATE
END_TIME	DATE
INPUT_BYTES	NUMBER
OUTPUT_BYTES	NUMBER
STATUS_WEIGHT	NUMBER
OPTIMIZED_WEIGHT	NUMBER
INPUT_TYPE_WEIGHT	NUMBER
OUTPUT_DEVICE_TYPE	VARCHAR2(17)
AUTOBACKUP_COUNT	NUMBER
AUTOBACKUP_DONE	VARCHAR2(3)
STATUS	VARCHAR2(23)
INPUT_TYPE	VARCHAR2(13)
OPTIMIZED	VARCHAR2(3)
ELAPSED_SECONDS	NUMBER
COMPRESSION_RATIO	NUMBER
INPUT_BYTES_PER_SEC	NUMBER
OUTPUT_BYTES_PER_SEC	NUMBER
INPUT_BYTES_DISPLAY	VARCHAR2(4000)
OUTPUT_BYTES_DISPLAY	VARCHAR2(4000)
INPUT_BYTES_PER_SEC_DISPLAY	VARCHAR2(4000)
OUTPUT_BYTES_PER_SEC_DISPLAY	VARCHAR2(4000)
TIME_TAKEN_DISPLAY	VARCHAR2(4000)

SQL> desc RC_RMAN_BACKUP_SUBJOB_DETAILS

Name	Null?	Type
DB_KEY		NUMBER
DB_NAME		VARCHAR2(8)
SESSION_KEY		NUMBER
SESSION_RECID		NUMBER
SESSION_STAMP		NUMBER
OPERATION		VARCHAR2(33)
COMMAND_ID		VARCHAR2(33)
START_TIME		DATE
END_TIME		DATE
INPUT_BYTES		NUMBER
OUTPUT_BYTES		NUMBER
STATUS_WEIGHT		NUMBER

OPTIMIZED_WEIGHT	NUMBER
INPUT_TYPE_WEIGHT	NUMBER
OUTPUT_DEVICE_TYPE	VARCHAR2(17)
AUTOBACKUP_DONE	VARCHAR2(3)
STATUS	VARCHAR2(23)
INPUT_TYPE	VARCHAR2(13)
OPTIMIZED	VARCHAR2(3)
AUTOBACKUP_COUNT	NUMBER
COMPRESSION_RATIO	NUMBER
INPUT_BYTES_DISPLAY	VARCHAR2(4000)
OUTPUT_BYTES_DISPLAY	VARCHAR2(4000)

SQL> desc RC_RMAN_BACKUP_TYPE

Name	Null?	Type
WEIGHT		NUMBER
INPUT_TYPE		VARCHAR2(13)

SQL> desc RC_RMAN_CONFIGURATION

Name	Null?	Type
DB_KEY	NOT NULL	NUMBER
CONF#	NOT NULL	NUMBER
NAME	NOT NULL	VARCHAR2(65)
VALUE		VARCHAR2(1025)
DB_UNIQUE_NAME		VARCHAR2(512)

SQL> desc RC_RMAN_OUTPUT

Name	Null?	Type
DB_KEY	NOT NULL	NUMBER
RSR_KEY	NOT NULL	NUMBER
SESSION_KEY	NOT NULL	NUMBER
RECID	NOT NULL	NUMBER
STAMP	NOT NULL	NUMBER
OUTPUT	NOT NULL	VARCHAR2(130)

SQL> desc RC_RMAN_STATUS

Name	Null?	Type
DB_KEY		NUMBER
DBINC_KEY		NUMBER
DB_NAME		VARCHAR2(8)
RECID		NUMBER
STAMP		NUMBER
RSR_KEY		NUMBER
PARENT_KEY		NUMBER
SESSION_KEY		NUMBER
ROW_TYPE		VARCHAR2(33)
ROW_LEVEL		NUMBER
OPERATION		VARCHAR2(33)
STATUS		VARCHAR2(33)
COMMAND_ID		VARCHAR2(33)
MBYTES_PROCESSED		NUMBER
START_TIME		DATE
END_TIME		DATE
JOB_KEY		NUMBER
INPUT_BYTES		NUMBER
OUTPUT_BYTES		NUMBER
OPTIMIZED		VARCHAR2(3)
OBJECT_TYPE		VARCHAR2(80)
SESSION_RECID		NUMBER
SESSION_STAMP		NUMBER
OUTPUT_DEVICE_TYPE		VARCHAR2(17)

SQL> desc RC_STORED_SCRIPT

Name	Null?	Type
DB_KEY		NUMBER
DB_NAME		VARCHAR2(8)
SCRIPT_NAME	NOT NULL	VARCHAR2(100)
SCRIPT_COMMENT		VARCHAR2(255)

SQL> desc RC_STORED_SCRIPT_LINE

Name	Null?	Type
DB_KEY	NOT NULL	NUMBER
SCRIPT_NAME	NOT NULL	VARCHAR2(100)
LINE	NOT NULL	NUMBER
TEXT	NOT NULL	VARCHAR2(1024)

SQL> desc RC_TABLESPACE

Name	Null?	Type
DB_KEY	NOT NULL	NUMBER
DBINC_KEY	NOT NULL	NUMBER
DB_NAME	NOT NULL	VARCHAR2(8)
TS#	NOT NULL	NUMBER
NAME	NOT NULL	VARCHAR2(30)
CREATION_CHANGE#	NOT NULL	NUMBER
CREATION_TIME		DATE
DROP_CHANGE#		NUMBER
DROP_TIME		DATE
INCLUDED_IN_DATABASE_BACKUP	NOT NULL	VARCHAR2(3)
BIGFILE	NOT NULL	VARCHAR2(3)
TEMPORARY	NOT NULL	VARCHAR2(3)
ENCRYPT_IN_BACKUP		VARCHAR2(3)

SQL> desc RC_TEMPFILE

Name	Null?	Type
DB_KEY	NOT NULL	NUMBER
DBINC_KEY	NOT NULL	NUMBER
DB_NAME	NOT NULL	VARCHAR2(8)
TS#	NOT NULL	NUMBER
TABLESPACE_NAME	NOT NULL	VARCHAR2(30)
FILE#	NOT NULL	NUMBER
CREATION_CHANGE#	NOT NULL	NUMBER
CREATION_TIME		DATE
DROP_CHANGE#		NUMBER

DROP_TIME		DATE
BYTES		NUMBER
BLOCKS	NOT NULL	NUMBER
BLOCK_SIZE	NOT NULL	NUMBER
NAME		VARCHAR2(1024)
RFILE#		NUMBER
AUTOEXTEND		VARCHAR2(3)
MAXSIZE		NUMBER
NEXTSIZE		NUMBER

SQL> desc RC_UNUSABLE_BACKUPFILE_DETAILS

Name	Null?	Type
DB_NAME		VARCHAR2(8)
DB_KEY		NUMBER
SESSION_KEY		NUMBER
RSR_KEY		NUMBER
BTYPE		CHAR(9)
BTYPE_KEY		NUMBER
ID1		NUMBER
ID2		NUMBER
FILETYPE		VARCHAR2(15)
FILETYPE_KEY		NUMBER
STATUS		VARCHAR2(1)
FILESIZE		NUMBER
DEVICE_TYPE		VARCHAR2(255)
FILENAME		VARCHAR2(1024)
MEDIA		VARCHAR2(80)
MEDIA_POOL		NUMBER

978-0-595-42027-8
0-595-42027-3